Travel with pleasure ... ship with confidence

Route of the *Vista-Dome* NORTH COAST LIMITED

	003	194120	3	2	PLACE OF ISSUE
	FORM NO.	TICKET NO.		CPN	

GREAT NORTHERN

SOLD WITH (FORM & NO.)

DATE ISSUED

COMMENCING DATE | PAID BY CHECK | BAGGAGE

TICKET

AREA BELOW FOR FAMILY PLAN, PARLOR OR SEAT CHARGE, IF COMBINATION SOLD, SEPARATE TICKET MUST BE USED FOR PARLOR OR SEAT CHARGE.

GOV'T.	2	8	EMPL.	HEAD OF FAMILY	NUMBER OF 1 PASSENGERS	FARE OR SPACE	SPACE
PP.O.	3	9	CHILD ½				
EXCH.	4	0	R.T.P.A.	WIFE OR CHILD 12-21 INCL.	NUMBER OF 1 2 3 PASSENGERS	FARE OR CAR	CAR
R.T.P.A.	5	1	CLERGY				
FURLO	6	R	R.T.C.				
R.T.P.A.	7	A	A.E.C.C.	CHILD 5-11 INCL.	NUMBER OF 1 2 3	FARE/TIME-DATE	TIME-DATE

ST. PAUL UNION DEPOT

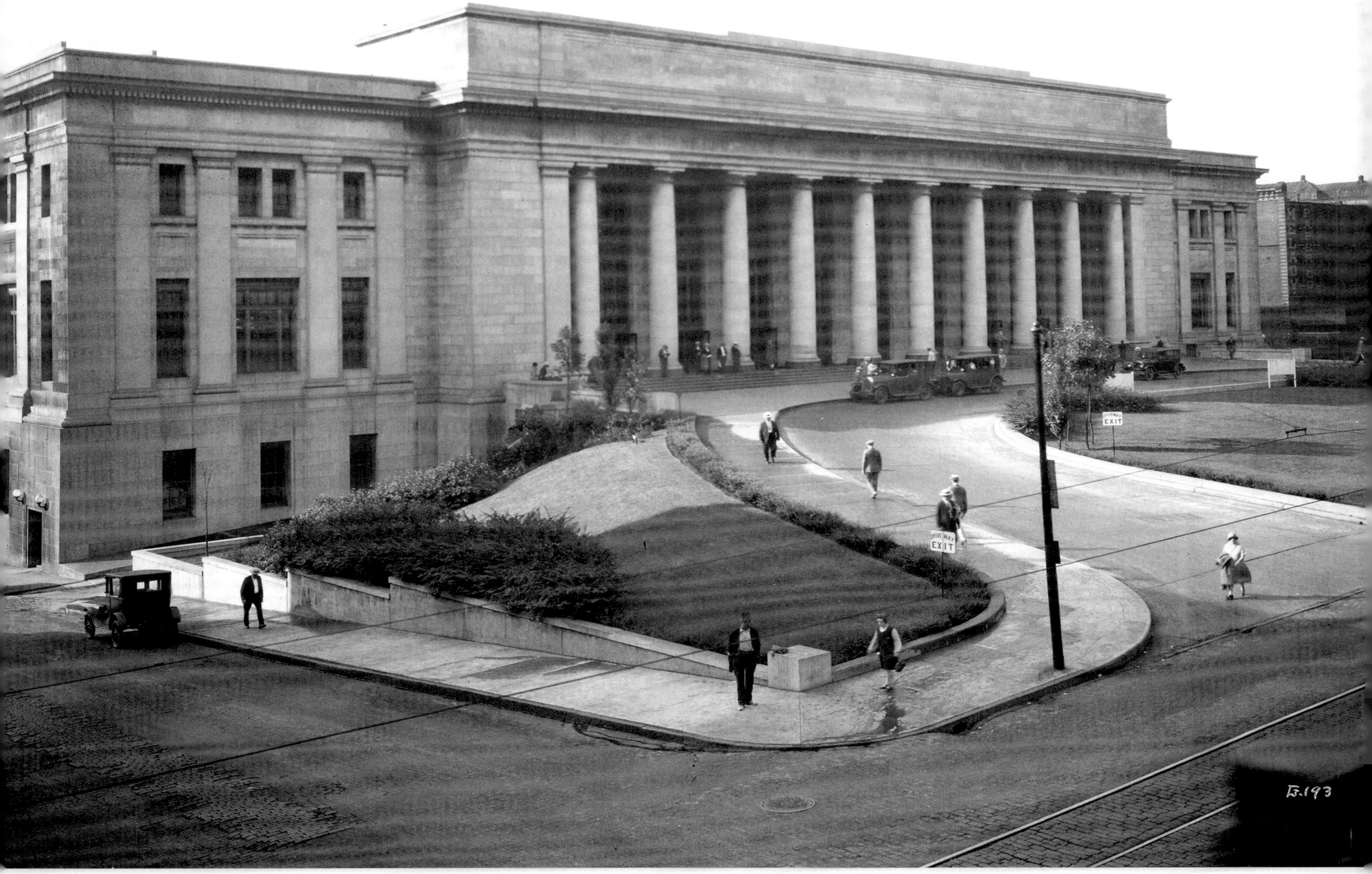
EXIT

ST. PAUL UNION DEPOT

※ JOHN W. DIERS

UNIVERSITY OF MINNESOTA PRESS
MINNEAPOLIS · LONDON

The University of Minnesota Press gratefully acknowledges financial assistance provided by Edward A. Burkhardt for the publication of this book.

Copyright 2013 by John W. Diers

All rights reserved. No part of this publication may be reproduced, stored in a retrieval system, or transmitted, in any form or by any means, electronic, mechanical, photocopying, recording, or otherwise, without the prior written permission of the publisher.

Published by the University of Minnesota Press
111 Third Avenue South, Suite 290
Minneapolis, MN 55401-2520
http://www.upress.umn.edu

Design and production by Mighty Media, Inc.
Interior/text design by Chris Long

Library of Congress Cataloging-in-Publication Data

Diers, John W.
   St. Paul Union Depot / John W. Diers.
   Includes bibliographical references and index.
   ISBN 978-0-8166-5610-3 (hardcover : acid-free paper)
1. St. Paul Union Depot (St. Paul, Minn.)—History.
2. Railroad stations—Minnesota—St. Paul—History.
3. Historic buildings—Minnesota—St. Paul—History.
4. Railroads—Minnesota—St. Paul—History. 5. St. Paul (Minn.)—History. 6. St. Paul (Minn.)—Buildings, structures, etc. I. Title. II. Title: St. Paul Union Depot.

TF302.S23D54 2013
385.3'1409776581—DC23

                                            2012048341

Printed in Canada on acid-free paper

The University of Minnesota is an equal-opportunity educator and employer.

20 19 18 17 16 15 14 13   10 9 8 7 6 5 4 3 2 1

For my wife, Marcia, the lady on the train

contents

ACKNOWLEDGMENTS ▪ IX

PROLOGUE: A NIGHT ON THE BUILDER ▪ XI

RAILROADS SERVING ST. PAUL UNION DEPOT ▪ XVIII

INTRODUCTION ▪ 1

1. RAILROAD AVENUE ▪ 11
2. ST. PAUL AND ITS RAILROADS ▪ 41

    LEROY BUFFINGTON ▪ 55

3. A NEW UNION DEPOT FOR ST. PAUL ▪ 89

    MILWAUKEE ROAD DEPOT ▪ 94

    GREAT NORTHERN STATION MINNEAPOLIS ▪ 96

    CHARLES SUMNER FROST AND THE FIRM OF FROST AND GRANGER ▪ 107

4. ARRIVALS AND DEPARTURES ▪ 131
5. MAIL AND EXPRESS ▪ 179
6. LAST CALL ▪ 209

EPILOGUE: WHITHER THE PASSENGER TRAIN? ▪ 259

APPENDIX: PASSENGER TRAIN DISCONTINUANCES IN MINNESOTA, 1950–1971 ▪ 270

BIBLIOGRAPHIC RESOURCES ▪ 274

ILLUSTRATION CREDITS ▪ 278

INDEX ▪ 280

acknowledgments

As a kid, I was a regular visitor to the St. Paul Union Depot. I loved the place, and I thought there would always be passenger trains and streetcars and steam locomotives. Today, in a world of exponential change, it is important that our memories and images and the memories and images of those who came before us are preserved for generations that will follow.

Many people helped, among them: Steve Glischinski, John Goodman, Dennis C. Henry, Don Hofsommer, Stuart Holmquist, Aaron Isaacs, John Luecke, Larry Millett, Steve Morris, and Byron D. Olsen. Special recognition is due the late William (Bill) Bannon, the last president of the St. Paul Union Depot Company, and John Jensen, its chief engineer. Both provided valuable insights into the day-to-day workings of the depot in the 1950s and '60s. I also want to thank the staff at the University of Minnesota Press including Todd Orjala, senior acquisitions editor; Kristian Tvedten, editorial assistant; and Nancy Sauro, copy editor. At the St. Paul Pioneer Press: Jason Melo, deputy photo director; Pat Thraen, newsroom researcher; and Frederick Melo, City Hall reporter. Organizations include the Andersen Library at the University of Minnesota, the John W. Barriger III National Railroad Library, Great Northern Railway Historical Society, Hennepin County Historical Society, Hennepin County Library, James J. Hill Reference Library, Kalmbach Publications, David P. Morgan Library, Minnesota Historical Society, Minnesota Streetcar Museum, Minnesota Transportation Museum, Museum of the Rockies, Newberry Library, Northern Pacific Railway Historical Association, Ramsey County Historical Society, St. Paul Public Library, Wayzata Historical Society, and Winona County Historical Society.

Finally, a special tribute to my grandfather and grandmother, August M. and Elsie Wallace; my parents, John C. and Helen B. Diers; and my uncle and aunt, Warner E. and Eleanor Anderson. They've been gone for many years, but their patience on our visits to the depot and innumerable train and streetcar rides gave me the interest and the inspiration for this book.

Bon voyage!

PROLOGUE
A NIGHT ON THE BUILDER

Growing up in St. Paul in the late 1940s, I was never a stranger to the St. Paul Union Depot. My grandfather worked for the Great Northern Railway, and my grandmother and I would accompany him on the streetcar when he went to the depot to go out on his run. Grandfather knew everyone and made sure I saw everything. For a five-year-old, the depot was a sea of legs and a din of train announcements. Steam locomotives were still in abundance. Their chuffing exhaust brought a faint scent of coal smoke drifting through open windows and stairwells on warm summer days. Then my dad's work, and a series of job transfers, took us away, and although I missed my grandparents, my melancholy was soothed by a series of wonderful train trips to visit them in St. Paul. At the time, I was much too young to travel alone, so my mother and often my grandmother came along.

Our first move was to Fort Dodge, Iowa. Fort Dodge was on the Omaha–Twin Cities line of the Chicago Great Western Railway. It was also served by the Minneapolis & St. Louis Railway, but we usually took the Great Western because it used St. Paul Union Depot and it was easier to take the streetcar from there to my grandmother's house. The Great Western was never a rich railroad. Our train was, typically, a collection of old coaches with red plush, straight-back seats, powered by a steam locomotive. It made every stop between Fort Dodge and St. Paul. It was slow, but I loved it. Unfortunately, railroad management didn't share that affection because it was discontinued not long after we moved from Fort Dodge to Philadelphia.

In contrast to Fort Dodge and the grubby trains of the Great Western, Philadelphia was my introduction to the streamline era and the premier trains of the late 1940s and early 1950s. My grandmother wouldn't fly, nor would she go coach on an overnight train trip. When I traveled with her, it was first class all the way. We always had parlor car seats on the *Hiawatha* or the *Zephyr* to Chicago, and a Pullman bedroom, or drawing room, on the *Broadway Limited* to Philadelphia. Breakfast, lunch, and dinner were always in the diner. Once, when she wanted to see some shows in New York, we traveled there, stayed for a couple of days, and then returned to Chicago on the *20th Century Limited*.

The *Broadway Limited* and the *20th Century Limited* were all Pullman, first-class trains that catered to business people, entertainers, and the carriage trade. Their observation cars were filled with gentlemen in suits and ties and ladies in feathered hats. It was a more elegant time, and in those days, before body scans, pat-downs, boarding cattle calls, and other indignities, you always dressed for travel. I was no exception, and grandmother, much to my objections, always made me wear a Little Lord Fauntleroy suit when we traveled.

There were amenities. If you needed a trim, there was a barber on board, and there was a lady's maid to assist women traveling with children. Did your suit need a press? Call the valet. Feeling ill? Call the nurse. There was a radiophone to keep in touch with the office and a train secretary, and, of course, there was the dining car and the steward who presided over his domain like the conductor of a symphony orchestra.

We moved back to the Twin Cities in 1952. My parents bought a home in suburban Bloomington, and train travel and the St. Paul Union Depot slowly retreated to childhood memories. Then, when I was a sophomore in high school, I saw a story in the newspaper about the Chicago & North Western Railway's efforts to discontinue its train to Omaha. It was called the *North American,* and it ran through Savage just across the Minnesota River from our house. I saw it quite often and mused that it might be fun to take a ride. It was summer and school was out, so I checked on ticket prices and assembled an itinerary that eventually grew into a circle trip from St. Paul to Omaha then Omaha to Chicago on the Chicago, Milwaukee, St. Paul & Pacific Railroad's *City of Denver,* and a return to the Twin Cities on the Chicago & North Western's *400*. My parents consented and even picked up part of the tab. My grandparents chipped in, and I was off on thirty hours of nonstop train riding. I was hooked, and for the next six years, I rode as many trains as I possibly could, usually just a few months ahead of a train off notice. These odysseys were a sampling of Americana and American history that are gone forever; I remember all of them to this day, but one final trip was very special.

It began at St. Paul Union Depot on a cold night a week before Christmas. I was a senior at the University of Minnesota. I had just turned twenty-one, and this was a birthday present to myself. I had saved up some money and purchased a first-class ticket and a Pullman bedroom on Great Northern's *Empire Builder* to Seattle with a return via Portland on the Northern Pacific Railway's *North Coast Limited*.

It was snowing that night as the taxi pulled up the driveway and stopped at the foot of the steps that led to the depot's entrance. I got out, paid the driver, then grabbed my suitcase and headed for the doors. Tugging at a well-worn handle, I stepped through an overheated vestibule into the lobby. I took a deep breath. Like all railroad depots, it smelled busy. That, along with the faint echo of hundreds of heels on the marble floors, the steady murmur of voices in the great hall, and the train announcements, confirmed the comings and goings of people and commerce. There were Christmas decorations and carols were playing on the PA system. I knew time was running out on the place as I looked wistfully around the lobby, but it was good to see that people had returned, if only for the Christmas rush.

The *Empire Builder* had just arrived from Chicago, completing its four-hundred-mile run in just under seven hours. Declining business had forced the Chicago, Burlington & Quincy to combine the *Empire Builder* with the Northern Pacific's *North Coast Limited* between Chicago and St. Paul, resulting in a huge train that stretched the full distance of the longest platform at St. Paul Union Depot. It was left to St. Paul Union Depot terminal forces to make two trains out of this behemoth, adding additional coaches and sleepers to both trains to accommodate passengers boarding in the Twin Cities. The rumbling noises beneath the waiting room served notice that this transformation was well underway.

Promptly at 8:15 an announcement echoed through the depot: "Your attention, please. Great Northern train number 31, the *Empire Builder* for Minneapolis, Willmar, Breckenridge, Moorhead, Fargo, New Rockford, Minot, Williston, Wolf Point, Glasgow, Havre, Chester, Shelby, Cut Bank, Whitefish, Troy, Spokane, Ephrata, Wenatchee, Everett, Portland, and Seattle now boarding on track 17."

I grabbed my suitcase and filed through the door to the escalator and the tracks below, into a world of cold drafts, swirling steam, and strange hissing sounds and groans, punctuated by the occasional shouting of a carman. The coach passengers headed toward the head end, where, in the distance, the railway post office crew was busy transferring a pile of mail sacks from a baggage cart. My bedroom space was in a Pullman near the rear of the train, and a trainman directed me to the left as I alighted from the escalator. Continuing on, I walked about a hundred feet to the open vestibule of my car, an all-room sleeper, number 1382, named *Inuya Pass*. A smiling, white-jacketed Pullman porter greeted me and inquired about my space. He then took my suitcase, and I stepped aboard, turned left, and walked down the hushed corridor to bedroom D.

Five minutes later, I heard a series of slams as the doors closed, followed by a slight tug. We were under way. Twenty-five minutes later we were standing in the Great Northern Station in Minneapolis. I decided to have a look and left my room and walked along the corridor to an open door. I stepped down to the platform and watched as passengers streamed aboard the coaches. The porter remarked that the sleepers were only half full, but the coaches were jammed, mainly students bound for Fargo and Minot going home for Christmas. He was a forty-year veteran, about to retire, and expressed how sad he was to see the sleeping-car business go away. "Everyone's in a hurry," he said, shrugging his shoulders, just as the conductor called out "Board" and highballed the head end.

These well-dressed passengers are enjoying the amenities of the observation car. The train is the 1951 *Empire Builder*, but the scene could have been on any of the great trains of that era. It was a time when comfort and class meant more than speed.

I decided to check out the diner. It was usually closed by this hour, but the porter said it was serving late because a large ski group for Whitefish, Montana, had just boarded in Minneapolis. The Ranch lounge car would remain open until well past midnight; it catered to the coach crowd, and they tended to be a boozy bunch. As we left Minneapolis, I walked forward through the next two sleepers, the dome lounge car, and stepped into the diner, a wonderful world of white tablecloths, china, heavy flatware, and waiters standing at attention. There were a few, perhaps a dozen, people scattered at separate tables. The steward, at the opposite end of the car, stood near the entrance to the pantry and kitchen. Menu in hand, he motioned to me and walked down the aisle to an empty table. As I approached, he pulled back a chair next to the window, placed a menu in front of me, and a check.

My waiter arrived. "Cocktail before dinner, sir?" he inquired. I paused a moment, realizing I'd just turned twenty-one and that this should be something of an occasion. Remembering the great

In the golden age of rail travel, these first-class passengers are enjoying first-class dining on the 1947 edition of the *Empire Builder*.

dining car scene in *North by Northwest*, I pictured myself as Cary Grant across the table from Eva Marie Saint and replied, "Yes, a Gibson, please." The waiter left my table and walked to the steward who returned carrying a serving tray with two glasses, one with shaved ice. Opening the cocktail bottle, he first poured the contents over the ice, then, placing a strainer over the glass, he poured the drink into the martini glass, adding a pearl onion.

I drank a silent toast to myself, appreciative of my good fortune at being aboard this grand conveyance—then stared out the window as the lights of Wayzata flashed by. There was a bump as we swung through a turnout and a dinging of crossing bells as we approached the Ferndale grade crossing where a queue of automobiles waited. It took mere seconds, but we slammed through the crossing, leaving the waiting autos in a swirl of snow. We were accelerating to sixty, seventy, now eighty miles per hour. We blasted through Long Lake, whistle blaring—more snow, and the distant lights of a farmhouse flashed by as we raced past automobiles on parallel Highway 12.

The waiter returned and inquired if I wanted to order. I said yes and began looking over the menu. I made my selection with difficulty. Closing the menu, I picked up the check and wrote out my order: prime rib, rare; baked potato; blue cheese dressing on my salad. Time passed. I was in no hurry and sipped my drink for a considerable time, perhaps expecting Eva Marie Saint.

Then she appeared. The steward seated a blond young woman at my table. She was attractive and laughed when I remarked about Cary Grant and *North by Northwest*. We spent the next forty-five minutes or so in pleasant conversation. Turned out she was getting off at Breckenridge and would be met by family from Battle Lake, a nearby town. She was going to stay at her grandmother's place. I didn't want to admit that I was riding the train just for the experience. It seemed so nerdy.

By then I had finished dinner. It was absolutely delicious. My waiter returned and looked at the check. Noting that I had forgotten to specify a choice for desert, he suggested, "We have Dutch apple or pumpkin pie, ice cream or sherbet." "Pumpkin," I replied. It was wonderful—served with a generous dab of whipped cream. Pushing back the plate, I poured another cup of coffee. My waiter asked, "How was everything?" "Great," I replied. The steward appeared, totaled my check, and placed it on a silver tray. I paid, and he returned my change. I took care to leave a generous tip. By this time my dining companion had finished, and as she got up, I stood and wished her a pleasant trip and a merry Christmas. As I departed the diner, I recoiled at how stupid I was not to find out more about her. Later, I spotted her on the platform at Breckenridge and waved at her as we pulled away.

Years went by, and the *Empire Builder* soldiered on, first under Burlington Northern and then

Amtrak, but it was a completely different train. I had revisited a few times and was not impressed. Gone were the Mountain series observation cars, the all-room Pullman sleepers, dome cars, the elegant diner, and five-star service. By then I had given up on passenger trains, thinking it was better to remember them as they once were rather than accept what they had become.

One day, I stopped by a friend's house on an errand, and as I walked into his living room, a woman got up from a chair. We were introduced. She was a teacher and the latchkey coordinator at a neighboring school. My friend served with her on the parent committee. The introduction turned out to be a formality because we had already met over dinner on the *Empire Builder* on a cold December night some twelve years before. I think we both pretended not to know each other. We married six months later and have been together for thirty-five years. ❈

Railroads Serving St. Paul Union Depot

NINE RAILROADS AND THEIR PASSENGER TRAINS used St. Paul Union Depot—eight after the Minneapolis & St. Louis Railway withdrew in 1933.

Chicago, Burlington & Quincy Railroad (Burlington)

The Chicago, Burlington & Quincy Railroad carried a high percentage of the Chicago–Twin Cities passenger traffic. Its principal trains were the morning and afternoon *Zephyr*s and the overnight *Blackhawk*. It also ferried the Great Northern's *Empire Builder* and *Western Star* and the Northern Pacific's *North Coast Limited* and *Mainstreeter* between the Twin Cities and Chicago. The latter were through trains originating in Chicago and Seattle–Portland. The Burlington's trains were noted for their speed and passenger comforts including full-service dining and lounge cars, Vista Dome coaches, parlor cars, and sleeping cars on the overnight and transcontinental runs. A number of its trains were discontinued or combined in the 1950s and 1960s, but a high quality of service was maintained until Amtrak took over on May 1, 1971.

Chicago Great Western Railway (Great Western)

The Chicago Great Western Railway ran some fine passenger trains in the first two decades of the twentieth century. They included the *Mill Cities Limited* between Minneapolis and Kansas City, the *Legionnaire* to Chicago, and other named trains between Minneapolis and Omaha. It also operated two local trains from Minneapolis to Rochester, Minnesota, with distinctive names, the *Red Bird* and the *Blue Bird*. The *Blue Bird* was a gasoline-electric motor train, a forerunner of the diesel-powered streamliners that would debut in the 1930s. The Depression and automobile competition hurt the

Great Western's passenger business. It withdrew most of its dining, lounge, and sleeping car services in the 1930s. By 1965 it was down to a pair of overnight trains between Minneapolis and Council Bluffs, Iowa. These were mostly mail and express trains with a single coach for the handful of remaining passengers. They were discontinued that same year.

Chicago, Milwaukee, St. Paul & Pacific Railroad (Milwaukee Road)

The Chicago, Milwaukee, St. Paul & Pacific Railroad was a major player in the Chicago-Milwaukee-Twin Cities passenger market, surpassing the Burlington in some years. The morning and afternoon *Hiawatha*s and the overnight *Pioneer Limited* were fine trains with first-rate diners, lounges, and sleeping cars (on the *Pioneer Limited*) and distinctive parlor cars (on the *Hiawatha*s). The Milwaukee also operated two transcontinental trains to Seattle, the *Olympian Hiawatha* and the *Columbian*. They were worthy competitors for Great Northern and Northern Pacific trains but served the same markets and suffered as air travel became more popular. They were gone by 1961. The Milwaukee's two mail and express trains between Chicago, Milwaukee, and St. Paul, trains 57 and 56, were among the heaviest in the entire United States. The Milwaukee's *Morning Hiawatha* lasted until Amtrak.

Chicago, Rock Island & Pacific Railroad (Rock Island)

The Rock Island's *Twin Star Rocket, Texas Rocket,* and *Zephyr Rocket* were its three principal named trains using St. Paul Union Depot. The *Twin Star* and the *Texas Rocket* ran via Des Moines, Iowa, and Kansas City to points in Oklahoma and Texas. They were streamliners with diners, sleeping cars, and observation lounge cars. The *Twin Star* carried a sleeping car for Los Angeles via a connection to its *Golden State* streamliner at Kansas City. The *Zephyr Rocket* was operated in conjunction with the Burlington via Cedar Rapids, Iowa, to St. Louis. It was an overnight train and came with a sleeping car, diner, and observation lounge. All these trains were gone by 1969. That year, the *Plainsman,* an abbreviated Minneapolis-Kansas City version of the *Twin Star Rocket,* was discontinued.

Chicago, St. Paul, Minneapolis & Omaha Railway (Omaha)

The Chicago, St. Paul, Minneapolis & Omaha Railway was a subsidiary of the Chicago & North Western Railway and kept its separate identity until it was folded into the Chicago & North Western in 1957. The Omaha was famous for its Chicago-Milwaukee-Twin Cities 400 streamliner and its overnight *North Western Limited*. The 400's name came from its Chicago-Minneapolis timing: four hundred miles in four hundred minutes. The *Viking* and the *Victory* were two secondary trains between Chicago and the Twin Cities via Madison rather than Milwaukee. They were mainly mail and express runs and operated on slower schedules. The Omaha also reached its namesake city, Omaha, Nebraska, via Mankato, Minnesota, and Sioux City, Iowa, with three named trains, the daytime *North American* and the overnight *Nightingale* and *Mondamin*. The *Nightingale* carried through sleeping cars for Los Angeles via a Union Pacific connection at Omaha. There were also several local trains out of Minneapolis and St. Paul for points in southern Minnesota and Wisconsin. The Omaha's trains were mostly gone by 1959. That year the *North American* and *North Western Limited* were discontinued, and in July 1963 the 400 made its final run.

Great Northern Railway

The Great Northern Railway anchored St. Paul Union Depot. Its transcontinental *Empire Builder* and *Western Star* trains served Glacier National Park and dominated the Chicago-Seattle-Portland market. Its *Fast Mail* was known as the Northwest's postman. Along with the *Winnipeg Limited* to Winnipeg; the *Dakotan* to Minot, North Dakota; the *Red River* to Grand Forks, Minnesota; and the *Badger* and *Gopher* to Duluth-Superior, they were among the finest trains to call on St. Paul Union Depot. Although several of these trains were discontinued in the mid- to late 1960s, the Great Northern upheld high standards to the end. The *Empire Builder* and the *Western Star* lasted until Amtrak.

Northern Pacific Railway

Northern Pacific Railway had two Chicago-Seattle-Portland runs, the *North Coast Limited*, via Butte, Montana, and the *Mainstreeter*, via Helena, Montana. Both trains served Yellowstone National Park. The Northern Pacific served larger population centers than those reached by the Great Northern, but they also had better roads, and automobile and bus competition drained away business. Besides its transcontinental service at St. Paul Union Depot, the Northern Pacific operated trains to Duluth, International Falls, and Winnipeg. The *North Coast Limited*, with its domes, dining and lounge cars, sleeping cars, and observation cars, was every bit the equal of the *Empire Builder*. The *Mainstreeter* carried a diner-lounge car, sleepers, and at one time, an observation car, but these disappeared as traffic fell off; the railroad substituted a self-service cafeteria car for the diner and a slumbercoach for the sleeper. Neither was popular with passengers. Both trains survived until Amtrak.

Minneapolis & St. Louis Railway

At one time the Minneapolis & St. Louis Railway had extensive passenger services in southern Minnesota, Iowa, and South Dakota. Its *North Star Limited* for St. Louis carried a diner, sleeping cars, and an observation car. It was a very fine train. However, the railroad was weak financially and was hit especially hard by the Depression. It vacated St. Paul Union Depot in 1933 and pulled all of its remaining trains back to Minneapolis.

Minneapolis, St. Paul & Sault Ste. Marie Railway (Soo Line)

As late as the 1940s the Minneapolis, St. Paul & Sault Ste. Marie Railway ran a number of passenger trains from St. Paul to points in northern Minnesota, Wisconsin, and Chicago. They included the *Winnipeger* to Winnipeg, Manitoba, and the *Laker* to Chicago. Through a Canadian Pacific connection at Portal, North Dakota, the Soo Line's *Dominion* and its summer-only *Mountaineer* ran from Chicago to Vancouver, British Columbia, via the Canadian Rockies. The Soo Line didn't purchase new passenger cars after World War II, preferring to modernize its older equipment. Only the *Winnipeger* was left by 1967, and it was discontinued that year.

It is 12:55 p.m. on a fall day in 1948, and the Milwaukee Road's *Afternoon Hiawatha* is ready to depart St. Paul Union Depot on a six-hour-twenty-minute dash to Chicago. Next to it, a Northern Pacific switch engine works a cut of mail cars and coaches on Northern Pacific's train 61, an all-stops local that just arrived after a four-hour trek from Duluth. In 1915, the depot's designers expected that there would be 300 arrivals and departures a day by 1950, an average of one train every 12.5 minutes, but in 1948 the nearly empty yards and tracks reflect a revised set of expectations. There will be 174 arrivals and departures this day and fewer still as the years go on.

INTRODUCTION

THIS BOOK IS ABOUT THE ST. PAUL UNION DEPOT—its history, its builders, and the railroads that served it. It is also about how it worked and how, like all railroad stations, its fortunes were inextricably linked to the rise and fall of the American passenger train. At the beginning of the twentieth century, in every small town and big city, the railroad depot was the community's gateway to the wider world. The railroads built Minnesota, and mile zero on most Twin Cities passenger timetables was St. Paul Union Depot because that is where it all began.

From 1868, when it was first published, until the arrival of Amtrak in 1971, railroad ticket and travel agents used the *Official Guide,* otherwise known as the ticket agent's bible, to route railroad passengers to their destinations. Published monthly, the *Official Guide*'s 1,224 consecutive issues carried every passenger train schedule on every railroad in America. A slim 280 pages in 1868, by 1913 it was three inches thick and 1,600 pages long and listed some 76,000 stations reached by passenger train.

Most of these 76,000 stations were modest brick or board-and-batten affairs, simple, functional structures befitting the small communities they served. But in the larger cities, between 1900 and 1920, the railroads displayed their vast wealth and power by constructing stations on an imperial scale, buildings so vast and of materials so rich that they rivaled the temples of ancient Rome.

It took four years and 1,800 workers to put together the 27,000 tons of steel; 64,000 barrels of cement; 17 million bricks; 660,000 cubic feet of granite, marble, and travertine; and 83,000 square feet of skylights that opened on August 1, 1910, as New York's Pennsylvania Station, then the largest passenger station in the world. A few blocks away Grand Central Terminal opened in 1913 at a cost of $72 million. In 1920 more than 37 million passengers passed through its doors. In Detroit, Reed & Stem and Warren & Whitmore, the architectural firms responsible for Grand Central Terminal, designed the magnificent, Beaux-Arts Michigan Central Station, which opened on December 27,

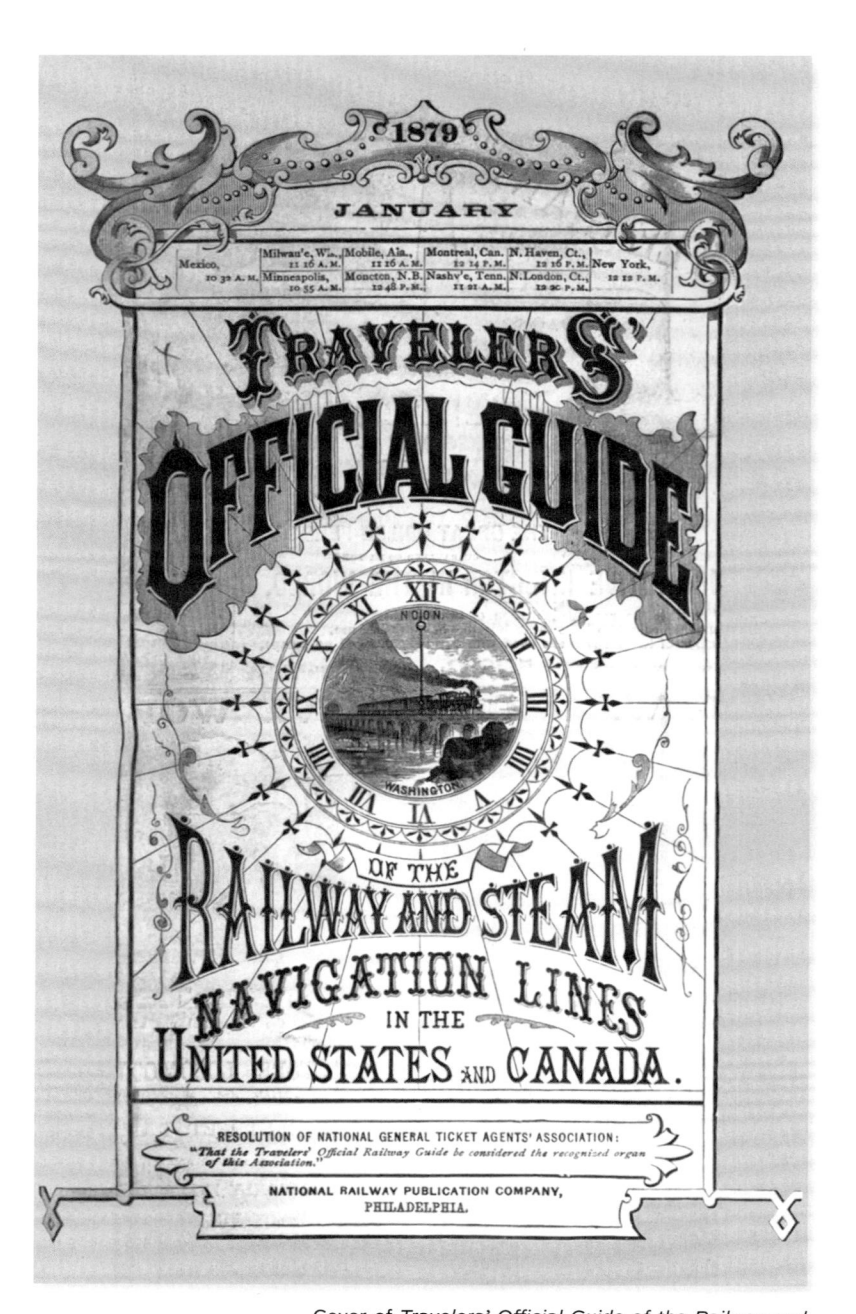

Cover of *Travelers' Official Guide of the Railway and Steam Navigation Lines in the United States and Canada* (Philadelphia: National Railway Publication Co., 1879). This came to be known as the ticket agent's bible because it contained the schedules for every passenger train on every railroad in the United States.

1913. There were others, among them Boston's South Station (1899); Nashville, Tennessee (1900); LaSalle Street, Chicago (1903); Atlanta Terminal Station (1905); King Street Station, Seattle (1906); Washington Union Station, Washington, D.C. (1907); Chattanooga Terminal Station (1909); North Western Terminal Station, Chicago (1911); Union Station, Seattle (1911); Kansas City Union Station (1914); Dallas Union Station (1916); Broad Street Station, Richmond, Virginia (1919); and Jacksonville Union Station, Florida (1919).

St. Paul's first union depot opened in 1881, replacing four smaller stations. It burned in 1884 and was rebuilt. By 1913 it had run out of capacity, and city fathers, envious of the grand stations going up in other cities, wanted something more befitting St. Paul's standing as a state capital and a major railroad hub. They got their chance late on the evening of October 3, 1913, when the old depot burned. Publicly, city fathers despaired the fire, but most of them privately rejoiced, thinking it a remarkable stroke of good fortune. They had complained about the old building for almost two decades, only to be frustrated by the railroads and their disagreements over the size of a new depot and how its construction costs would be financed and apportioned among them. St. Paul Union Depot was used, and jointly owned by, the nine railroads serving the city. They were tough competitors in the finest traditions

INTRODUCTION   3

Boxcars, grain elevators, water tank, windmill, train order signal, and kids on the platform were standard for a small town depot such as Pierz, Minnesota, on the Soo Line between Brooten, Minnesota, and Superior, Wisconsin. It hosted one passenger train and a local freight each way, every day in 1915.

of the Gilded Age, but they could also cooperate as long as it was in their interests. Passenger stations were expensive, and one station was cheaper than nine.

But defining and sharing costs and benefits proved elusive, and cooperation faded as prosperous roads, like the Great Northern, or those with extensive passenger services, like the Chicago, Milwaukee & St. Paul, tried to leverage weaker roads, like the Chicago Great Western or the Minneapolis & St. Louis, to share the expense of a much grander passenger station. James J. Hill's Great Northern and the City of St. Paul wanted a civic monument worthy of a state capital and a city at the center of railroad wealth and power. Hill complained that railroads were unwilling to invest and provide for growth and future needs. On the other hand, a colleague, Samuel Felton, president of the Chicago Great Western, a less robust railroad with fewer passenger trains, bluntly told the city that if it wanted a civic monument, it should pay for one.

St. Paul Union Depot served as headquarters for the Tenth Division of the U.S. Railway Mail Service, and it was the third-busiest mail terminal in the country. Clerks load a mail car prior to its departure.

Still, as much as railroad officials squabbled over money, none of them disputed that something had to be done. St. Paul's growth was outstripping its existing rail passenger facilities. In 1899, 107 depot employees sold 350,000 tickets and handled 45,000 tons of mail and express. By 1913, the year of the fire, depot employment had tripled, and 302 employees sold almost three-quarters of a million tickets and loaded and unloaded 280,000 tons of mail and express from arriving and departing passenger and mail trains. Each day, 30,000 people passed through the depot destined for towns and cities in Minnesota and across the country. There was direct service to Chicago, Omaha, Kansas City, Seattle, Portland, and Winnipeg, among other destinations. With connections, it was possible to go anywhere in the United States, Canada, and Mexico. Travelers could purchase space in a Pullman sleeping car in St. Paul and stay aboard all the way to Los Angeles, San Francisco, Boston, or Montreal. More traffic was expected with the recent completion of the Milwaukee Road's line to Puget Sound.

Across the Mississippi in Minneapolis, James J. Hill's Great Northern was putting the finishing touches on its new Great Northern Station, which hosted tenants Chicago, St. Paul, Minneapolis & Omaha; Chicago Great Western; Northern Pacific; Minneapolis & St. Louis; and the Chicago, Burlington & Quincy. Hill's Minneapolis station replaced an earlier 1885 depot that had grown progressively inadequate as the city's industry prospered and more people arrived to work in its factories and mills. When it was replaced in 1914, the old Minneapolis station was handling 115 trains and 11,000 passengers each day during the peak summer travel months, half as many as St. Paul's. Yet Minneapolis, where Hill had a free hand and could do as he pleased, now had a beautiful new station. St. Paul, with twice the traffic, was stuck with a temporary depot that the press described as "unsanitary, inadequate, and unsuitable."

The outrage of St. Paul politicians and business leaders was predictable and overwhelming. Why should St. Paul settle for a burned-out shell of a building and a warehouse as its passenger station when other cities, especially rival Minneapolis, gained impressive new facilities? That was the question asked by the St. Paul Citizens Terminal Depot Committee, representing fourteen St. Paul civic and business organizations, in a July 31, 1914, letter to Edmund Pennington, president of the St. Paul Union Depot Company. The letter complained of four years of delay and great inconvenience and a facility completely unable to handle the 10,000,000 people who had passed through its doors in 1913. It noted a 45 percent increase in passenger traffic during the previous ten years and a 207 percent increase in the volume of mail and express. In 1913 a total of 73,373 trains used the station, an increase of 3,119 over 1912 and an average of one train every six minutes day and night.

Very bluntly the committee stated, "The interests of the City of St. Paul in the new terminal are greater than that of all the railroads combined." It was a final call for action, and it worked.

Ten years and $15 million later, St. Paul had its depot, the largest construction project in downtown St. Paul in the twentieth century. Built in phases, the new depot went up on the site of the old, permitting the railroads to maintain full service while the new facilities were under construction. Work commenced on the head house building in 1917 with the demolition of several warehouses fronting on Fourth Street between Wacouta and Sibley Streets. Delayed by World War I, the head house was completed in 1920. All work was finished in 1926 with completion of the waiting room, track approaches, platforms, and a roundhouse building and locomotive servicing facilities.

The ticket office, baggage room, passenger waiting room, a large restaurant, a drugstore, and other shops were located on the main floor. Offices for the depot company, an infirmary, playrooms for children, and a women's retiring room with couches, tables, and baths occupied the second. The largest tenant in the building was the U.S. Post Office, which maintained a huge mail-sorting operation. St. Paul was headquarters for the Tenth Division of the U.S. Railway Mail Service. Next to New York and Chicago, it was the third busiest in the country.

Practical rather than pretentious, St. Paul Union Depot was no Grand Central Terminal or Penn Station. It never fulfilled the expectations of its builders or paid off its construction debt, but it was the largest and most important rail passenger station west of Chicago. For fifty-one years, millions of people bought tickets and walked through its lobby and concourse to board waiting trains. Others came to send off friends and family or welcome them home. It sent children off to summer camp and school and young men and women off to war—many never to return. It hosted U.S. presidents and presidents-to-be, royalty, authors, movie stars, the rich and famous, but it also sheltered the homeless and the troubled seeking a warm space on a cold night. It was a place of sounds and smells and every possible emotion and experience. It was built to last forever, and it still stands, but its trains are gone as are the people who rode them.

When planning for St. Paul's new depot got under way, the railroads were moving virtually all of the nation's intercity passenger traffic and most of its freight. A fresh wave of immigration was settling the American West. Yellowstone National Park was attracting eastern tourists—most of them traveling through St. Paul Union Depot—and the Great Northern and Northern Pacific, the two transcontinental roads headquartered in St. Paul, were vying for passengers with two new trains, the *North Coast Limited* on the Northern Pacific and the *Oriental Limited* on the Great Northern.

Prosperity for the passenger business seemed permanent and assured. W. C. Armstrong, chief engineer for the St. Paul Union Depot Company, in a report to the president and board of directors, concluded that, based on the 500,000 passenger cars passing through the depot in 1915 and current trends, the new station could expect 850,000 cars by 1933 and 1,100,000 cars by 1955, when it would reach capacity. The board adopted these projections, but they proved far too optimistic. By the time all work was finished in 1926, the passenger train and the great downtown stations, including St. Paul Union Depot, were already in decline.

There were 200 automobiles licensed in Minnesota in 1900 and no paved roads. By 1913, the year the old depot burned, the number of autos had grown to 37,000, and the good roads movement was well under way. By 1920, the same year that Northwest Airlines won its first airmail contract, there were 320,000 automobiles in the state. Seven years later, in 1927, the year after the depot was completed, there were 648,000 automobiles in Minnesota, and Northwest Airlines had begun scheduled passenger service to Chicago. The following year Northwest Airlines entered into a transcontinental air–rail travel compact with the Great Northern, Baltimore & Ohio, and New York Central railroads providing for rail transportation between St. Paul and Seattle, and Chicago and New York, with connecting air service between St. Paul and Chicago.

When the Bureau of Railway Economics published *A Statistical Review of the Railroad Year 1924*, it noted there were 15 million automobiles in the United States and commented, prophetically: "The American people will have their passenger transportation in the form in which they want it. Although long distance automobile travel is frequently more expensive than travel by rail, even when the latter is undertaken with the most luxurious conditions and environment, yet the pleasure of traveling as a free agent in an individual unit of transportation seems to outweigh, in the minds of many, the comfort, speed and convenience of travel by passenger train."

The intercity passenger train stopped making money in the 1920s, shriveled in the 1930s, and only briefly returned to profitability during World War II. Thereafter, the railroads spent over $500 million of private capital on improved infrastructure and fleets of streamlined trains that were the envy of the world, only to see them bested by Chevrolets and Boeing 707s. By May 1, 1971, when

A grandmotherly farewell, as a young man prepares to board the Milwaukee's *Hiawatha* for Chicago in 1948. Was it his first train trip? Scenes like these were repeated every day for fifty years.

Will it be Eisenhower or Stevenson? The policeman's expression gives it away. Dwight and Mamie Eisenhower on a 1952 campaign stop at St. Paul Union Depot.

Amtrak took over, Minnesota's rail passenger network was down to a handful of intercity trains arriving and departing from a vast, empty St. Paul Union Depot, an expensive reminder of a vanished era.

This book is about the St. Paul Union Depot, but it is also about what economists call *creative destruction,* the process by which technology and innovation drive out the old and bring in the new. Creative destruction is about change. It is relentless, unforgiving, and blind. It has no respect or reverence for the past. However, it is susceptible to perverse public policy, and it is public policy—not technology or market forces—that directed government subsidies to highways and airports and taxed railroads and railroad passenger terminals, which, along with stubborn unions, archaic and often discriminatory government regulation, fickle politicians, and shortsighted management, combined to empty the American passenger train and the great stations, St. Paul Union Depot among them. What the process will bring to rail passenger service in the twenty-first century is unknown. With energy increasingly expensive, there could, and should be, a large-scale revival of the intercity passenger train and a bright future for the St. Paul Union Depot.

The trains are gone, and weeds grow between the rails at St. Paul Union Depot. Soon the tracks will be taken up. Three years after it closed in 1971, St. Paul Union Depot awaits an uncertain future.

In 1912, fifty years after its first trip, the *William Crooks*, Minnesota's first locomotive, rests on display outside the train shed at St. Paul Union Depot. The Great Northern Railway saved the *William Crooks* from the scrapper and brought it out for special occasions. It was put on display inside the depot in 1954 and rested there until it was moved to the Lake Superior Museum of Transportation in Duluth, following the depot's closure.

1
Railroad Avenue

THE SIMPLE, SEVEN-BY-NINE-FOOT FRAME STRUCTURE at the mouth of Phalen Creek went unremarked and unnoticed by the large crowd that had gathered near the levee the morning of June 28, 1862. It was the first railroad station in St. Paul and in Minnesota, but on that day it was an accessory to a more important event. The star was Minnesota's first steam locomotive, the *William Crooks,* about to depart St. Paul for St. Anthony, some ten miles to the west. Governor Sibley and Lieutenant Governor Ignatius Donnelly were there, along with Edmund Rice, president of the St. Paul & Pacific Railroad Company, the mayors of St. Paul and St. Anthony, and Colonel William Crooks, the railroad's chief engineer. Then there was James J. Hill, who would help load freight cars when regular service began three days later. Hill was an associate in the wholesale grocery and freight-forwarding firm of Borup and Champlin. He was seventeen years away from the presidency of the St. Paul, Minneapolis & Manitoba Railway, the future Great Northern, but he already had his sights on the railroad business. In four years Hill would construct a warehouse at the levee and go into business for himself, acquiring adjoining property that would one day be the site of the St. Paul Union Depot.

Shortly before noon the dignitaries boarded the cars, engineer Webster Gardner tugged at the throttle, and the *William Crooks* pulled away from the diminutive depot and commenced its assault on the long grade out of the Mississippi River valley toward St. Anthony. It took a little more than an hour to complete the trip. Scheduled service began on July 2. By October there were four trains each way, daily. A one-way ticket cost 60 cents.

Webster Gardner, the *William Crook*'s first engineer (left), and James J. Hill (right) stand in the cab of the *William Crooks* at St. Paul Union Depot. In 1912 it was a special reunion for two men who were there for the first train in Minnesota. Gardner had a long career with Great Northern. Hill went on to become known as the "Empire Builder," the mightiest railroad baron of the Gilded Age.

This was St. Paul's first railroad, but by 1862 St. Paul was already a gateway city and a transportation hub. In 1835 St. Paul was joined to settlements and trading posts in the Red River Valley by the Red River trails. One trail followed the west side of the Red River to the headwaters of the Minnesota River, then downstream to St. Paul. A second, northern trail was established in the 1840s, running from the vicinity of what is now Breckenridge to St. Cloud, then downriver to St. Paul. Farther north, a third trail, the Woods Trail, extended from the trading post of Crow Wing in the vicinity of Brainerd to the area of today's Detroit Lakes, then northwest to the Red River Valley.

By 1857 some five hundred oxcarts were moving goods to and from the steamboats at St. Paul on a thirty-to-forty day overland trek to the Kittson Trading Post at Pembina. The Red River trails, along with an expansion of steamboat service on the Mississippi, caused the Hudson's Bay Company to divert its European shipments from Hudson Bay to the Red River Trail and a connection with the Mississippi River steamboats at St. Paul. By now, the Mississippi was the Midwest's corridor to the outside world, linking St. Paul to St. Louis, New Orleans, and cities on the Ohio River. In 1844, forty-one steamboats called on St. Paul. Regular service began in 1852. By 1857 there were over a thousand. Beyond St. Paul, there was heavy steamboat traffic on the Minnesota River as far as Mankato. Over four hundred boats plied the Minnesota River to St. Paul in 1862.

The 1850 census found only 6,077 people in the Minnesota Territory, but Indian treaties in 1851, 1854, and 1855 opened most of Minnesota west of the Mississippi to settlement, and people rushed in to make claims. Preemption laws provided that only surveyed lands could be occupied, but the laws were largely ignored and unenforced as thousands of newcomers from eastern states swarmed into the territory. An estimated 20,000 people had arrived by 1852, most of them traveling

Red River oxcarts from the Kittson Trading Post in Pembina rest in downtown St. Paul in 1860. For three decades they linked the steamboats at St. Paul with the hinterlands of Manitoba, the Dakota Territory, and Minnesota. In two years the *William Crooks* will make them obsolete.

by steamboat to St. Paul, where hotels and lodging houses were so overcrowded that people camped in the streets. An 1857 census, taken in anticipation of statehood, identified 150,037 inhabitants in the territory.

Other than the Red River trails, which were little more than ruts on the prairie, 1830s Minnesota had few improved roads. The army built a road between Fort Snelling and Lake Calhoun and another to St. Anthony Falls, and by the time Minnesota became a territory in 1849, there were primitive roads from St. Paul to Fort Snelling, St. Anthony, and Stillwater. Another road ran east to the St. Croix and then south in Wisconsin. A stage road was built in 1848 from Stillwater down the east side of the Mississippi via Prairie du Chien, Wiconsin, to Galena, Illinois, but it was only used in the winter when the Mississippi was impassable.

Congress passed a Minnesota Road Act in 1850, along with a $40,000 appropriation to build a network of military roads in the territory, and in 1851 the Territorial Legislature passed a law requiring able-bodied men between twenty-one and fifty to spend three days a year building roads. But

In 1857 travelers from Chicago and the East could travel by rail as far as Prairie du Chien, Wisconsin. A steamboat was required to journey the rest of the way to St. Paul. The first all-rail route to St. Paul via Prairie du Chien and Austin, Minnesota, opened ten years later.

progress was slow, and settlers and stagecoach companies grew increasingly restless as more people moved into the territory. Taking matters into their own hands, in 1852 settlers in the Minnesota River valley organized a road-building project under the leadership of William Dodd and Auguste Larpenteur with the objective of building a road from St. Paul to St. Peter.

The proposed network of military roads was unfinished in 1858 when Minnesota's statehood ended the federal government's responsibility for roads. Thereafter, state government and local communities and counties became responsible for road construction. The U.S.–Dakota War of 1862 and the Civil War further slowed expansion of the road network, and dray and stagecoach service suffered. At the end of the Civil War, there were some 1,200 miles of stage road in the state.

Railroads seemed to be the answer, and there was no shortage of plans to build them. An 1847 proposal called for the construction of a line from St. Paul and another from Lake Superior. Both were to converge and meet at a point near the Red River and today's Fergus Falls. Territorial governor Alexander Ramsey, speaking to the legislature in 1853, addressed the importance of building lines that would connect the Mississippi River with Lake Superior and the Red River of the North. To further demonstrate the need for railroads, in 1854 promoters organized the widely publicized Great Railroad Excursion from Chicago to St. Paul by way of the just completed Rock Island Railroad to Rock Island, Illinois, then by steamboat to St. Paul. Of greater significance, however, was congressional passage of the Minnesota Enabling Act on February 26, 1857, which allotted government lands in alternate odd-numbered sections within six miles on both sides of a railroad's right-of-way. Speculators took it from there, and within the year the Minnesota Territorial Legislature had given away charters to twenty-seven companies, only to see none of them lay a foot of track. The financial panic of 1857 intervened, land values collapsed, and Minnesota's railroad boom went bust.

Statehood came in 1858, and it brought a revival. Forty-six new charters were awarded, many to holders of the original twenty-seven. Among these ventures were the Minneapolis & Cedar Valley Railroad Company, the Root River Valley & Southern Minnesota Railroad Company, the Minnesota & Pacific Railroad Company, and the Transit Railroad Company. The Minneapolis & Cedar Valley managed to grade about seventy miles of right-of-way south from Minneapolis to Owatonna. The Root River Valley & Southern Minnesota did some preliminary work between Grand Crossing and Houston, and the Minnesota & Pacific graded a short distance between St. Paul and St. Anthony and St. Anthony and St. Cloud. But the effects of the panic lingered, and there were other complications.

To front the cost of construction, the state presented a constitutional amendment to the voters in 1858 that provided for the issuance of Minnesota bonds in an amount not exceeding $1,250,000

The Lower Levee, the future site of St. Paul Union Depot, is a busy place in this 1865 view. St. Paul was at the head of navigation on the Mississippi River. Everything that moved by boat transferred here—to oxcarts and later to trains. The St. Paul & Pacific depot is the small structure to the left of the elevator and James J. Hill's warehouse. Hill saw the future was in railroads, and in a few years he would take control of the St. Paul & Pacific. On the extreme left is a sign for what could be the Minnesota Central's ticket office, presumably for connecting steamboat passengers. The Minnesota Central's depot was then across the Mississippi. It will be four more years before it bridged the river and built its own station on the Lower Levee.

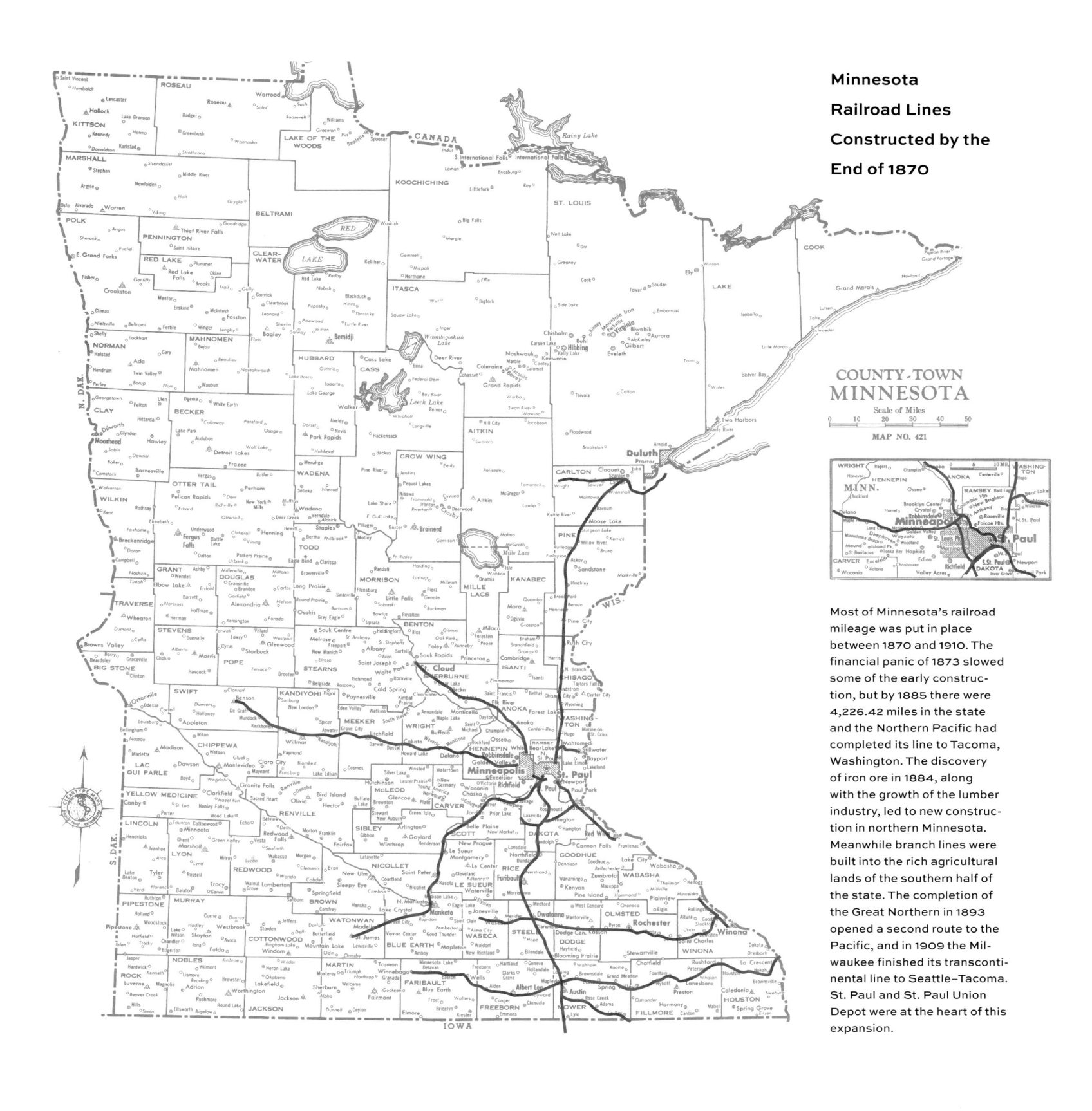

Minnesota Railroad Lines Constructed by the End of 1870

COUNTY-TOWN
MINNESOTA
Scale of Miles
0 10 20 30 40 50

MAP NO. 421

Most of Minnesota's railroad mileage was put in place between 1870 and 1910. The financial panic of 1873 slowed some of the early construction, but by 1885 there were 4,226.42 miles in the state and the Northern Pacific had completed its line to Tacoma, Washington. The discovery of iron ore in 1884, along with the growth of the lumber industry, led to new construction in northern Minnesota. Meanwhile branch lines were built into the rich agricultural lands of the southern half of the state. The completion of the Great Northern in 1893 opened a second route to the Pacific, and in 1909 the Milwaukee finished its transcontinental line to Seattle–Tacoma. St. Paul and St. Paul Union Depot were at the heart of this expansion.

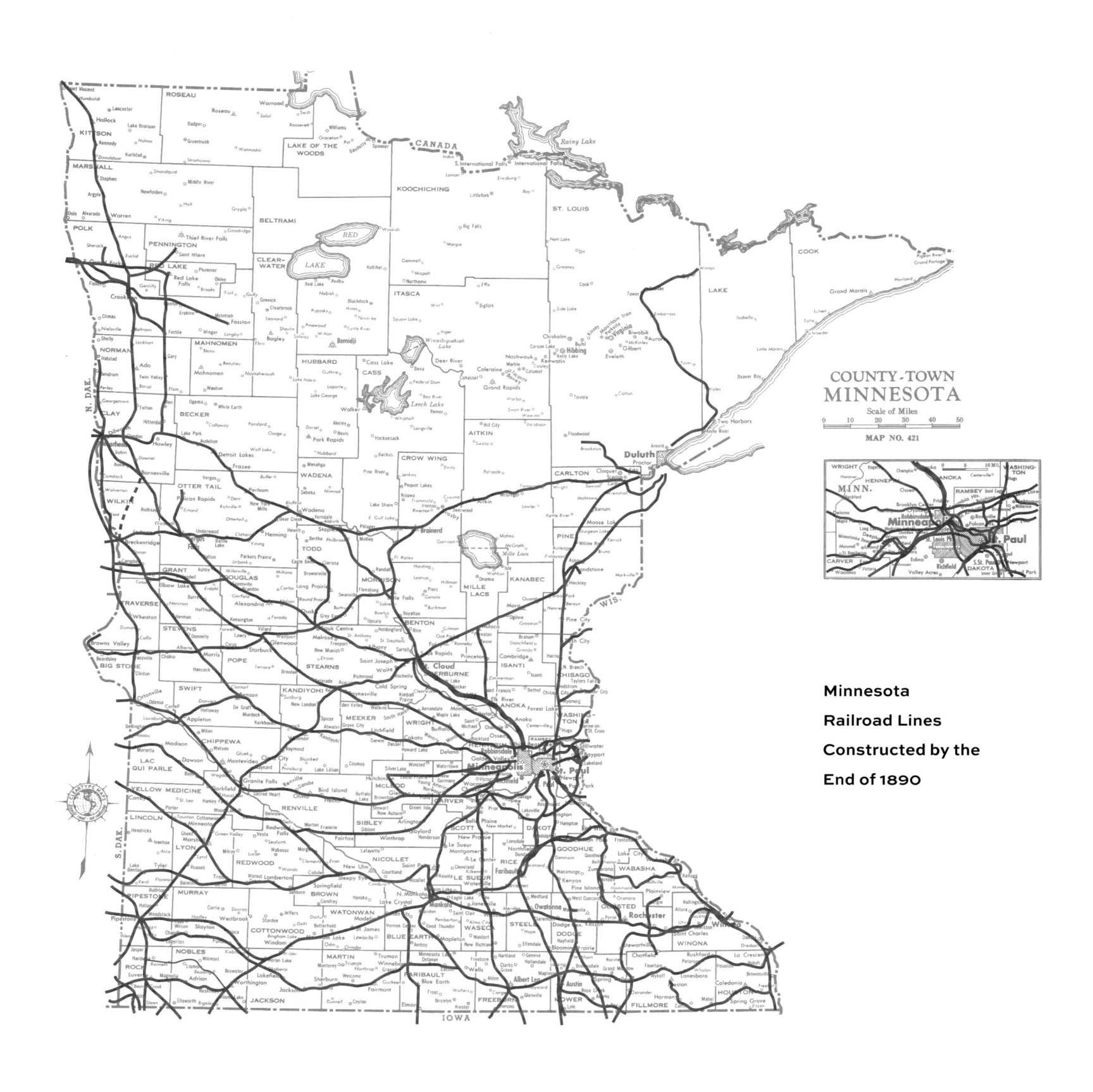

COUNTY-TOWN
MINNESOTA
Scale of Miles
0 10 20 30 40 50

MAP NO. 421

Minnesota Railroad Lines Constructed by the End of 1890

County-Town Minnesota

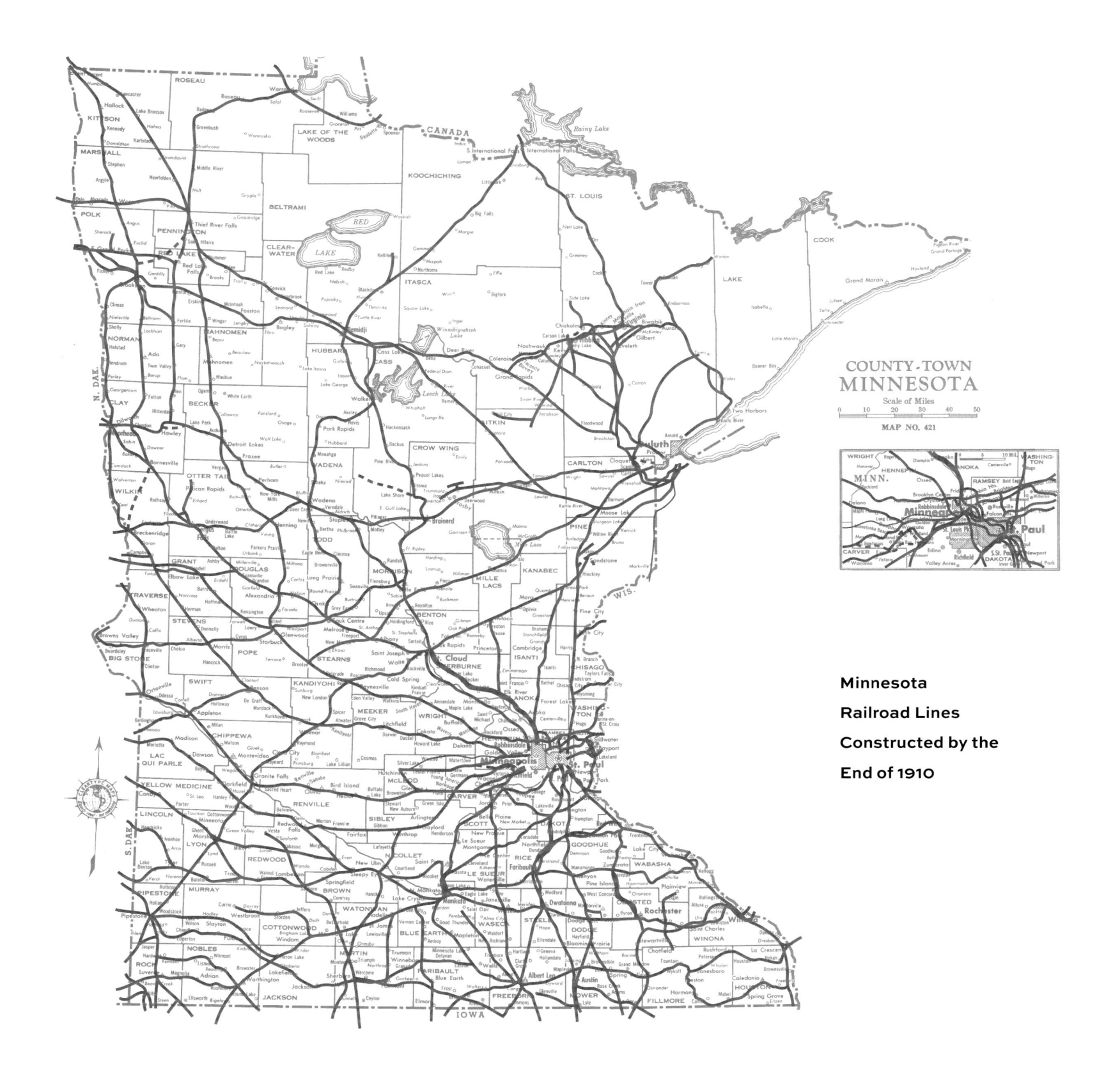

Map No. 421

Minnesota Railroad Lines Constructed by the End of 1910

to each of the four companies. The amendment passed and the bonds were issued, but none of the companies were able to complete construction and commence operations within the time limits specified in the bonds or their charters. Worse, the amendment provided that the railroads themselves were to guarantee the bonds by mortgaging their assets. The state had appropriated no money to secure them. When the companies failed to perform, their assets became worthless, as did the bonds, and the entire financing plan collapsed.

It would take four more years to finish the first ten miles while promoters and financiers struggled to raise capital amid the economic turmoil at the start of the Civil War. Frustrated, the state revoked the charter of the Minnesota & Pacific, and a new venture, the St. Paul & Pacific, took over and finally completed the line to St. Anthony. Rails reached Anoka in 1864, and as the Civil War came to an end and capital became available, a building boom got underway that would, by 1885, see four thousand miles of track put down in Minnesota, along with a Pacific extension to Tacoma and connecting lines to adjoining states. Minnesota became a state in 1858, but it was the railroads that brought it into the Union.

Minnesota had almost half its railroad mileage in place by 1885, just twenty-three years after the *William Crooks* covered the first ten miles between St. Paul and St. Anthony. But there was more work to be done, and the rail network would eventually grow to 9,400 miles as the iron ore lines were completed in northern Minnesota and a web of branch lines blanketed the state.

Consolidation came in the 1880s and 1890s as the railroads, confronting competitive pressures and the need to raise fresh capital, looked for operating efficiencies to improve earnings and pay off debt. Twenty-five railroad companies reported to the Minnesota Railroad and Warehouse Commission in 1890. Through consolidations, that number eventually declined to nine large systems and a handful of shorter lines. All nine were centered on the Twin Cities. Three of them—the Great Northern, the Northern Pacific, and the Chicago, St. Paul, Minneapolis & Omaha Railway (controlled by Chicago & North Western)—had their corporate headquarters in St. Paul. Two—the Minneapolis & St. Louis and the Minneapolis, St. Paul & Sault Ste. Marie (Soo Line)—were headquartered in Minneapolis. The other four—the Chicago, Burlington & Quincy (Burlington); Chicago Great Western (Great Western); Chicago, Milwaukee & St. Paul (Milwaukee Road); and the Rock Island—located major yards and shop facilities in the area.

Between 1880 and 1910, Minnesota's population jumped from 780,000 to more than 2,000,000, and railroad traffic followed apace. Tonnage in all commodities doubled and even tripled. Trains handled 5 million passengers in 1900, 14 million in 1910. Railroad revenues more than

Between 1880 and 1910, thousands of European arrivals passed through St. Paul and St. Paul Union Depot on their way to a new life in Minnesota and the Dakotas. There were no amenities on these immigrant trains. People, sometimes their animals, and all their worldly goods traveled together, hoping for a brighter future and a fresh start. Engraving circa 1886.

doubled, from $44,950,093 in 1900 to $99,804,007 in 1910. A great railroad avenue had emerged that brought prosperity to every town and hamlet, and whether it was a crate of freight or a trip to the big city, the journey along that avenue began at the depot.

Depot Place

Few communities prospered without a rail connection, and as the system expanded and towns grew up along the railroad network, the railroad depot competed with the general store, the feed mill, the post office, and even the church as the center of town life. The relative importance and wealth of a community were reflected in the size and splendor of its depot, which ranged from the grand new terminals that would be erected in St. Paul, Minneapolis, and Duluth to a portable depot set on a gravel foundation. The latter was often an ordinary boxcar that had been shorn of its wheels and trucks and then dropped along the right-of-way at some new town site. If the community grew, and with it railroad revenues, the temporary structure might be replaced with a larger building of standard design. Some small stations were never staffed, and trains stopped only if they were flagged or signaled to stop by a waiting passenger. These flag stops were listed in the public timetables but were nothing more than open shelters with three sides and a roof. The Twin City Rapid Transit Company, the Minneapolis, Northfield & Southern (Dan Patch Line), and other roads with suburban commuter service built dozens of them around the Twin Cities. Other flag stations in rural areas were fully enclosed buildings but went unstaffed except for the occasional trackman or caretaker who came by to clean it.

For convenience and safety, railroads took care to site station buildings along single-track lines on the side of the track where most of their business originated. This minimized the need for people and wagons to cross the tracks at grade in front of approaching trains. On double-track lines, station buildings were usually erected along the track where the greatest number of passengers boarded. Thus, stations were typically constructed along the inbound track on lines approaching the Twin Cities.

Railroad depots were always busy places at train time, but this Winona crowd, boarding a Chicago-bound train, is exceptionally large, suggesting it is a special trip. The clothes and the automobiles suggest it may have been a group traveling to Chicago for some special event sometime around 1929 or 1930.

RAILROAD AVENUE   23

"Form follows function." In the 1920s this simple shelter greeted arriving and departing campers at Lake Hubert, north of Brainerd, on the Northern Pacific's line to International Falls. Today, the railroad line is the Paul Bunyan State Trail, and the shelter survives for the benefit of hikers and cyclists.

The depot reflected the aspirations of the community, but it was also there to do the business of the railroad. Whether it was a boxcar at a new town site or a big city terminal, the depot was there to serve the needs of the railroad and its customers.

At the depot travelers could inquire about schedules, purchase tickets, and wait for trains, or for friends and relatives to gather to greet arrivals. At larger stations, the American Railway Engineering Association recommended, and Victorian custom required, that there be separate waiting rooms so women and children could retire from the boisterous, cigar-smoking, snooze-chewing male passengers. Restrooms had to be provided, and at a time when most households made do with outdoor privies, the depot might be one of the few buildings in town with indoor plumbing.

Depots in smaller towns might be open only ten to twelve hours a day. Others operated twenty-four hours a day, seven days a week, and were staffed around the clock, sometimes with both a telegrapher and a station agent on duty at any given time. More often it was a single agent on duty, and it was this agent who confronted multiple tasks, from planning travel itineraries and selling tickets to checking baggage and handling express, all the while with an ear to the telegraph wire.

The depot might be a quiet place for most of the day, but train arrivals and departures turned quiet to chaos. There would be a queue at the ticket window and baggage to be checked in the baggage room and then piled aboard a wagon, along with bags of mail and express. The wagon then had to be towed to the platform to be positioned for loading in the baggage car. There might be orders telegraphed from the dispatcher that had to be copied and handed off to the train crew. Once the train departed, the agent noted its arrival and departure time on a "train sheet" and telegraphed the times back to the dispatcher. The lone agent had a day's work packed into the half hour before train time, and with several arrivals and departures each day, the hours in between offered a welcome rest.

But there were other things to do. There were floors to sweep, and in the winter, the platform had to be kept clear of snow and ice. Freight, mail, baggage, and express business occupied a considerable part of the agent's day. Before there were paved roads, everything moved in and out of town by rail, and the agent was responsible for every shipment, whether it was a carload of canned goods or a sack of mail. Carload shipments required that the consignee be notified and arrangements made for unloading the car, which was usually spotted on a siding adjoining the depot. Less-than-carload freight was another matter. The agent, or sometimes a paid helper, would unload the contents for storage in the baggage room. At larger towns, or where there was enough business, there might be a freight agent, and freight and express shipments would be handled in a separate building.

Then there were the inevitable reports and paperwork. Ticket sales had to be recorded and waybills completed. The dispatcher had to be notified when there were cars to be picked up, and if a shipper needed a car, the agent had to order one.

In small-town Minnesota the agent was the official representative of the railroad, and the position was held in high regard. The agent was expected to know all aspects of the railroad's operation and the territory it covered including passenger train schedules, freight routings and tariffs, as well as the schedules and routings of connecting carriers. The agent was also expected to be informed about local business and economic conditions, crop and agricultural reports, and any other matters that might affect railroad business and report them to the railroad's traffic departments.

The long-distance telephone did not come into widespread practical use until after World War I, and in an era when all long-distance communication was by telegraph or U.S. mail, the agent was the town's only link with the outside world. Each station had its own call sign, and the agent-operator had to be alert for those two or three letters, amid the constant clicking of the sounder, that indicated there was incoming traffic for his station. It might be routine railroad business like a train order, a switch list, or a confirmation of a Pullman reservation. But there was other traffic and business to be done as well. The depot was usually the local Western Union office. Town residents would go to the depot to send personal and business messages. The local newspaper relied on the depot telegraph for news reports, election results, and market quotations. Official time signals were sent out on the telegraph wire. To get the exact time, one would check with the depot agent.

There was always something happening at the depot. Old-timers congregated on benches on the station platform to swap stories and reminisce. Traveling salesmen compared notes and bragged about their latest big business deal or romantic conquest. There was a map on the wall near the

Great Northern agent Harry Ellis relaxes in the office of the Solway, Minnesota, depot. A typewriter, used for copying train orders and telegrams, rests to the left of the telephone and telegraph instruments on the table. A hoop for handing up orders to passing trains hangs on the wall. A time signal was transmitted over the telegraph line every day to check the station clock for accuracy. The cabinet behind Ellis held forms and tariff books.

Every depot was a gathering place to wait for trains or, in the case of these old-timers at North Redwood, Minnesota, just to pass the time of day.

ticket office that displayed the extent of the railroad system and its connections along with racks of brochures and timetables. Children, especially young boys, would gather to listen to the telegraph or observe the work of the agent. A few lucky ones might be invited into the office to learn telegraphy or perhaps earn a dime or two running errands. When a train arrived, they could watch the engineer as he came down from the cab to oil around the huge, panting steam locomotive. If it needed water, the fireman would climb up on the tender, swing the long spout from the water tank into position, and let hundreds of gallons of water spill into the tender. If it overflowed, and it usually did, everyone got a good soaking—welcome on a hot summer day.

Train time meant welcoming hugs, tearful good-byes, and strangers to watch, and the local newspaper editor would be sure to have a young spotter at the depot to search out stories. Then there were special trains. Politicians would show up to electioneer and make speeches from the open platform of an observation car. A circus or carnival might come to town by train, unload at the depot, and then parade down the main street. There were special trains for revivalists, immigrants, and agricultural exhibits.

By the end of the 1900s, Minnesota's railroads evolved a series of standard depot designs, specific to each company, and replicated in the various communities served by each railroad. These combination depots accommodated both freight and passenger services. They varied in size, depending on the volume of business, but they typically featured a freight and baggage room at one end of the building with a scale for weighing shipments. Sometimes a separate, insulated room might be provided for temperature-sensitive or perishable commodities such as milk or cream.

The passenger waiting room was either in the middle of the building or at the end opposite the freight and baggage room. Entrance was usually by a doorway to the train platform, but often a separate entrance was provided leading to the street or, in larger stations, a covered carriageway. Accommodations were simple in small stations—nothing more than a few wood benches, a train bulletin board showing arrival and departure times, and a clock. A large wood or coal stove provided heat. There was no indoor plumbing.

Larger stations offered more amenities. There was central heat, indoor plumbing, electric lighting, terrazzo or tile floors, plastered walls, and wainscoting. There might be a large wall map of the railroad system and a rack with travel brochures and railroad timetables.

The agent's office was located trackside at the center of the building with a bay window arrangement permitting a clear view in both directions up and down the tracks. Entrance to the office was through a door to the waiting room, although there was sometimes a separate office entrance from the station platform—a considerable convenience for the agent, trainmen, or others who had business in the office.

Outside the agent's office, mounted on a pole or attached to the side or roof of the building, was a train order semaphore (or light) that could be controlled by the agent inside the office. Its purpose was to advise approaching trains to stop for passengers or to pick up orders from the dispatcher. Such orders, for example, might advise of track conditions or instruct the crew to take a siding to clear an opposing train. These form 31 orders required the signatures of the conductor and the engineer. Another class of train order, form 19, did not require the train to stop or the crew's signatures and were handed up on a hoop by the agent as the train passed the station at speed.

The ticket window opened into the waiting room, except where there were separate waiting rooms for men and women. Then it typically faced a passageway opposite the men's and women's restrooms.

Some ticket forms were preprinted, and the agent simply validated the ticket with a date stamp. This made for a very simple transaction providing the destination was on the same line and no more than one train was involved. But ticketing could be involved and time-consuming, especially for

Depots often had second-floor living quarters for agents and their families. In 1910, the agent at Solana, Minnesota, on the Soo's Brooten–Duluth line, stands on the station platform with his two young children.

long-distance travel where more than one railroad was involved. For example, if one was traveling from Sauk Centre on the Great Northern to Philadelphia via the Pennsylvania Railroad, complexities multiplied. Between Sauk Centre and St. Paul, a standard Great Northern ticket form sufficed. Beyond St. Paul the agent would have to write up separate ticket forms for each railroad. Between St. Paul and Chicago, it might be the Burlington, the Milwaukee Road, or the Omaha. Beyond Chicago it would be the Pennsylvania. If a Pullman reservation was desired between Chicago and Philadelphia, the agent would have to wire the Pennsylvania's reservation bureau in Chicago and secure the space before writing up a separate Pullman ticket. Travel plans had to be made well in advance so that there would be sufficient time to complete the ticketing process.

Railroads occasionally provided living quarters in the depot for the agent and the agent's family. This was more common in the West, such as in the Dakotas or Montana, where communities were more isolated and suitable living arrangements more difficult to come by. However, there were a number of them in Minnesota, and all of the major carriers had them. As employers, the railroads felt that married agents with families were more stable and dependable and better representatives for the company, particularly in newly developed frontier settlements where saloons outnumbered other businesses. A live-in employee also meant that someone would be available around the clock

A train arrives at the Redwood Falls, Minnesota, depot. The mighty Sears retail empire got started here in 1886, when agent Richard Sears began selling watches to other station agents up and down the line. The business was so good that Sears began selling other items and was soon making more money as a retailer than as a railroad station agent. The building was moved to the Redwood County Fairgrounds but was destroyed in an accidental fire in 1961.

should some special need or emergency arise. The railroads frequently kept large cash receipts on hand, and having someone on the premises discouraged burglary. Thus, the railroads were willing to make the extra investment in a larger building, typically by adding a second story to accommodate living quarters, although some designs had them on the ground floor.

One such station was at Redwood Falls in Minnesota on the Minneapolis & St. Louis line to Watertown, South Dakota. In 1886 its agent, Richard Sears, took to supplementing his railroad income when the town jeweler refused a shipment of watches. Sears bought them and began selling them, along with other items, to station agents in other towns. The watches were popular and sold quickly. Sears contracted with the watchmaker for more and then began taking out advertisements in town newspapers. The orders kept coming, leading to what would eventually become the giant mail order firm of Sears Roebuck & Company.

Whether it was a small town or a terminal in a major city, the depot was the gateway to the community, and residents always wanted to give travelers the best impression. When this desire coincided with the business interests of the railroad, the result was a handsome building that satisfied everyone's needs. When it didn't, there were complaints. Letters of protest were written to railroad officials, government regulators, and elected representatives. The most frequently expressed concern was that the depot was too small—although in fairness, a railroad typically sized a depot according to the volume of business. Stone or brick construction was always preferable to wood because it presented a look of permanence and durability. Sometimes there was dissatisfaction with maintenance. Public spaces were often dirty due to male passengers smoking cigars or chewing tobacco and spitting on the floor. While public behavior was not the responsibility of the railroads, they did nonetheless incorporate separate waiting rooms for men and women in their larger stations.

The depot's location sometimes aroused the ire of town officials, especially if it was a considerable distance from the principal business district. Town elders, for obvious reasons, always wanted it as close to the main street as possible. New towns generally grew up around the railroad, but in established communities natural features and construction costs more often determined the routing of a line through or around a community and, with it, the placement of the railroad depot. A somewhat perverse exception occurred at Wayzata, just west of Minneapolis. Wayzata grew up as a fashionable resort community on Lake Minnetonka. The St. Paul & Pacific built a line through Wayzata in 1867, locating its tracks and the depot along the lakefront on the town's main street. As time passed, Wayzata and Lake Minnetonka became extremely popular with tourists, who flocked to lakefront hotels and businesses. It was only then that local officials began complaining about

The first St. Paul & Pacific train arrived at Wayzata in 1867. Wayzata was already a resort community when the railroad came in 1867, and over the years, its proximity to the Twin Cities made it even more so. This photograph was taken looking east on the lakefront, near where today's downtown Wayzata is located, to the left.

the noise and disruption created by the comings and goings of trains on its main street. Getting no satisfaction from the railroad, Wayzata sued, and in 1883 a court ordered the railroad to relocate its tracks. Furious, Manitoba president James J. Hill complied with the court ruling and ordered the tracks moved, but in a blow to Wayzata, he directed that the depot be relocated a mile out of town. Hill finally relented in 1906 and returned the depot to its original site. For twenty-three years Wayzata had to endure the inconvenience, although Hill ultimately redeemed himself with a fine new building that fronted on the downtown and the lake.

The new Wayzata depot exemplified an evolution in the thinking of railroad executives about the role of the depot in the community and the image that it projected for the railroad. The distinctive English Tudor-style depot, which stands today and is home to the Wayzata Historical Society, was designed by St. Paul architect Samuel Bartlett, whose work for the Great Northern railroad included the lodges at Glacier National Park. Its overall size and floor plan is that of a typical combination depot, but the type and use of materials set it apart. By 1900 Minnesota railroads were turning away from wood-framed structures and constructing new or replacement depots of brick, stone, or stucco with tile roofs. Wood floors disappeared, replaced by tile or terrazzo. Central heat and indoor plumbing replaced the stove and outhouse. Landscaping became important. Lawns, flowers, hedges, and ornamental plantings created parklike settings. The former Northern Pacific depot in Little Falls, Minnesota, is another example of this trend. In 1899 the railroad commissioned architect Cass Gilbert to design a new depot as part of a line relocation project, replacing a structure destroyed in an 1897 fire. Built at a cost of $12,000, the Tudor-Craftsman-style building of brick and sandstone construction is today home to the Little Falls Chamber of Commerce. There are more. The Chicago, St. Paul, Minneapolis & Omaha constructed substantial new depots in Mankato and Worthington. Just across the state line in Fargo, North Dakota, the Great Northern erected a large passenger station in 1906–7 to replace an 1881 structure deemed inadequate. Topped by a thirty-five-foot clock tower, the all-masonry Richardsonian Romanesque structure, which stands today, is 240 feet long and 40 feet wide. As built, it featured separate men's and women's waiting rooms, a ticket office, and a baggage room. A lunch counter and a separate express building were added in later years. It was one of the finest stations on the Great Northern system.

Larger facilities were typically found at division points where engine and/or train crews were changed and the railroads maintained shops and roundhouses. Fargo was one such location. In Minnesota, others were Mankato, St. James, Waseca, Worthington, Montevideo, Tracy, St. Cloud, Glenwood, Albert Lea, Brainerd, Breckenridge, Barnesville, Willmar, and Staples. At division points

James J. Hill, president of the Great Northern, ordered this beautiful English Tudor–style depot, which is shown with a train arriving sometime after it opened in 1906. Today, the building is preserved and is home to the Wayzata Historical Society.

Wayzata station agent Bob Rossler is shown at work transmitting a message on the telegraph key in the station office. Before and during World War II the depot was staffed twenty-four hours a day, seven days a week. A station baggage man was available during the summer months to handle the additional tourist traffic. When the Great Northern installed centralized traffic control west of Wayzata after World War II, there was no longer a need for the depot to remain open continuously as a train order office. Thereafter, the depot went to a five-day-per-week schedule. It was closed in the 1970s and the building was given to the Wayzata Historical Society, which has preserved it as a museum. The building is open to visitors during the summer months.

NORTHERN PACIFIC DEPOT, LITTLE FALLS, MINN.

Famed architect Cass Gilbert designed Little Falls's 1899 depot, replacing an earlier structure that was destroyed by fire. Little Falls became a busy junction point once the Northern Pacific completed its Staples cutoff between Little Falls and Staples in 1886. The new main line bypassed Brainerd, considerably shortening the route between the Twin Cities and points west. The old line through Brainerd, however, remained an important link to northern Minnesota's lake country and International Falls. With passenger and freight trains diverging in both directions, Little Falls saw dozens of passenger and freight trains every day. Passenger trains no longer stop in Little Falls, and while the cutoff is among the busiest lines on the Burlington Northern Santa Fe system, train dispatching is centralized and depots are no longer needed. Today the depot has been beautifully restored and is home to the Little Falls Chamber of Commerce.

the depots, besides the regular passenger and freight functions, might house administrative offices of the division superintendent, who was responsible for all operations within that division, the division dispatcher, the roadmaster (track maintenance), and the road foreman of engines (who supervised all locomotive engineers in the division). They were kept open twenty-four hours a day, seven days a week, with a staff of passenger and freight agents, telegraphers, and express and baggage handlers. Some had station restaurants that accommodated waiting passengers or provided meal

St. Cloud, Minnesota, was a division point on the Great Northern Railway and home to a large car repair shop. Its depot was at the center of a wye track formed by the junction of its east–west and north–south lines. This view, dating from about 1905, shows an early automobile and a horse-drawn omnibus, presumably awaiting the passenger train that has just pulled to a stop.

Mankato's Chicago, St. Paul, Minneapolis & Omaha depot housed offices of the division superintendent and dispatcher on the second floor and a large waiting room and lunchroom on the ground floor. Shown here around 1910, it was a division point with passenger trains arriving and departing for the Twin Cities; Omaha; Sioux City, Iowa; Chicago; and Rapid City, South Dakota.

stops for those trains that didn't offer dining cars. In Minneapolis and St. Paul the railroads maintained centrally located downtown ticket offices as a convenience for business travelers.

By the early 1870s, Minnesota railroads came to recognize the operational advantages and economies that could be had by consolidating terminal operations for both passenger and freight services. Why have three or four separate depots when one would better serve the needs of the traveler and the railroad companies and do so far more cost-effectively? In smaller town and cities that were served by two or more railroads, this was not as important an issue, but in St. Paul, Minneapolis, and Duluth it became a matter of some urgency for the railroads as well as the political and the business community.

A small town, especially if it was on a branch line, had less frequent passenger service—typically two trains in each direction each day. If it was served by two railroads, there was virtually no economic incentive for the competing roads to merge operations at one depot, even where their tracks were side by side. There were exceptions. At Shakopee, the Omaha and the Milwaukee Road initially built separate stations even though their tracks were parallel and eventually crossed. Then in 1914 the Omaha constructed a new depot, and the Milwaukee Road moved in. The same was true in nearby Chaska, where the Minneapolis & St. Louis and Milwaukee Road tracks crossed not far from the center of town. Both originally had separate depots. The Milwaukee Road closed its station and moved into the Minneapolis & St. Louis's. In both instances, the Milwaukee Road became a tenant of the owning railroad.

The owner-tenant relationship at these joint facilities was the same as at the larger passenger stations that were erected in Minneapolis, Duluth, and Mankato. In Minneapolis the Great Northern owned its namesake Great Northern Station, which hosted trains of the Northern Pacific; Chicago, Burlington & Quincy; Chicago Great Western; and the Minneapolis & St. Louis. Similarly, the Milwaukee Road's new Minneapolis depot, constructed in 1900, accommodated its trains along with those of the Rock Island and the Soo Line. Here, as was the case in Shakopee and Chaska, the tenant railroads paid the owning road for the use of its station. At Shakopee and Chaska, where the Milwaukee Road furnished its own agent, it paid a fee for use of the space. At the Great Northern and Milwaukee Road stations in Minneapolis, where the owning road provided staff and support facilities, the tenants paid a usage fee according to a formula that took into consideration the number of cars and locomotives handled at the station, tickets sold, and the volume of mail and express moved by depot employees. Duluth's Union Depot was a separate company, totally controlled by its owner, the Northern Pacific, with tenants Great Northern and Duluth, Missabe & Iron Range. Chicago, St. Paul, Minneapolis & Omaha owned and controlled Mankato's depot, with the Chicago & North Western as a tenant.

In St. Paul the railroads formed a union depot company that was owned and controlled by all of the railroads serving the city—an arrangement that was not the first choice of its principal sponsor but one that would be associated with him and his railroad until the final Burlington Northern passenger train departed St. Paul.

Union Station

James J. Hill led the St. Paul, Minneapolis & Manitoba and the Great Northern from 1879 to 1914. Hill instinctively understood how to run a railroad. From his surveyors and engineers he demanded "the best possible line, shortest distance, lowest grades and least curvature that we can build." From his operating and mechanical departments, he demanded trains that moved tonnage at the lowest possible expense. His distaste for inefficiency was exceeded only by his disdain for organized labor and the Northern Pacific. The former wanted more money—in his view—for less work. The latter stole business from his St. Paul, Minneapolis & Manitoba. He was an immovable object against irresistible forces, whether it was employees competing for a share of company profits or rivals poaching traffic from the Manitoba. But he was also a pragmatist who understood when it was time to compromise and do business with his rivals.

Hill arrived in St. Paul in 1856. Then a young man, just eighteen years old, he had aspired to seek his fortune in the Orient but quickly grasped the burgeoning opportunities in the steamboat business, which had seen the number of boats on the upper Mississippi grow from 85 in 1849 to 837 in 1856. His first job was with the firm of Brunson, Lewis & White, agents for the Dubuque Packet Company, followed by several years at the firm of Borup & Champlin, wholesale grocers. Hill learned the intricacies of the shipping and freight-forwarding business and advanced himself in St. Paul's growing business community, making important connections with prominent and influential entrepreneurs of the day. By 1874 Hill was in the coal business, owned a warehouse on St. Paul's levee, from which he ran his own freight-forwarding company, and, along with his partners, Chauncey and Alexander Griggs and Norman Kittson, acquired a monopoly on the Red River steamboat trade. He was also involved in the affairs of several smaller St. Paul businesses.

Hill knew the future was in railroading and had a careful eye on the struggling St. Paul & Pacific, which had come under the influence of the Northern Pacific, after one of its two constituent companies defaulted on the interest on its bonds. That was in 1872. A year later, financier Jay Cooke, the Northern Pacific's chief financial backer, ran aground when his bank, Jay Cooke and Company, failed, bringing on the financial panic of 1873 and forcing the Northern Pacific itself into bankruptcy. Hill saw an opportunity. The St. Paul & Pacific was in receivership and effectively under the thumb of a consortium of Dutch bondholders, and they wanted to get their money out of the railroad. There was no way that he could possibly arrange the necessary financing on his own, but Hill had wealthy, powerful friends who had confidence in him and were willing to take the risk. After six years of complicated financial maneuvering, Hill and his associates—John S. Kennedy, Norman Kittson, Donald Smith, and George Stephen—took control of the St. Paul & Pacific and reorganized it as the Minneapolis, St. Paul & Manitoba.

The Manitoba was one of seven railroads that showed St. Paul on its passenger timetables. Their trains arrived and departed from separate stations that mixed passengers with the handling of freight. The stations were small and crowded, located on or near the levee, an arrangement that was unsatisfactory and unsustainable, especially as traffic grew and St. Paul changed from river town to railroad hub. The railroads wanted to expand and improve their passenger facilities at the lowest possible expense. A shared terminal was clearly the best option, but agreement proved difficult. Hill supported a shared facility, but he wanted one under his control and that of the Manitoba. However, he was distracted by the reorganization of the Manitoba and needed funds to support that reorganization and sustain his investment, which consisted of his entire personal fortune. Reluctantly, he agreed to a jointly owned union depot and pledged to sell to the union depot company the land at the foot of Sibley Street where his career began some twelve years before. He wrote to his friend and associate George Stephen: "I assure you that it was the hardest thing I have had to do in the whole enterprise . . . to forever part with terminal property, knowing that my views might not prove to be as advantageous as I now believe them to be. The price is a very large one and the money will be of great use to us, and I believe we have everything left which our line can possibly want even if it were 2,000 miles long."

Designed by local architect Leroy S. Buffington, St. Paul's first union depot opened in 1881. It replaced the four separate stations then used by the railroads serving the city. The building sustained massive damage in an 1884 fire but was rebuilt using the same plans and specifications. There were further improvements in subsequent years, but the building was again claimed by fire in 1913. The present depot took its place.

2

St. Paul and Its Railroads

President Abraham Lincoln signed the Homestead Act on May 20, 1862, granting 160 acres of undeveloped government land to anyone who was willing to settle, improve, and live on it. Two years later on July 2, 1864, he signed the charter of the Northern Pacific Railway, the nation's second transcontinental railroad. The rush was on. By 1873 the Northern Pacific had stretched its line to the Missouri. The year before it had opened a colonization office in Europe to lure newcomers to the prairies. Over the next three decades, other railroads, notably the Minneapolis, St. Paul & Manitoba, would do the same. Between 1870 and 1890 the population of Montana, the Dakotas, Minnesota, and western Wisconsin grew from 700,000 to nearly 3 million, an increase of some 2.2 million people, of which 1.5 million were immigrants, half coming from the eastern United States and the other half from Europe, mainly Germany and Scandinavia. Of these, half would settle and develop new farms while the rest moved into rural towns and hamlets that followed the expanding railroad web. This was one of the greatest migrations in recorded history, and the railroads made it happen. In the twenty years between 1870 and 1890, some 5 percent of the hot-rolled iron and steel production of the United States was used to lay rails from St. Paul to the west. Mark Twain had observed that St. Paul was a city of commerce, and so it was, as St. Paul began its transition from a gateway city for oxcarts and steamboats to its new preeminence as a gateway city for the railroads that would replace them.

The Civil War slowed new railroad construction. The St. Paul & Pacific managed to replace its original St. Paul depot with a larger structure and extend its line to Anoka by 1864, but material and capital shortages and the U.S.–Dakota War of 1862 slowed further new railroad construction out of St. Paul and elsewhere in the state.

The end of the Civil War brought the Minnesota Valley Railroad (the future Omaha) and the Minnesota Central (the future Milwaukee Road) onto the scene. Both roads did some preliminary work in 1864. The Minnesota Valley line set about arranging financing and acquiring its first locomotive, while the Minnesota Central began grading and laying track from Mendota north toward

The Minnesota Valley Railroad (later the Omaha) reached Mendota from Savage in 1865 and continued on to West St. Paul via Mendota in 1866. It was in Mankato by 1868 and St. James in 1870. Its first locomotive was this rather odd-looking combination steam engine and passenger car named the *Shakopee*. The *Shakopee* was loaned to the Northern Pacific in 1870 and used as a pay car. It was scrapped in the late 1870s.

Minneapolis and south toward Northfield and Faribault. There was more progress in 1865. The Minnesota Central opened its line to Faribault on October 18, 1865. A December 1865 timetable showed a passenger train departing Minneapolis at 7:10 a.m. and returning to Minneapolis from Faribault at 9:20 p.m. Stagecoaches from Faribault allowed travelers to reach points in southern Minnesota. Meanwhile, the Minnesota Valley began construction at a point near Credit River (today's Savage), building north toward Mendota and south toward Shakopee and Mankato, reaching Mendota in October 1865. There, a connection was made with the Minnesota Central.

Both railroads subsequently signed an agreement providing that the Minnesota Valley would construct a line from Mendota to West St. Paul that would be used jointly with the Minnesota Central. In exchange, the Minnesota Valley would have rights into Minneapolis over the Minnesota Central. The line from Mendota to West St. Paul was completed in August 1866. Until then, passengers had to use stagecoach and/or steamboat service to reach St. Paul from Mendota. By August 1866, three railroads and two depots served St. Paul. One, the St. Paul & Pacific's, was on the levee at St. Paul; a second, across the Mississippi in West St. Paul, was used jointly by the Minnesota Central and the Minnesota Valley.

The joint agreement between the Minnesota Valley and the Minnesota Central was the first of its kind in Minnesota. They followed it in 1869 with a second agreement that provided for construction of a bridge over the Mississippi south of Mendota and a joint line and depot facilities on the levee in St. Paul. By 1870 the Minnesota Valley reached St. James, Minnesota, becoming the St. Paul & Sioux City that same year.

Meanwhile the Minnesota Central was pushing its line south from Faribault, reaching Owatonna in August 1866 and a connection with the Winona & St. Peter. In October 1867 the Minnesota Central reached Austin, Minnesota, meeting the McGregor Western, which had built north from the Iowa border. Both railroads had earlier come under the control of the Milwaukee & St. Paul. One month later, just five years after the *William Crooks* made its first trip and some ten years after the Great Railroad Excursion from Chicago to St. Paul, the railroad inaugurated the first through passenger train between the Twin Cities and Chicago and St. Paul's first all-rail link to markets and manufacturing centers in the East. By 1869 the *Eastern Express* was advertising through sleeping cars to Chicago. This route would lose some of its importance and passenger traffic just three years later in 1872, when the Milwaukee & St. Paul acquired the St. Paul & Chicago Railroad Company, which had just completed a line up the west bank of the Mississippi River from La Crescent, Minnesota, opening a much faster route to the east.

The Minnesota Central built north from Mendota up the Mississippi River toward Minneapolis and south toward Faribault in 1864, reaching Faribault in 1865 and Austin in 1867. That year it was acquired by the Milwaukee & St. Paul, opening a through route to Chicago. This 1880 view shows the Milwaukee & St. Paul tracks below Fort Snelling. A small depot and siding for the fort are visible, as is the Minnesota River bridge in the distance. Today the line is the Minnehaha Trail, connecting Fort Snelling State Park to Minnehaha Park in Minneapolis.

The Milwaukee & St. Paul became the Chicago, Milwaukee & St. Paul in 1874. That year a Chicago-bound train *(right)* and two locals wait at the Austin, Minnesota, depot.

Milwaukee & St. Paul's *Eastern Express*, the first through train between St. Paul & Chicago, stands at the Milwaukee depot on the St. Paul Lower Levee in 1869. The *Eastern Express* took a southern route through Faribault, Owatonna, and Austin, Minnesota, then swung east, crossing the Mississippi at Prairie du Chien. It was slow and circuitous but faster than the stagecoaches and steamboats that travelers used just ten years before.

In 1904 a Chicago, Milwaukee & St. Paul express heads north along the Mississippi bluffs near Wabasha, Minnesota. This line, opened in 1872, offered a more direct route to Chicago.

Yet another St. Paul–Chicago route emerged in 1869 with the incorporation of the St. Paul, Stillwater & Taylors Falls Railway. Backed by St. Paul and Sioux City, Iowa, interests, the company built east from St. Paul in 1871 with the goal of reaching Stillwater and Hudson, Wisconsin, where a connection would be made with the West Wisconsin, which was completing its line from Tomah via Eau Claire to the St. Croix River. Work on the St. Paul, Stillwater & Taylors Falls finished in February 1872 when the two roads met at the Hudson crossing, opening a third route to Chicago and the east. The St. Paul, Stillwater & Taylors Falls entered into an operating agreement with the recently incorporated Chicago, St. Paul & Minneapolis, successor to the West Wisconsin, but remained independent until 1880 when it was acquired by the St. Paul & Sioux City. In 1881 both roads were consolidated under the Chicago, St. Paul, Minneapolis & Omaha (the Omaha), which itself was controlled by the Chicago & North Western. Stock ownership of the Omaha was acquired by the Chicago & North Western in 1904, but it continued to operate independently until 1957.

Promoters had long dreamed of a rail connection between Lake Superior and the Mississippi and Missouri Rivers. Thus, in 1857 they organized the Nebraska & Lake Superior Railroad with the objective of linking Duluth and Lake Superior with the Mississippi River at St. Paul and the Missouri River at Omaha. The financial panic of 1857 wiped out any hope for construction; however, the road reemerged in 1861 as the Lake Superior & Mississippi Railroad. The outbreak of the Civil War stalled further work, but in 1864 crews were in the field grading up Phalen Creek with the goal of reaching Wyoming, Minnesota, by year's end. Unfortunately, funds ran out, and the railroad lay dormant for almost two years. When financier Jay Cooke determined its importance as a connection for the Northern Pacific, took interest in the project, and provided financial support, work resumed. By the end of 1868, rails had reached White Bear Lake and a twenty-by-sixty-foot passenger depot had been erected in St. Paul at the foot of Third Street. The railroad reached Hinckley before the end of 1869. On August 22, 1870, a great celebratory excursion marked the official opening of the line between St. Paul and Duluth. Four months later, in December 1870, a subsidiary company, the St. Paul & Stillwater, completed its line to Stillwater from White Bear Lake and a connection with the Lake Superior & Mississippi. The Lake Superior & Mississippi eventually became part of the Northern Pacific.

In February 1870, the Northern Pacific broke ground for its transcontinental route to the Pacific coast at a point near what is today Carlton, Minnesota. The completion of the Lake Superior & Mississippi line to Duluth just three months before was important for the Northern Pacific because it opened an all-rail route for the shipment of supplies to the advancing railhead. The Northern Pacific

Looking east toward Superior Street in 1873, the Lake Superior & Mississippi's freight and passenger terminal stands on the Duluth lakefront. The railroad was an important supply route for the Northern Pacific, then building its line to the Pacific.

In February 1870 ground is broken near Carlton, Minnesota, for the Northern Pacific, America's second transcontinental railroad. St. Paul Union Depot was the eastern terminal for its line that reached Tacoma, Washington, in 1883.

had advanced as far as the Missouri River when the financial panic of 1873, brought on by the collapse of Jay Cooke's bank, caused businesses and railroads everywhere to fall into bankruptcy, including the Northern Pacific. It would be six years before the railroad could its resume its westward extension.

The Northern Pacific coveted the advancing lines of the St. Paul & Pacific through Willmar and St. Cloud. Control over them would give the Northern Pacific important access to Minneapolis and St. Paul, the Mississippi River, and Chicago, creating a monopoly of all-rail transportation in the region. That opportunity came in 1870, when the Northern Pacific acquired a majority of the St. Paul & Pacific stock. It then moved to take control of the Lake Superior & Mississippi; the Stillwater & St. Paul, which had built from Stillwater to White Bear Lake in 1870; and the Minneapolis & Duluth, which had built from Minneapolis to White Bear Lake in 1871. It even leased the Minneapolis & St. Louis, which had yet to lay its first rail south to the Iowa border. But it was a house of cards, and the whole enterprise collapsed during the panic of 1873, taking with it a line the St. Paul & Pacific had under construction between Sauk Rapids and Brainerd, which, if completed, would have given Northern Pacific direct access to Minneapolis and St. Paul. James J. Hill recognized the importance of this connection and, even then, eyeing possible control of the St. Paul & Pacific, formed his first railroad venture, the Western Railroad of Minnesota, in 1874, with the goal of completing the Brainerd cutoff. Hill, however, was unable to finish the work, and in 1877, an impatient Minnesota Legislature revoked the charter, giving it to the Northern Pacific, which by then had regained its footing. The line was completed and opened to traffic in November 1877. That, along with a trackage rights agreement with the St. Paul & Pacific, which granted the Northern Pacific running rights over the St. Paul & Pacific's line between Sauk Rapids and St. Paul, finally gave the Northern Pacific its route to St. Paul and the east. November 1877 newspaper ads proclaimed, "Through trains from St. Paul to Bismarck daily—making close connections at St. Paul with trains from Chicago and all points south—No delays! Continuous Run." This arrival of the Northern Pacific affirmed St. Paul's standing as the rail gateway to the Northwest.

Railroad construction transformed the area near the Mississippi River and Lowertown. Marshes at the mouth of Phalen Creek were filled, and the surrounding land was raised to provide better access for railroad tracks, previously carried through the area on trestlework. Dayton's Bluff was cut back, and the bluff between the upper and lower river landings was reduced to provide more room for tracks. The Lowertown neighborhood took on a distinctly commercial character as large stone and brick commercial structures replaced smaller wood-framed buildings, many of them residences.

This is an early 1870s view of St. Paul and the Lowertown area from Dayton's Bluff. Tracks in the foreground are those of the Lake Superior & Mississippi. Much of the area has yet to be filled, but in just twenty years railroad yards and freight houses will dominate the scene.

City fathers were enthusiastic about railroads and encouraged their development, helping to sell bonds to promote construction and giving away land to construct warehouse buildings and elevators on the levee where railroads and steamboats could exchange traffic. There were ten thousand people in St. Paul in 1870. By 1872 St. Paul had its first horse-car line running from Lowertown to Seven Corners. The city was spreading beyond the river, reaching west toward what would be the Midway District.

The 1878 edition of the *Official Guide* found seven railroads and thirty-eight daily passenger trains arriving and departing from four depots crowded on or near the Mississippi levee. The St. Paul & Pacific; St. Paul & Sioux City; Chicago, Milwaukee & St. Paul; and St. Paul & Duluth (which acquired the Lake Superior & Mississippi in 1877) had separate stations. The Northern Pacific was a tenant at the St. Paul & Pacific depot. The St. Paul, Stillwater & Taylors Falls, along with the West Wisconsin, used the St. Paul & Sioux City's station facilities.

None of these stations were adequate for the hundreds of people passing through them every day, not to mention the volume of baggage, mail, and express that had to be loaded and unloaded or carted from one station to another. There was also the matter of switching cars and locomotives as trains

The Chicago, Milwaukee & St. Paul completed its Mississippi River line from St. Paul to La Crescent in 1872, creating a faster, more direct route to Chicago. Its first line, in 1867, through southern Minnesota and Prairie du Chien, Wisconsin, was longer and more time consuming and would eventually host just one through passenger train a day. The River Line, on the other hand, went from two trains a day in 1878 to seven in 1956 and saw its nineteen-hour running time in 1878 cut to six and one-half hours in 1956.

In 1878 James J. Hill had yet to take command of the St. Paul & Pacific. It was in financial trouble, and its lines went no farther than Breckenridge and Melrose, Minnesota. Two years later, with Hill in charge, it emerged as the St. Paul, Minneapolis & Manitoba. In 1890 it became the Great Northern and, in 1893, completed its line to Seattle and the Pacific Coast. With its headquarters in St. Paul and its passenger trains anchored at St. Paul Union Depot, the Great Northern was the most prosperous of all the western railroads.

arrived and departed, made even more difficult by the shortage of track capacity. Railroad managements foresaw that a growth in traffic was inevitable once the Northern Pacific finished its Pacific extension and the St. Paul & Pacific moved into the Red River valley and to the Canadian border. The need was obvious but the solution less so. There were disputes among the various railroads over ownership and access to terminal facilities. Should it be a union depot company owned by all the railroads, or should one railroad own the depot with the other railroads as tenants in a joint facility arrangement? More land would be needed, and it would have to come from adjoining businesses or steamboat interests at the levee—the latter watching their business shrink as the rail network expanded.

James J. Hill and the St. Paul & Pacific much preferred a joint facility controlled by the St. Paul & Pacific with the other roads as tenants, an arrangement Hill achieved in Minneapolis when his station opened there in 1884, but Hill had little bargaining power, given the financial weakness of the St. Paul & Pacific, and he reluctantly agreed to a union depot company while cannily securing preferential use of certain depot trackage and access for the St. Paul & Pacific.

The First Union Depot

"The name of this Corporation is The Saint Paul Union Depot Company. The general nature of the business of said corporation is to build, purchase, or lease and operate transfer tracks on railways in the city of St. Paul in the State of Minnesota, open alike to the use (under proper regulations) of all railroads now constructed or which may hereafter be constructed into the said city of St. Paul to and between each of said roads and to and between each and all of said roads and each and all important industries in the said city of St. Paul whose business requires special rail accommodations by means of transfer tracks, side tracks, or railways and in connection therewith to build, lease or otherwise provide and maintain in said city of St. Paul a union passenger depot and proper tracks for access thereto, and to that end to construct, purchase, lease or otherwise secure and to maintain and operate lines of railway in the said city of St. Paul."

On January 24, 1879, Sherburne S. Merrill, Judson W. Bishop, James J. Hill, George H. Smith, Homer E. Sargent, Alpheus B. Stickney, and Frank B. Clarke, all general managers of the railroads then serving St. Paul, signed the articles of incorporation of the St. Paul Union Depot Company and set its capital stock at $250,000. Six months later on June 13, 1879, the board of directors met and elected Alpheus B. Stickney as its first president.

The Union Depot Company was wholly owned by the railroads, each of them subscribing to shares of its capital stock and holding a seat on its board of directors. The board elected officers from among its members, and they in turn hired its managers. An operating agreement among the owning companies governed day-to-day operations and how the costs of those operations were apportioned.

Elsewhere, there was mixed enthusiasm for the project. While the city quickly passed the necessary ordinances enabling the closure of certain city streets at the levee, a group of property owners and steamboat interests—today we might call them NIMBYs—filed suit to block construction.

The November 19, 1879, *Minneapolis Tribune* commented cynically, "It is unfortunate for St. Paul that her location is so wretched that it is impossible for a railroad to enter the city without obstructing her riverfront. By repeated concessions the railroads have come to almost monopolize the levee, to the prejudice of navigation interests and of the owners of the adjoining property." It went on to suggest, "Of course this litigation will put a stop for some time to the union depot project. Meantime, wouldn't it be well for the railroad companies to avoid trouble by abandoning the project which finds so many obstacles to its consummation in St. Paul and locate the great union depot in Minneapolis, where plenty of available ground for it can be obtained without interfering with anybody's vested rights."

While the *Tribune*'s unsympathetic tone betrayed its biases, the site of the proposed union depot came with problems that would linger for decades. St. Paul was then a growing river town set atop a cliff overlooking a bend in the Mississippi River. At the base of the cliff the river scoured out a narrow strip of land that formed a natural levee and a convenient spot for steamboats to tie up. Tributary valleys, eroded by small streams, made it easy to move goods and people up the hill. When the railroads, forever seeking the easiest grade, followed the river into St. Paul, they, too, occupied the levee. It was close to the commercial center of St. Paul and offered a good connection with the steamboats. But there wasn't enough room for both, and as railroad traffic increased, steamboat interests came under increasing pressure to yield to the railroads. The steamboat interests filed suit.

Had it succeeded, the lawsuit would have enjoined the railroads from constructing a depot at the levee and would have required them to abandon one of the three tracks that already crossed it. However, the lawsuit failed, and the court allowed construction to proceed. But the ruling couldn't overcome geography, and the new depot and its successors were confined by the river on one side and a growing city on the other. Future expansion meant acquiring developed property to the north or filling the river channel and the marshy Phalen-Trout Brook area to the east, all expensive undertakings. The site was also subject to flooding and had terrible soil conditions. St. Paul would have its new union station, but the railroads would have a whole new set of issues to face in future years.

Local architect L. S. Buffington was hired to design the building. Work commenced on the foundation on June 1, 1880, but a year was consumed improving the site, which was boggy and subject to flooding. Finally, on the evening of August 21, 1881, the first passenger trains departed the new station. Built at a cost of $250,000, the building and grounds covered nine and one-half acres. Beginning at Third and Sibley Streets, the property line continued 208 feet along Sibley toward the Mississippi River. To the east it extended to Willius Street, curving northward until it intersected Third Street. Its eastern and southern boundaries were, respectively, the tracks of the St. Paul & Duluth and the Milwaukee Road, the latter's running parallel to the Mississippi River. Within these boundaries were the depot building, a coach storage yard, a roundhouse, and locomotive coaling and watering facilities.

Nine tracks served the first depot. Six of them were stub tracks terminating at a cross platform, or concourse, thirty feet wide and covered by an iron porch roof. Three tracks ran through along the south side of the building, parallel to the river, connecting with a tenth through track used for interchange business. The tracks were arranged in pairs and accessed by covered platforms, 475 feet long and 17 feet wide, extending from the concourse. This arrangement was designed to accommodate seventy-five trains a day, a number that soon proved grossly inadequate.

LEROY BUFFINGTON

Leroy Sunderland Buffington was one of Minnesota's most important nineteenth-century architects. Born in Cincinnati, Ohio, in 1849, Buffington trained at the Cincinnati architectural firm of Hannaford and Anderson. He moved to St. Paul in 1871 and took up a partnership with Abraham Radcliffe. In 1874 he opened his own office in Minneapolis and by 1885 had built one of the largest and most successful architectural practices in the Twin Cities.

Buffington worked in the heavy Romanesque style then favored by Victorian swells, designing mansions for some of the most prominent local figures of the Gilded Age. Among them were Thomas Lowry, president of the Twin City Rapid Transit Company, Governor John S. Pillsbury, and George Pillsbury. Besides the first St. Paul Union Depot, his other commissions included the Pillsbury A Mill and the West Hotel in Minneapolis, the 1882 State Capitol in St. Paul, Pillsbury Hall at the University of Minnesota, the Hotel Lafayette and Lake Park Hotel on Lake Minnetonka, Yellowstone Hotel at Mammoth Hot Springs in Yellowstone Park, and the Twin City Rapid Transit Company's Big Island amusement park on Lake Minnetonka.

He became the official architect of the St. Paul, Minneapolis & Manitoba Railway in 1880 and designed many of its depots.

Buffington was an early developer of steel-skeleton construction for high-rise buildings, for which he received a patent in 1887. That patent, however, was challenged in a lawsuit, and he lost.

Buffington died in 1931.

Leroy S. Buffington, circa 1895.

Still standing despite structural problems that appeared within a few years of its 1881 completion, the Pillsbury A Mill is perhaps Buffington's most durable creation. Charles Pillsbury claimed it was the largest flour mill in the world. The mill is on the National Register of Historic Places. Plans are underway to convert it to apartments.

Fire destroyed the first union depot in 1884. It was rebuilt that year using the same plans and specifications. Here it hosts a passenger train awaiting departure.

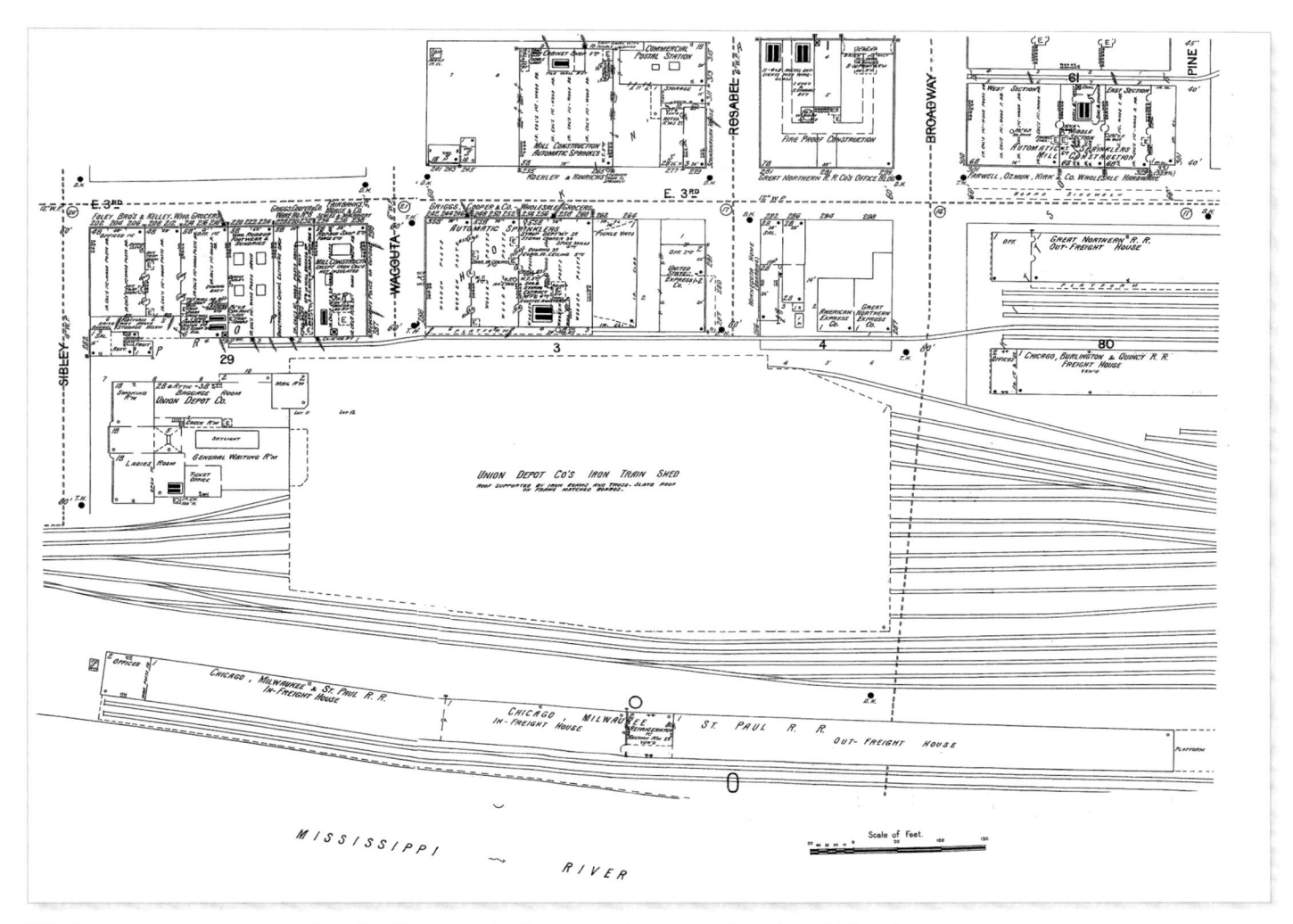

This 1904 Sanborn Insurance map shows the 1884 depot after improvements were completed in 1900. These improvements included an expansion of the train shed, more storage tracks for arriving and departing trains, and an addition to the waiting rooms. Ten years later, buildings north of the depot head house between Sibley and Wacouta became a temporary depot following the 1913 fire. They in turn, along with the other structures paralleling Third Street next to the train shed, were demolished after 1917 to make way for the new facility.

This is the entrance and central hall of the 1884 depot. The women's waiting room is on the left, men's on the right. Depot offices are on the second floor.

Fronting on Sibley Street, the depot building measured 130 feet wide by 150 feet deep. It was two stories tall with two wings connected by a central hall that opened all the way to the second-floor ceiling, which had skylights and two circular windows at either end. Entering the hall through a vestibule on Sibley Street, on the right was the women's waiting room and on the left the men's. Both had adjoining restrooms. Farther down the hall, beyond the women's waiting room, was an eighteen-by-twenty-two-foot ticket office with a large window fronting on the main hall and a smaller window opening into the women's waiting room. The main hall, in turn, advanced to a cross hall that divided the building into two halves. On one side there was a commercial telegraph office, on the other a parcel checkroom, a stairway to the second floor, and beyond a lunchroom, baggage room, and space for the U.S. mail service. The second floor was given over to a kitchen, the main dining room, an immigrant room, and depot offices. An employee dormitory room was located in the attic.

The exterior walls were of pressed brick set atop a granite base over a limestone foundation.

View of the women's waiting room in the 1884 depot. Victorian custom required that women and children be secluded from the smoking, tobacco chewing, drinking, and bad language of male travelers.

Interior finishes were all hardwood, oak and ash. Some door panels were finished with bird's-eye maple. Moldings were applied to ornament the stairways and wainscotings, and the ceiling of the main waiting room was divided into rectangles by intersecting oak ribs. The building was heated by steam and lighted by gas, with provision for electric lighting once it became available.

Mark Twain in an 1882 visit to St. Paul commented in his *Life on the Mississippi*, "There is an unusually fine railway-station; so large is it, in fact, that it seemed somewhat overdone, in the matter of size, at first; but at the end of a few months it was perceived that the mistake was distinctly the other way."

It took some forty years to make the correction, and by then the passenger train was in decline. But in 1882 it was about manifest destiny, the pending completion of the Northern Pacific's line to

Taxis await arriving passengers at the Sibley Street entrance, 1893.

the Pacific, and the sure and inevitable growth in passenger and freight traffic to follow as thousands of immigrants passed through St. Paul and its depot on their way to settle the Dakotas, Montana, and the Pacific Northwest.

Shortly after midnight on June 11, 1884, a fire was discovered in the restaurant kitchen. The great central hall provided a convenient draft, spreading flames throughout the building. The *Railway Gazette* of June 13, 1884, reported a $200,000 loss. Temporary sheds were constructed for passengers, and the Union Depot Company immediately set about rebuilding and expanding its facilities. Among the improvements was a three-hundred-by-thirty-foot, two-story building designed to free up space in the head house. The ground floor was used for baggage, mail, and express. The second floor provided accommodations for emigrants. A thirty-foot addition at the rear of the depot allowed

The 1889 train shed is under construction. Train sheds were a hallmark of nineteenth-century railroad depots. They were supposed to protect passengers from inclement weather but instead trapped smoke, soot, and gases from steam locomotives and were expensive to maintain. St Paul's survived the 1913 fire but was torn down to make way for the new depot.

Steamboats are still calling on St. Paul in this 1898 view taken from the Robert Street Bridge. Although river traffic held up for a number of years, it was freight, not people, that brought these boats to St. Paul. Passengers had long since deserted the levee in favor of St. Paul Union Depot, and as more and more goods went into boxcars, still fewer boats would call. In a few years, barges carrying bulk commodities will have the river largely to themselves.

other improvements, including a doubling of the size of the men's and women's waiting rooms and the ticket office. The rebuilt and remodeled station opened for business in the fall of 1884.

1889 brought construction of a 120,960-square-foot train shed that covered all nine tracks and five boarding platforms. Extending 640 feet in length and 189 feet in width, the shed's superstructure consumed some 1,690,00 pounds of iron and steel and cost $123,000, nearly the cost of the depot itself. It was the largest in the state, outclassing similar structures at the Great Northern Station in Minneapolis, Duluth Union Station, and the Milwaukee's soon-to-be-completed (in 1899) depot in Minneapolis.

The great arched train shed was a hallmark of Victorian station architecture. Railroads lavished great sums on their construction and even more, much to their discomfort, on their maintenance. Some of the more spectacular included the first Grand Central Terminal in New York City, St. Louis Union Station, the Pennsylvania's Broad Street Station in Philadelphia, and the New Haven's South Station in Boston—the latter's shed spanned twenty-eight tracks. But imposing as they were, they were still dark, gloomy places that required constant maintenance. The comings and goings of steam locomotives deposited layer after layer of soot and cinders, which in turn made their way into every nook and cranny of the station building. Locomotive exhausts bathed the roof with an acid steam that attacked and corroded the deck and its structural supports. St. Paul's building was ventilated by a series of wood louvers located near the center of the roof that extended the entire length of the shed. The louvers were supplemented by four large ventilators and ten smoke jacks. Skylights and electric lights provided illumination. While impressive in scale, it had all the deficiencies of those in other cities, and it would come down during construction of the present depot.

Between 1889 and 1910, there were changes under the shed. Passenger traffic doubled. Five railroads joined the depot company, others merged, and three finished lines to the Pacific, essentially completing the network of rail lines entering St. Paul Union Depot.

The Chicago, Burlington & Northern created another link to Chicago and the East when it finished its line on the east bank of the Mississippi from 1886 to 1889. The Chicago, Burlington & Quincy acquired the Chicago, Burlington & Northern in 1899.

The Chicago Great Western purchased the Chicago, St. Paul & Kansas City in 1893. The latter had (in 1887) acquired the Minnesota & Northwestern Railroad Company, which had completed a line from St. Paul to the Iowa border in 1885. It reached Dubuque, Iowa, the following year and by 1888, Chicago. The Great Western would stretch its lines into southern Minnesota, Iowa, Illinois, and Missouri, reaching Omaha, Kansas City, and Chicago.

The Minneapolis & St. Louis gained entry to St. Paul in 1886 under an agreement with the Northern Pacific for use of its just completed "A" line between the two cities. However, the animus of James J. Hill kept it out of St. Paul Union Depot until 1902, and it was forced to use a temporary depot adjoining the Northern Pacific's freight house.

The Minneapolis, St. Paul & Sault Ste. Marie, with lines to North Dakota and Wisconsin and connections with the Canadian Pacific at Portal, North Dakota, and Sault Sainte Marie, Michigan, came together in 1888 from the merger of the Minneapolis & Pacific; the Minneapolis, Sault Ste. Marie & Atlantic; the Minneapolis & St. Croix; and the Aberdeen, Bismarck & Northwestern. In 1909 the Soo Line took over operation of the Wisconsin Central, which arrived in St. Paul in 1885.

The Rock Island gained entry to St. Paul in 1903 when it purchased the Burlington, Cedar Rapids & Northern Railway. Prior to 1901-2, the Burlington, Cedar Rapids & Northern had used the Minneapolis & St. Louis to reach the Twin Cities from a connection at Albert Lea. However, as the result of a dispute with the Minneapolis & St. Louis, it constructed its own line between Albert Lea and Comus, and a second line between Rosemount and Newport. It had trackage rights over the Milwaukee between Comus and Rosemount and over the Chicago, Burlington & Quincy between Newport and St. Paul.

There were several mergers and acquisitions. The St. Paul, Stillwater & Taylors Falls Railroad was sold to the St. Paul & Sioux City Railroad in 1880, which in turn was acquired by the Chicago, St. Paul, Minneapolis & Omaha in 1881. The Omaha in turn came under the control of the Chicago & North Western in 1882. The St. Paul & Duluth (the former Lake Superior & Mississippi) was sold to the Northern Pacific in 1900.

The Northern Pacific finished its transcontinental line to Tacoma-Seattle in 1883. In 1889 it opened a more direct route to the Twin Cities with the completion of a cutoff between Little Falls and Staples, Minnesota, thus bypassing the longer, less direct line through Brainerd.

The Great Northern Railway Company came into being in 1890 under the terms of a special charter granted by the Minnesota Legislature. It subsequently took over operations of the St. Paul, Minneapolis & Manitoba, which it leased for ninety-nine years. It completed its transcontinental line to Seattle in 1893, and under the auspices of the Eastern Railway Company of Minnesota, it built a new direct route to Duluth via Coon Creek Junction and Cambridge, Minnesota, in 1899.

The Chicago, Milwaukee & St. Paul finished its short-line, direct route between Minneapolis and St. Paul via the Midway in 1880. In 1909 it opened its Pacific extension to Seattle-Tacoma, the third transcontinental line to the coast, becoming the Chicago, Milwaukee, St. Paul & Pacific.

The Great Encampment

The Grand Army of the Republic, a fraternal organization of Union Army veterans numbering in the tens of thousands, descended on St. Paul for its annual encampment from August 31 to September 5, 1896. The depot and the railroads serving St. Paul had never seen such crowds, and it tested their abilities. According to accounts of the day, depot forces carried it off with aplomb, but it was also a caution to the railroads that the 1884 depot was running out of room and that expansion would be needed soon.

The numbers are amazing. Between August 31 and September 5, 1896, 1,172 trains and 8,074 passenger and baggage cars moved in and out from under the great train shed. Some 200,000 people, equaling 403,000 arrivals and departures, attended the encampment and moved through the depot on these trains. All the passengers were preticketed, the great majority using special trains in addition to those regularly scheduled through the depot. At the conclusion of the encampment, trains were reportedly dispatched from the depot at the rate of one per minute. It was an incredible feat, especially given the available technology. St. Paul Union Depot had no signal towers or interlocking plants. Train directors and switchmen used hand signals to control all movements.

In an earlier article in 1895, the *St. Paul Pioneer Press* called the depot a "wonder" allowing that it was second only to Philadelphia's Broad Street Station in business handled and that railroaders across the country looked to St. Paul as the leader in depot operations. St. Paul was proud of its railroads, its fine Union Depot, and its standing as the railroad hub of the upper Midwest, and the *Pioneer Press* was unabashed in its praise of the 110 employees who shepherded some 150 passenger trains and 800 freight cars through the depot every day. This was a decline, the *Pioneer Press* admitted, from the 362 passenger trains and 1,500 freight cars handled in 1886-87. It attributed the drop to the 1890 debut of the electric streetcar, which displaced more than 150 commuter trains that had once moved a quarter of a million annual riders between Minneapolis and St. Paul—a loss of business that was seen by the greater community as a sign of urban progress. The electric cars were cleaner and offered much better service to the neighborhoods that were rapidly filling the empty land between the two cities.

Just five years after this article appeared, the *Pioneer Press* turned from praise to complaint and lobbied for further improvements. At issue was capacity. The depot company's 1899 annual report showed 353,583 tickets sold in 1899 compared to 237,389 in 1898. There was a similar striking increase in the total annual number of passenger trains arriving and departing the depot.

Grandees of the Gilded Age, President William Howard Taft *(center)* came to St. Paul for a visit in 1911 and was greeted by Governor Adolph O. Eberhart *(right)*. They shared a carriage at St. Paul Union Depot.

NUMBER OF TRAINS USING ST. PAUL UNION DEPOT

Railroad	1898	1899	Increase (%)
Milwaukee	5,693	6,830	20
Omaha	9,127	10,405	14
Great Northern	4,972	5,113	2.8
Northern Pacific	2,119	2,234	5.4
Burlington	4,816	4,852	0.75
Great Western	2,582	8,165	316*
Totals	29,309	37,599	28.3

*Chicago Great Western had the largest increase because it moved its local Inver Grove and South St. Paul commuter trains to the depot.

The frontier may have closed, but more and more people were moving to the West and Midwest as cities and towns filled in and the country recovered from the financial panic of 1893. *Source:* St. Paul Union Depot Company annual reports.

Twin Cities Suburban Passenger Trains

From the 1880s through the early 1920s, the railroads serving the Twin Cities operated an extensive network of steam-powered suburban trains. All eventually succumbed to streetcar and auto competition, but in their day they were the best and, in many instances, the only way to move around the region. From St. Paul Union Depot they extended to Stillwater, North St. Paul, White Bear Lake, St. Paul Park, South St. Paul, and Inver Grove. From Minneapolis there was service to White Bear Lake, Mendota, and Lake Minnetonka. Three railroads ran competing trains on four different routes between downtown Minneapolis and St. Paul Union Depot. The Minnesota Belt Line Railway & Transfer ran a connecting passenger service from the Great Northern's station at St. Anthony Park to the New Brighton stockyards, primarily for stockyard workers.

Mostly these were Monday-through-Saturday commuter services with trains scheduled in the morning and afternoon and a few in the middle of the day. On Sundays, schedules were adjusted to better serve recreational venues. There was frequent service between Minneapolis and St. Paul. The railroads serving Lake Minnetonka ran additional trains on weekends during the summer months. Special weekend excursion trains to Stillwater, White Bear, and Taylors Falls were popular. Extra trains from downtown Minneapolis and St. Paul ran to the Minnesota State Fair. There was even a special Opera Train between the two cities.

This map shows the network of commuter trains that once connected downtown St. Paul and adjoining communities. Most were victims of the electric streetcar and vanished between 1890 and 1900. The remainder couldn't compete with automobiles and improved roads and were mostly gone by 1925. A few struggled into the late 1940s and early 1950s.

It's 1890 and a Great Northern commuter train from St. Paul speeds across the Stone Arch Bridge on its way to the Great Northern Station. The banks of the Mississippi River upstream from the bridge were dominated by sawmills utilizing the waterpower of St. Anthony Falls. The St. Anthony depot can be seen in the far distance to the left of the Stone Arch Bridge.

In St. Paul these suburban services strained the capacity of the 1881 St. Paul Union Depot and were a factor in the improvements carried out in 1889-90. In 1888 some 221 trains moved through St. Paul Union Depot. Half of them were suburban runs. Suburban trains were also a factor in the 1915-17 planning for the new depot, and a separate concourse was built to accommodate them. However, by the time the new depot opened, the trains were largely gone, and the arrival concourse, as it was called, was never used for its intended purpose.

The following is a summary of the various services between St. Paul and Minneapolis and the suburbs of the Twin Cities.

Trains between St. Paul and Minneapolis

In 1878 the St. Paul & Pacific was running three extra trains via its Midway line between St. Paul and Minneapolis. The Milwaukee also scheduled Minneapolis-St. Paul trains via its Fort Snelling and Mendota route. By 1888 there were dozens of trains running throughout the day on three routes between the two cities. Several factors were at work. Minneapolis and St. Paul were prosperous cities; the population and the economy were growing. The Milwaukee and the Northern Pacific opened new lines between Minneapolis and St. Paul, and there were new station facilities in both cities. Also, the Great Northern had completed its Stone Arch Bridge, affording a more direct route into downtown Minneapolis.

By 1893 competition from Twin City Rapid Transit's streetcar line on University Avenue put an end to commuter service on the Great Northern, Northern Pacific, and the Milwaukee's Short Line. The trains were faster, but the streetcars ran more frequently and made more stops. They were also much closer to the residential areas and businesses that were developing in what would become St. Paul's Midway neighborhood. By then, the Milwaukee's trains via Fort Snelling and Mendota were actually separate sections of long-distance trains to southern Minnesota and Iowa that met at Mendota. All service on the Fort Snelling line was gone by 1926. Although the Great Northern's intercity commuter trains disappeared, the railroad continued to offer summer-only excursion trains from St. Paul Union Depot to Lake Minnetonka destinations until the World War I era.

Trains Operating via the Great Northern Line

Great Northern, Omaha, and Great Western all offered services via the Great Northern's line.

1883   Sixteen eastbound and twenty westbound trains; travel time thirty to forty minutes

1890   Eighteen round trips; travel time twenty-five minutes

1891   Fifteen round trips; travel time twenty-five minutes

1894   Thirty trains each way, all long distance; operated by Great Northern, Omaha, and Great Western; only four eastbound trains and three westbound trains make intermediate stops—at Como, Hamline, and St. Anthony Park stations

1910   Only one Hutchinson train each way with stops at Como and Hamline stations

1917   Forty-seven long-distance trains with no intermediate stops

Trains Operating via the Milwaukee Road's Short Line

The Milwaukee opened its Short Line through what would be the St. Paul Midway in 1880 and shifted most of its long-distance trains to this new, more direct route. It also began commuter service between Minneapolis and St. Paul. All of the commuter runs were discontinued by 1893, victims of streetcar competition. Its long-distance trains remained, together with those of the Soo Line and Rock Island, which also used the Short Line.

1881   Twelve trains each way Monday–Saturday, four on Sunday; travel time thirty minutes

1883   Seventeen trains each way with hourly service; travel time thirty to forty-five minutes

1884   Nineteen trains each way with hourly service; travel time thirty minutes

1885   Twenty trains each way with hourly service; travel time thirty minutes

1890   Nineteen trains each way with hourly service; travel time twenty-five minutes

1891   Eighteen trains each way with hourly service; travel time twenty-five to thirty minutes

1892   Twelve trains each way; several are long distance

1917   Twenty-one trains each way; all are long distance

Trains Operated by the Milwaukee Road via Fort Snelling and Mendota

Constructed in 1865 by a predecessor company, Minnesota Central, this was the Milwaukee's original line out of Minneapolis. By 1869 it had become part of a circuitous route between Minneapolis and St. Paul. Long-distance trains originated in both cities and were combined at Mendota. These were supplemented by a limited local service until the Short Line opened in 1880. Then, the locals were taken off and the remaining through service was provided solely by long-distance trains.

MANITOBA SHORT LINE.

MINNEAPOLIS TO ST. PAUL.

Corrected to Jan. 5, 1890.

TRAIN. See Foot Note.	Days.	Leave Minneapolis.	East Minneapolis.	State University.	St. Anthony Park.	Hamline.	Como.	Arrive St. Paul.
St. P. M. & M	Daily	6 25am	6 29		6 35	6 40		6 55
Nor. Pac	Daily	6 35 "						7 05
East'n Minn	Daily	6 40 "						7 10
C. B. & N	Ex Sun.	6 45 "	6 49					7 15
Soo Line	Daily	6 55 "	6 59					7 25
C. St. P. & K. C	Daily	7 05 "	7 09					7 35
St. P. M. & M	Daily	7 30 "	7 34	7 35	7 39	7 42	7 45	7 55
do	Daily	8 30 "	8 34	8 35	8 39	8 42	8 45	8 55
C. St. P. M. & O	Daily	8 53 "						9 23
St. P. M. & M	Daily	9 00 "	9 05					9 30
C. St. P. M. & O	Ex Sun.	9 20 "	9 24					9 50
St. P. M. & M	Daily	9 30 "	9 34		9 39	9 42	9 45	9 55
do	Daily	10 30 "	10 34		10 39	10 42	10 45	10 55
do	Ex Sun.	10 45 "	10 49					11 10
do	Daily	11 30 "	11 34		11 39	11 42	11 45	11 55
do	Daily	12 30pm	12 34	12 35	12 39	12 42	12 45	12 55
Wis. Cent'l	Daily	12 45 "	12 49					1 15
St. P. M. & M	Daily	1 30 "	1 34	1 35	1 39	1 42	1 45	1 55
C. St. P. M. & O	Daily	2 20 "						2 50
St. P. M. & M	Daily	2 30 ',	2 34		2 39	2 42	2 45	2 55
do	Daily	3 30 "	3 34	3 35	3 39	3 42	3 45	3 55
C. St. P. & K. C	Daily	4 15 "	4 19					4 45
St. P. M. & M	Daily	4 30 "	4 34	4 35	4 39	4 42	4 45	4 55
do	Daily	4 40 "						5 10
Nor. Pac	Daily	5 30 "	5 34	5 35	5 39	5 42	5 45	5 55
St. P. M. & M	Ex Sun.	5 45 "	5 49					6 15
do	Ex Sun.	5 52 "						6 20
East'n Minn	Ex Sun.	6 00 "	6 04			6 15		6 30
St. P. M. & M	Ex Sun.	6 20 "						6 45
Nor. Pac	Daily	6 25 "	6 29					6 50
Wis. Cent'l	Daily	6 30 "	6 33	6 34	6 39	6 42	6 45	6 55
St. P. M. & M	Daily	6 35 "	6 39					7 03
C. St. P. M. & O	Daily	6 40 "	6 44					7 10
C. B. & N	Daily	6 50 "						7 20
C. St. P. M. & O	Daily	7 00 "	7 04					7 27
C. St. P. & K. C	Daily	7 30 "	7 34		7 39	7 42	7 45	7 55
St. P. M. & M	Daily	8 30 "	8 34	8 35	8 39	8 42	8 45	8 55
do	Daily	10 00 "	10 04					10 30
C. St. P. M· & O.	Daily	10 30 "	10 34		10 39	10 42	10 45	10 55
St. P. M. & M	Daily	11 30 "	11 34		11 39	11 42	11 45	11 55

All tickets reading over St. P., M. & M. R'y between St. Paul and Minneapolis, are good on any of above trains, excepting that Commutation Tickets are not honored on Northern Pacific trains.

This January 1890 timetable published by the St. Paul, Minneapolis & Manitoba (the future Great Northern) shows the schedules of the nine railroads running commuter service between Minneapolis and St. Paul. All of these trains disappeared following the opening of Twin City Rapid Transit's interurban streetcar line in December 1890.

MILWAUKEE SHORT LINE.

ST. PAUL TO MINNEAPOLIS.

Leave St. Paul,	Chestnut St.	Murray Hill.	Ridgewood Park.	Macalester.	Merriam P'k	Desnoyer Park.	South Minneapolis.	Arrive Minneapolis.
Ex Sunday 7 00 am	7 03	7 06	7 08	7 14	7 16	1 18	7 24	7 30
Daily 7 40 am								8 10
do 8 00 am	8 03	8 06	8 08	8 14	8 16	8 18	8 24	8 30
do 9 00 am	9 03			9 10	9 12	9 14	9 19	9 25
do 10 00 am	10 03			10 10	10 12		10 19	10 25
Ex Sunday 10 30 am	10 33	10 36		10 34	10 46	10 48	10 54	11 00
Daily 11 00 am	11 03				11 12		11 19	11 25
do 12 00 m	12 03	12 06	12 08	12 14	12 16	12 18	12 24	12 30
do 1 00 pm	1 03	1 05		1 10	1 12	1 14	1 19	1 25
do 2 00 pm	2 03				2 12		2 19	2 25
do 2 05 pm								2 35
do 3 00 pm	3 03	3 05		3 10	3 12	3 14	3 19	3 25
do 3 25 pm								3 50
do 4 00 pm	4 03		4 06		4 12		4 19	4 25
do 5 00 pm	5 03	5 06	5 08	5 14	5 16	5 18	5 24	5 30
do 6 00 pm	6 03	6 06	6 08	6 14	6 16	6 18	6 24	6 30
do 7 00 pm	7 03	7 06	7 08	7 14	7 16	7 18	7 24	7 30
do 7 15 pm	7 18			7 29	7 31		7 39	7 45
do 8 00 pm	8 03			8 10	8 12		8 19	8 25
do 10 00 pm	10 03	10 06	10 08	10 14	10 16		10 24	10 30
Ex Sunday 11 10 pm	11 13				11 22		11 29	11 35
Daily 11 30 pm	11 33	11 36	11 38	11 44	11 46	11 48	11 54	12 00

MINNEAPOLIS TO ST. PAUL.

Leave Minneapolis.	South Minneapolis.	Desnoyer Park.	Merriam P'k	Macalester.	Ridgewood Park.	Murray Hill.	Chestnut St.	Arrive St. Paul.
Ex Sunday 6 45 am	6 51		6 57	7 12	7 14	7 20	7 06	7 10
do 7 00 am	7 06	7 10	7 12	7 14	7 20	7 22	7 26	7 30
Daily 8 00 am	8 06	8 10	8 12	8 14	7 20	8 22	8 26	8 30
do 8 10 am	8 16		8 22				7 36	8 40
do 9 00 am	9 06		9 12	9 14	9 17	9 18	9 21	9 25
do 10 00 am	10 06	10 10	10 12	10 14		10 18	10 21	10 25
do 11 00 am	11 06		11 12	11 14			11 21	11 25
do 12 00 m	12 06	12 10	12 12	12 14			12 21	12 25
do 1 00 pm	1 06		1 12	1 14	1 20	1 22	1 26	1 30
do 2 00 pm	2 06	2 10	2 12	2 14		2 18	2 21	2 25
do 2 20 pm							2 45	2 50
do 3 00 pm	3 06		3 12	3 14	3 17	3 18	3 21	3 75
do 4 00 pm	4 06		4 12	4 14			4 21	4 25
Ex Sunday 4 30 pm	4 36		4 42	4 44			4 51	4 55
Daily 5 00 pm	5 06	5 10	5 12	5 14	5 20	5 22	5 26	5 30
do 6 00 pm			6 10	6 12			6 21	6 25
do 6 10 pm							6 67	6 30
Daily 6 50 pm							7 15	7 20
do 7 00 pm	7 06	7 10	7 12	7 14	7 20	7 22	7 26	7 30
do 8 00 pm	8 06		8 12	8 14			8 21	8 25
do 10 00 pm	10 06	10 10	10 12	10 14	10 20	10 22	10 26	10 30
do 11 30 pm	11 36	11 40	11 42	11 44	11 50	11 52	11 56	12 00

The Milwaukee Road opened its new Short Line between St. Paul and Minneapolis in 1880. It replaced a slower, indirect route through south Minneapolis that bridged the Minnesota River below Fort Snelling, then doubled back to St. Paul via Mendota and a Mississippi River crossing at Lilydale. The Short Line left St. Paul Union Depot, climbed out of the Mississippi River Valley, then headed west through the Midway District, crossing the Mississippi River just north of Lake Street on a bridge that is still used today. The new route was a huge timesaver, and the Milwaukee Road immediately began commuter service with trains running every hour in the midday and every thirty minutes during morning and afternoon rush hours. The trains made intermediate stops and used the Milwaukee Depot in Minneapolis. Streetcar competition ended the commuter trains, but the Short Line is still used for freight and by Amtrak from its Midway station.

ST. PAUL AND ITS RAILROADS   □ □ □   73

Service between Minneapolis and Mendota had ended by 1926.

1879   Eight round trips Monday through Saturday, five on Sunday; travel time fifty minutes

1884   Two round trips betweem St. Paul and Minneapolis; three round trips between St. Paul and Mendota; four round trips between Minneapolis and Mendota

Trains Operated by the Minneapolis & St. Louis via the Northern Pacific "A" line

The Northern Pacific opened a new main line between Minneapolis and St. Paul in 1886. As part of a trackage rights agreement to use the line to access St. Paul, the Minneapolis & St. Louis ran hourly commuter trains from 6:15 a.m. to 6:15 p.m. between the cities from 1886 until 1892, when they were discontinued due to streetcar competition. Capacity issues and railroad politics—James J. Hill disliked the competing Northern Pacific and Minneapolis & St. Louis—kept these trains out of St. Paul Union Depot. Instead, they were routed to a passenger depot in the Northern Pacific's freight house just east of Fourth Street and Broadway.

Rattan seats and gas lamps greeted patrons in Burlington's commuter coaches on the run between St. Paul Union Depot and Pullman Avenue. The cars were all-wood hand-me-downs, bumped from upgraded main-line trains, and were much like those used in its Chicago commuter service at the time. They were rough to ride, hot in summer and cold in winter, and were a good reason to go buy a Model T and drive downtown.

Minneapolis and St. Paul to White Bear and Stillwater

One of the longest-lived suburban services, and probably the most complex, was the Northern Pacific's (originally the Lake Superior & Mississippi and then the St. Paul & Duluth) service to White Bear, Stillwater, and Taylors Falls. The Lake Superior & Mississippi opened its line from St. Paul to Duluth in 1870. It also built the Minneapolis & Duluth from Minneapolis to White Bear and the Stillwater & St. Paul from White Bear to Stillwater. Another branch was subsequently constructed between Wyoming, Minnesota, and Taylors Falls by the Taylors Falls & Lake Superior Railroad. All of these companies were absorbed into the Northern Pacific by 1900.

There were several route combinations over the years. Some suburban trains originating at White Bear or on the Stillwater and Taylors Falls branches were scheduled to run directly from

It's June 30, 1948, and locomotive 328 departs the Wyoming, Minnesota, depot and crosses Highway 61, leading the final run on Northern Pacific's Taylors Falls branch. In a few weeks the scrapper will call and begin pulling up the tracks, ending forever this remnant of Northern Pacific's suburban services to White Bear, Stillwater, and Taylors Falls. In the 1890s the Taylors Falls branch hosted several passenger trains a day to St. Paul Union Depot via White Bear Lake. Taylors Falls was a popular weekend picnic destination, with even more trains running on Saturdays and Sundays, but the automobile took away most of the business. The through trains became local mixed-freight and passenger runs between Taylors Falls and Wyoming. With the passengers gone and no local freight customers, the Northern Pacific called it quits and filed for abandonment. The Taylors Falls depot survives as a community center.

White Bear to Minneapolis, others to St. Paul, and still others to Minneapolis via St. Paul. Some branch-line trains transferred their passengers to main-line Duluth trains at White Bear. There was even a shuttle on the Stillwater branch between White Bear and Mahtomedi.

Service frequencies varied over the years. In 1886 there were ten daily round trips between Minneapolis and Stillwater. By 1900 these trains had disappeared. Elsewhere, the Northern Pacific fielded a robust schedule well into the 1920s. The 1920 timetable shows three pairs of trains from St. Paul to Taylors Falls, four trains between Stillwater and White Bear, and eight between Mahtomedi and White Bear, with three of them running through to St. Paul Union Depot.

The Twin City Rapid Transit Company began streetcar service from downtown St. Paul to Stillwater in 1899, Mahtomedi in 1891, and White Bear in 1904, but evidently it wasn't able to woo all the business from the Northern Pacific because the suburban trains kept right on running. The suburban trains were faster, twenty-two to thirty minutes for the trains to White Bear versus sixty-two minutes for the streetcars, and thirty-five to forty minutes by trains to Mahtomedi versus fifty-three minutes by streetcar. The trains also provided the only direct service to the north shore of White Bear Lake, offering multiple local stops.

St. Paul to North St. Paul and Stillwater

From 1887 to 1891, the Wisconsin Central fielded several daily suburban trains from St. Paul to stations in North St. Paul. When Northern Pacific controlled Wisconsin Central, the trains were extended to Stillwater via a connection with Northern Pacific at Stillwater Junction. Running time was forty-five to fifty minutes one way.

The steam-powered narrow-gauge North St. Paul railroad initiated a competitive service in 1890 with hourly trains running from the end of the East Seventh Street cable-car line at Duluth Avenue. The line was electrified and standard-gauged in 1892 and acquired by Twin City Rapid Transit in 1898.

St. Paul to Lake Elmo and Stillwater

The St. Paul, Stillwater & Taylors Falls built into Stillwater in 1872. It subsequently became part of the Omaha. Local service was a mixture of through Stillwater runs and shuttles to main-line trains at Stillwater junction. At the peak there were six daily pairs of suburban trains from St. Paul Union Depot and three pairs of shuttles to Stillwater Junction. As late as 1926 there were still six eastbound and four westbound shuttles to Stillwater Junction. The line from Stillwater Junction to Stillwater was abandoned in 1935, but service on its line between Stillwater and Hudson, Wisconsin, and a connection with main-line trains continued until after World War II.

St. Paul to St. Paul Park

The Chicago, Burlington & Northern—later Chicago, Burlington & Quincy—opened its Mississippi River line between St. Paul and Aurora, Illinois, in 1887 and immediately began a local suburban service between St. Paul Union Depot and Pullman Avenue in St. Paul Park. The trains lasted until September 1924.

1887   Six daily round trips

1890   Eleven round trips weekdays and Saturdays, eight on Sunday; thirty-five minutes running time to Pullman Avenue

1900   Five round trips on weekdays, six on Saturday, one on Sunday

In 1900, Pullman Avenue in Inver Grove was the last station on Burlington's commuter service from St. Paul Union Depot. This group appears ready to board a departing train for St. Paul.

St. Paul to Inver Grove

Chicago, St. Paul & Kansas City, predecessor to Chicago Great Western, began running commuter trains between St. Paul and Inver Grove in 1886 using a pair of bidirectional 2-4-2T tank engines, which it dubbed "motors." The service ran hourly, seven days a week, primarily serving the large workforce at the South St. Paul stockyards. These trains were scheduled separately and did not appear in the regular timetable or the *Official Guide*. They ran from a small suburban station at the foot of Jackson Street until 1899, when they were moved to St. Paul Union Depot. Streetcar competition appeared in 1905 when Twin City Rapid Transit built out Concord Street to South St. Paul. The trains were gone by 1912.

St. Paul, Cardigan Junction, and Minneapolis

The Soo Line had a number of suburban stations on its lines from Minneapolis to Cardigan Junction

The Chicago Great Western ran commuter trains to South St. Paul using a bidirectional steam locomotive termed a "motor." This photograph shows one of the trains at South St. Paul circa 1900. The Twin City Rapid Transit Company extended its electric line to South St. Paul in 1905. The commuter trains were gone by 1912.

and from St. Paul through Cardigan Junction to White Bear Beach. They were used for freight and for main-line local passenger trains. By 1912 only three—Bulwer Junction (New Brighton), Cardigan Junction, and Bald Eagle Junction—were still in use, and they were served by a lone local passenger accommodation. Train 94 left St. Paul Union Depot at 7:55 a.m. Monday through Saturday, running to Cardigan Junction, where it became train 111 to Minneapolis, and arriving in Minneapolis at 8:35 a.m. The train retraced its steps in the evening, departing Minneapolis at 5:50 p.m. In Minneapolis it terminated at the old Soo Line Minneapolis depot on Second Street at Fifth Avenue North, not the Milwaukee depot on Washington Avenue. One of the Soo Line's Duluth trains and a day train from Ladysmith, Wisconsin, also used this depot. This train was also a convenient way to deadhead passenger equipment between St. Paul Union Depot and the Soo Lines's Shoreham Shops. It is not known when it was discontinued, but it probably did not survive the 1920s.

Mail on the Suburban Trains

Besides commuters, the suburban trains were used to carry the U.S. mail between and for local destinations. Frequencies between stations in 1891 were as follows:

Hourly between Minneapolis and St. Paul

Five times daily between Stillwater and St. Paul

Four times daily between Stillwater and Minneapolis

Three times daily between St. Anthony Park and St. Paul and between Merriam, Macalester, and Minneapolis via the Milwaukee

Twice daily between St. Anthony Park and Minneapolis; Hamline and Minneapolis and St. Paul; Merriam Park and Minneapolis; Fort Snelling, Minneapolis, and St. Paul

Once daily between Fort Snelling, Minnehaha, and Minneapolis

The Sperry Report

The increase in traffic from the Great Encampment prompted the board of directors to retain Henry M. Sperry, an engineering consultant, to study the situation and make recommendations for improvements. Writing in his 1901 report, Sperry found, "The capacity of the station is now taxed to the utmost during the busy hours, making it impossible to handle any additional trains without great delays." Fundamental was a shortage of track space. Moreover, expansion would require acquiring developed property on the north or filling the river channel on the south. The depot timetable of March 6, 1901, showed the nine railroad companies scheduling 202 arrivals and departures

Sometime around 1910 a distinguished-looking group crowds the observation platform of an unidentified Soo Line train as it awaits departure beneath the 1889 train shed of the St. Paul Union Depot.

daily. The heaviest hour was from 8:00 to 9:00 a.m., when 96 trains entered and left the station. Ten tracks were available to handle this traffic, nine of them stub tracks under the station shed. Only one was a through track running parallel to the river, and it was also used for freight-car transfers.

From Broadway, at the east end of the shed, to Willius Street, the right-of-way owned by the depot company was wide enough for only three of the ten tracks, creating a serious bottleneck at busy times when multiple trains were moving in and out of the depot. Of the three, the north and the middle tracks were typically used for westbound departures and the south track for those to the east and south. A fourth track to the north of the three was owned and controlled by the Great Northern and reserved for its trains—a stipulation demanded by James J. Hill in the original operating agreement.

On account of the narrow right-of-way from Broadway east, all tracks in the shed were short; the longest, tracks 8 and 9, were 650 and 700 feet in length, respectively. By comparison a ten-car passenger train of that era, including its locomotive, was typically 740 to 750 in length, putting it on the crossovers at the terminal throat and thereby blocking access to the other tracks. The alternative was to split the train and spot it on two tracks, but that required additional switching moves and even more congestion and delay.

Complicating matters, the railroads were loath to cooperate in scheduling their trains in and out of the depot. A timetable from 1901 found six trains given the same time as six other trains moving over the same track entering or leaving the station. In one incident a special train scheduled to arrive at 9:00 a.m. showed up at 7:50 with scant notice to the terminal superintendent. Once

Looking east at the yard and approach tracks from the roof of the 1889 train shed. The Great Northern's coach yard and other railroad freight houses are on the left; the Mississippi River is on the right. The Third Street viaduct is visible on the far left.

As more trains were added to their schedules, railroads struggled to find the space to store passenger cars for inspections and maintenance. In this photograph taken about 1900, the coach yards east of the depot are packed with cars.

assigned to a track, it was discovered that the passengers were not up and dressed and ready to deboard. As a result, the train sat in the shed for some forty minutes, delaying six other trains waiting to arrive or depart. The terminal's timetable, which in railroad parlance is "the authority for the movement of regular trains subject to the rules," was completely at the whim of the railroads. It was not unusual for as many as five timetables to be issued in just forty-two days.

Freight-train transfer movements created still more issues. Besides passenger trains, one of the depot's through tracks was used by freights of the tenant railroads to transfer cars. On one typical day in 1901, 106 freight transfers moved through the terminal consuming six hours and ten minutes. The trains were slow and were required to make a complete stop at Third Street before entering one of the main-line tracks. Any delay or mishap could tie up the entire terminal.

The depot coach yard was located east of the train shed. Because of its limited capacity, it was used only for short-term storage of cars and the makeup of trains. The movement of cars to and from the station and the coach yard caused considerable congestion because it required use of one of the three approach tracks. There was no separate switching, or drill, track for shunting cars and locomotives.

In 1901 the depot was a terminal station for all Northern Pacific trains except those from Duluth and certain other stations on the Lake Superior Division. These trains terminated at Minneapolis. Empty trains were backed to and from the railroad's Mississippi Street coach yard and engine terminal. Lake Superior Division trains headed in and out with the road engine running around its train and turning on the depot turntable. White Bear suburban trains terminated at the depot and used the depot coach yard and turntable.

The coach yard was just east of the depot. Trains were moved between the yard and the depot by Union Depot switch engines. For the Chicago, St. Paul, Minneapolis & Omaha Railway, the depot was a through station for trains coming from Wisconsin and the east. Trains headed into the depot, then the road engine was cut off, turned on the depot turntable, and returned to its train, which continued on the Great Northern's line to Minneapolis.

Chicago, Milwaukee & St. Paul trains coming from the east on the Mississippi River line (River Division) ran through the depot and continued on the Short Line to the Milwaukee depot in Minneapolis. Trains from the west on the Hastings and Dakota Division and those from the south on the Iowa and Minnesota Divisions that were not continuing on to Minneapolis terminated at the depot and used the depot coach yard.

The depot was a through station for the Chicago Great Western Railway except for commuter trains, which began using the depot after 1898. Long-distance trains entered the depot from Great Western's Mississippi River bridge and proceeded on to Minneapolis via the Northern Pacific's "A" line to its own station on Washington Avenue.

Chicago, Burlington & Quincy through trains to Chicago arriving from Minneapolis via Great Northern's line backed into the station using one leg of the Burlington's wye track. Westbound trains typically ran in and backed out. Suburban trains from St. Paul Park terminated at the station.

Minneapolis, St. Paul & Sault Ste. Marie trains from the west operated through Minneapolis (using Great Northern's station) and reached St. Paul via Northern Pacific's "A" line. They terminated at the depot and used the depot coach yard. Trains originating in Minneapolis and going to or from the east headed into the depot, with the engine turning on the depot turntable. All Wisconsin Central trains were either turned on the wye track at Trout Brook Junction and then backed in or headed out of the station, or they ran into the station and their engines were turned on the depot turntable. (The Soo Line subsequently moved to the Milwaukee depot in Minneapolis and began using the Short Line for its trains.)

In 1901 the Minneapolis & St. Louis was still using its station at Broadway and Fourth, but it moved to St. Paul Union Depot in 1902.

In 1901 the Burlington, Cedar Rapids & Northern was still constructing its new route into the Twin Cities and would, within the year, lose its identity to the Rock Island, which subsequently used St. Paul Union Depot as a through station, operating its trains to and from Minneapolis via the Milwaukee's Short Line.

The depot building was similarly inadequate for the traffic it was expected to handle. Over 1 million pieces of baggage were moved through the depot each year, some 2,216 pieces a day. (By comparison, Grand Central Terminal in New York, one of the busiest stations in the country, was handling an average of 2,654 pieces per day in a baggage facility twice the size of St. Paul's.) The ticket office was small, prompting long lines at the windows at busy times, and the waiting rooms were overcrowded. Of greater concern were the through tracks that passed by the depot at grade, creating a serious hazard for pedestrians and wagons on Sibley Street.

Sperry's report foresaw a 60 percent increase in traffic and noted that it was safe to predict "that with the growth of the Northwest, St. Paul, located as it is at the center of North America, will move forward at a pace so rapid that transportation facilities not even dreamed of will be demanded."

Sperry's recommended improvements called for an expansion of the train shed, four additional tracks and the lengthening of tracks already in use, the separation of passenger from freight traffic through the terminal, a switching lead, or drill, track for the coach yard, and the construction of three interlocking plants to control switches and signals and the movement of trains in and out of the depot. The station building should be remodeled and enlarged. There was no need to construct a new head house or acquire additional property. All passenger facilities could be relocated to the second floor of the depot with the ground floor turned over completely to baggage, mail, and express and an immigrant waiting room. To provide additional room, an addition could be constructed over the through tracks. The use of the second floor for all waiting rooms, the ticket office, and a restaurant would require that Sibley Street be brought up on an elevated roadway from Third Street to the new depot entrance on the second floor. Access to all platforms and trains would be by stairway.

A switch engine pushes a cut of cars toward the old train shed. It's 1915 and construction on the new facility has yet to begin as railroad officials haggle over costs. The semaphore signal on the right governs access to the Chicago Great Western's Mississippi River bridge.

Recommended Interlocking Plants and Track Work

Sperry's report envisioned four interlocking plants as follows: a yard tower controlling all switches leading to the terminal throat; the crossing of the Chicago, Burlington & Quincy and Chicago, Milwaukee & St. Paul, and the coach yard and freight transfer tracks; Sibley Street and the connections with the Chicago Great Western and Chicago, Milwaukee & St. Paul; and Third Street and the junction with the Great Northern and Northern Pacific main lines.

The plants would be electro-pneumatic, using electricity to activate signals and a display or mimic board in the towers, showing the position of switches and signal aspects, and compressed air to power switch motors. Semaphore-type signals would be mounted on signal bridges above the track governed or on a mast to the right of the track. All tracks in the depot would be wired with electric track circuits to detect the presence of a train and display it on a signal board in the yard tower. Electric push buttons would be located on the platforms for conductors to signal the yard tower when their train was ready to depart.

A train director located in the yard tower would control all train movements through the depot yard. The director would be linked to the Sibley Street and Third Street towers by telephone and telegraph as well as the dispatchers of the tenant railroads and the towers at West St. Paul (Chicago Great Western), Chestnut Street (Chicago, Milwaukee & St. Paul), Mississippi Street (Northern Pacific), East Seventh Street (Northern Pacific), Westminster Street (Great Northern), and Dayton's Bluff (Chicago, Burlington & Quincy).

A force of twenty-two employees per shift would have been required to operate and maintain the three interlocking plants, the same number then employed to manually switch the depot yard. However, it would have vastly improved the efficiency of depot operations at peak times.

1901–1902 Improvements

The recommendations in Sperry's report demanded money, lots of it, but more than money, they required cooperation, a commodity forever in short supply among the owning railroads. Sperry's report noted that the Union Depot Company had no authority over the railroads in scheduling their trains and that the railroads turned a deaf ear when there were protests from the terminal superintendent. Sperry admonished the roads to follow the example of the Terminal Railroad Association of St. Louis, operator of St. Louis Union Station. There the timetable was subject to the approval of the terminal company, not the tenant lines. Sperry warned, "If the interests of all concerned cannot be properly provided for, then, in turn, all must suffer. A union station should be all that the name implies."

That message was only partially heeded. The railroads agreed to expand the train shed and rearrange the depot's trackage with some filling of the river, but there was no consensus on other recommended improvements. The head house, with the exception of a small addition, remained unchanged, and the interlocking plants, which would have vastly improved terminal efficiency, were never built, even though the proposal would resurface many times. As late as the 1950s studies were underway to install an automated interlocking to govern train movements. All agreed to the advantages, but when it came time to vote the money, the board could never bring itself to support the project by appropriating funds for the work.

None of this pleased James J. Hill and the Great Northern; by 1909 the railroad had acquired all of the property along Third Street north of the existing depot from Sibley Street to the bluff at the eastern end of the railroad yards. This land, together with the property already owned by the Union Depot Company, would permit construction of a grand station equal to any in the United States, with sufficient room for more than thirty tracks and a head house with waiting rooms, dining rooms, ticket offices, and other public spaces and amenities together with baggage and mail facilities worthy of a city that had become the railroad gateway to the Northwest.

Louis Hill, James J. Hill's son and then president of the Great Northern, issued a statement in the July 22, 1909, *St. Paul Dispatch* that the Great Northern would use its land to construct its own station if the railroads owning the existing station would not agree to a plan that would give the city adequate facilities. Hill went on to say: "The Great Northern has made every effort to increase the facilities here and we are ready to begin actual work on a new building. There has been constant pressure brought to bear on the owners of the union station to have it rebuilt on better lines, but there are too many owners interested. Nine railroads own shares in the depot, and each are afraid to move alone. The Great Northern will have a depot of its own unless a new one is built. We are ready to meet the present owners in any plan that is mutually attractive and have been for the past twenty-five years. The present station has been rebuilt three times in the past twenty-five years, but has not been bettered to any great extent. And the recent agitation begun by business interests of the city is causing some stir among the directors of the station. None of the directors is willing to move alone and the talk of getting nine men representing as many different companies, has been too great to be accomplished to date."

Individually, the railroads were in favor of a grand new station, but collectively there was no agreement. It would take a catastrophe to force it on them. ❊

Overcrowded yards and approach tracks as seen from Dayton's Bluff in 1918. The old depot burned in 1913. Five years later there was very little change as disputes and World War I stalled work on the new facility.

St. Paul Union Depot was among the last of the great stations. Finished in 1926 at a cost of $15 million, it was the largest construction project in downtown St. Paul in the twentieth century.

3
A NEW UNION DEPOT FOR ST. PAUL

Finding Consensus

Firefighters were summoned to the old depot late on the evening of October 3, 1913. A small fire smoldering in the second-floor restaurant kitchen, undetected for perhaps an hour, had burned its way through an inside wall, found a draft, and exploded, enveloping the entire upper half of the building. Stationmaster B. J. Thorpe gave the alarm and ordered an immediate evacuation of the approximately two hundred employees and waiting passengers. Everyone got out safely, even Sarah the depot cat, but by the time firemen arrived, the fire had gone through the roof, and it was hopeless. It was the second fire in the depot in thirty years, and it left St. Paul and over two hundred daily passenger trains without a rail station.

The railroads responded to the emergency with their usual efficiency. Officials of every stripe descended on St. Paul. Even retired Great Northern president James J. Hill, traveling in the west, returned by special train. There was no interruption in service. The charred rubble of the old depot was cleared within forty-eight hours while trains continued to arrive and depart on schedule from beneath the undamaged train shed. Coaches and baggage cars were converted to temporary waiting rooms and ticket offices. Park benches were brought in from Phalen Park to accommodate waiting passengers. Meanwhile, a nearby warehouse was rebuilt as a temporary depot, and what was left of the ruined building became a baggage room.

The front (Sibley Street) side of the 1884 depot received an addition in 1900 enlarging both men's and women's waiting rooms. It's visible behind the gentleman in the buggy. A larger steam heating plant was also installed (the stack on the side of the building). Ironically, when the depot burned in 1913, only the addition survived.

Planning for a new depot was already under way when the old depot burned. The board of directors had formed an engineering committee and appointed W. C. Armstrong, then chief engineer of the Union Depot Company, as engineer for the project. But there was mixed enthusiasm, especially over the extent and the cost of the new facility. The Great Northern and the Northern Pacific, both with corporate headquarters in St. Paul, were enthusiastic backers as were the Milwaukee and the Omaha, the latter having a large passenger presence in St. Paul. The Burlington was similarly inclined; it enjoyed a healthy passenger traffic base and was controlled by Great Northern and Northern Pacific. The Soo Line, the Rock Island, and the Minneapolis & St. Louis operated fewer passenger trains but were persuaded of the need for a new terminal and were sensitive to the public interest.

That left the Chicago Great Western and its president Samuel Felton. Much of the public frustration over delays rested squarely on his shoulders. Felton was a difficult man with an even more

The October 1913 fire consumed the upper floors, leaving only a shell of the 1884 building. Thoughts of repair were set aside as railroad officials resumed planning for a new depot. Remains of the old building became a baggage room. The train shed survived, and a nearby warehouse was remodeled as a waiting room and ticket office. Days after the fire, workers picked through the rubble.

The Sibley Street side of the station after the fire. The 1899–1900 addition survived and would become the baggage room. The rest of the building would be demolished.

After the fire a temporary waiting room and ticket office were constructed in a nearby warehouse. This stairway and concourse led from the train shed to the interim facilities.

difficult challenge, rescuing the Chicago Great Western. The Great Western was the creation of Minnesota railroader Alpheus B. Stickney, a personal friend of James J. Hill. Stickney acquired a number of smaller railroads and knitted them together with new main lines, transforming the Great Western into a scrappy, Midwestern powerhouse and a thorn in the side of established players Chicago & North Western, Milwaukee Road, and the Rock Island. The Great Western reached the Twin Cities, Des Moines, Omaha, Chicago, and Kansas City, but unfortunately, so did its competitors, and the financial panic of 1907 pushed it, along with fifty-one other railroads, into receivership. On August 21, 1909, it was sold at auction for $12,000,000 to a financial syndicate controlled by J. P. Morgan. Felton was subsequently hired as a consultant to evaluate the property. Impressed, Morgan made him president. Felton, then fifty-seven, had made a reputation as a doctor of sick railroads. Edward H. Harriman had earlier made him president of the Chicago & Alton when that road was in need of a turnaround. In eight years he almost doubled its earnings.

A NEW UNION DEPOT FOR ST. PAUL

Chicago Great Western president Samuel Felton *(front row, far left)* joined other railroad executives at a 1921 White House meeting. Felton thought plans for the new depot were far too ambitious and expensive. He argued for a smaller facility, possibly in St. Paul's Midway District. History would prove him right.

Felton was gruff, humorless, and arrogant and cared little about anything except efficiency and the bottom line. But he got results. Subordinates were given no quarter. In one famous incident he dressed down Walter P. Chrysler, the road's superintendent of motive power, over a hotbox that had caused a three-minute delay on the *Great Western Limited*. Chrysler had enough and resigned, moving on to found the Chrysler Corporation, builder of automobiles and trucks that ultimately put the Great Western out of business for good.

MILWAUKEE ROAD DEPOT

In 1898 the *Minneapolis Tribune* called it "a splendid structure, one of the finest buildings of its kind in the Northwest and an ornament to the city." The *Tribune* was referring to the new Chicago, Milwaukee & St. Paul passenger station. Designed by architect Charles Frost, the depot and its train shed stand today, despite several attempts at demolition in the 1970s.

The depot replaced an earlier (1877) structure on the same site. By the turn of the century, Minneapolis had become the flour- and lumber-milling capital of the nation, and its growth had outpaced St. Paul's. The Milwaukee made Minneapolis its Minnesota headquarters city and constructed a large shop complex in south Minneapolis near Twenty-Eighth Street and Hiawatha Avenue South. Now it needed a new passenger station to enhance its standing.

The three-story rectangular building (130 by 120 feet) that went up at the corner of Washington and Third Avenues South is a blend of Renaissance and Victorian architectural styles. The first story is pink Ortonville granite, the same material that is used on the Minneapolis city hall. The upper stories are faced with yellow brick. A square yellow brick tower faces Third Avenue. That tower was originally 140 feet high and capped by an ornate cupola. It was shortened to 100 feet in 1941 following damage in a windstorm. The depot was built as a stub end station with a 100-foot-wide, 600-foot-long train shed spanning five tracks. A 225-foot baggage, mail, and express building stood north of the shed. The ticket office, waiting room, and a station restaurant were on the ground floor. The upper floors were offices.

In its heyday the Milwaukee hosted twenty-nine trains a day in and out of the station, along with trains of tenant roads Soo Line and Rock Island. Among the Milwaukee's named trains were the overnight Chicago–Twin Cities *Pioneer Limited*, the *Morning Hiawatha* and *Afternoon Hiawatha*, and the *Olympian* and the *Columbian* to Seattle–Tacoma. The Soo Line fielded the *Winnipeger* to Winnipeg, Manitoba, and the *Mountaineer* to Vancouver, British Columbia, along with trains to Duluth, Chicago, and Sault Sainte Marie, Michigan. The Rock Island's Rockets headed south for Des Moines, St. Louis, Kansas City, and Dallas–Fort Worth with through Pullmans for Los Angeles via a connecting train at Kansas City.

The interior was remodeled in 1939. Individual padded chairs replaced the wood benches. A drop ceiling was installed along with fluorescent lighting and a modernized ticket office.

Passenger traffic declined during the Depression but rebounded during World War II. Peacetime conditions brought back the passenger losses, and they accelerated rapidly in the late 1950s and early 1960s. First to exit the depot was the Soo Line in 1967, followed by the Rock Island in 1969. When Amtrak took over, only one train remained, the Milwaukee's *Morning Hiawatha* to Chicago.

The Milwaukee depot at the corner of Washington and Third Avenues as it appeared in 1924. It was designed by architect Charles Frost and built in 1898–1899, replacing a late 1870s facility at the same location. The cupola atop the clock tower was damaged in a 1941 windstorm and subsequently removed. The depot closed when Amtrak took over in 1971. It was used as an office building by the Milwaukee until 1978, when the railroad filed for bankruptcy. Years of neglect and vandalism followed until the City of Minneapolis bought it for redevelopment in 1992. In 2012 it is part of a Radisson Marriott Hotel and restaurant complex.

MILWAUKEE ROAD DEPOT   ☐ ☐ ☐   95

There followed some thirty years of neglect and decay. The Milwaukee used the building for offices until it filed bankruptcy in 1978. Thereafter it sat empty. The station tracks were ripped out, and the area under the shed was used for parking until the roof deteriorated so badly it became unsafe. In 1978 it was placed on the National Register of Historic Places. The City of Minneapolis acquired the property for redevelopment in 1992. Today, it is The Depot, a Marriott Renaissance hotel and restaurant.

Passengers await their trains in this 1925 interior view of the Milwaukee depot. A later remodeling project brought dropped ceilings, fluorescent lighting, and a more modern look.

The Milwaukee's *Afternoon Hiawatha* is about to board passengers as it awaits an 11:15 a.m. departure for Chicago. The solarium in its Skytop observation-parlor car gave wonderful views of the Mississippi River, Lake Pepin, and the bluff country of western Wisconsin. Sadly, the train disappeared from the Milwaukee's timetable in January 1970.

GREAT NORTHERN STATION MINNEAPOLIS

The Great Northern Station, located at the foot of Hennepin Avenue, replaced an 1885 building on the same site. It was designed by architect Charles Frost and opened in 1914. The depot was located about a mile from the downtown business district in an area that, by the Depression, had deteriorated to mostly cheap hotels and bars frequented by panhandlers and derelicts. Urban renewal cleared the area in the 1960s, and the depot was sandblasted and cleaned. It was the Twin Cities Amtrak station from 1971 until 1978 when Amtrak moved to a new station in St. Paul's Midway district. It was subsequently razed to make way for the Federal Reserve Bank.

James J. Hill disdained jointly owned passenger terminals. He wanted to own what he built, and his own experience confirmed the benefits. While railroad officials squabbled in St. Paul, Hill's Great Northern gave Minneapolis a fine new passenger station, replacing an older 1885 terminal on the same site at the foot of Hennepin Avenue opposite High Street and the Mississippi River. It was an excellent location, close to downtown businesses and the mill district and on a major thoroughfare with extensive streetcar service to all parts of the city.

As in St. Paul, constructing the new terminal with no interruption to traffic, which at the time was considerable, was a difficult problem. Each day 115 trains and some 11,000 passengers visited the depot during the peak summer months. That, along with 1,700 pieces of baggage and 8,200 sacks of mail, made for a very busy place. Like St. Paul, the majority of arrivals and departures occurred during early morning and early evening hours, with mostly local trains coming and going during the middle of the day.

Besides the owner, Great Northern, four other roads used the station: the Northern Pacific; the Chicago, Burlington & Quincy; the Chicago Great Western; and the Chicago, St. Paul, Minneapolis & Omaha. The Minneapolis & St. Louis moved in after completion of the new building. These tenant roads paid Great Northern for use of the station according to a formula that considered the number of tickets sold, the number of cars passing through the depot, and the volume of mail and express handled.

The old station was located on the south side of Hennepin Avenue with a train shed covering its six through tracks. Except for inadequate track capacity, it was an excellent arrangement. All of the coach yards and locomotive servicing facilities were located north or east of the depot. Since most of them departed to the south, they could be assembled in the coach yards and brought down by the road engine, which greatly minimized switching in the makeup of trains originating at the station.

Plans called for erecting the new station on the north side of Hennepin Avenue directly opposite the old. This was advantageous because it eliminated most of the interference to existing passenger traffic. The old depot remained open and in full operation until the new building was ready. Then it was razed to make way for a new mail and express building.

The new layout provided for twelve through tracks with the new head house directly above the station tracks and the Hennepin Avenue viaduct covering the platforms.

The project architect was Charles Frost, with the work carried out initially under the supervision of A. H. Hogeland and subsequently by Ralph Budd, both chief engineers for the Great Northern Railway. The total cost was $1.9 million.

The building was a rectangle, 155 by 300 feet, of steel-beam construction with brick walls faced by Kettle River sandstone. The two main entrances passed through massive arches at opposite ends of the building and thence through outer and inner vestibules leading to the main waiting room. The upper floors extended around three sides of the building; the central portion was the roof of the main waiting room. The station restaurant was located on the second floor on the west side of the building with windows looking out on the main lobby. The remainder of the upper floor space was used for offices and mechanical equipment for the building.

Butterfly-type train sheds covered the platforms, and a system of elevated trucking passageways led from the baggage room and the mail and express building across Hennepin Avenue to elevators at the end of the station platforms. A conductor signal system and telephones connected the platforms with the concourse gates. A separate powerhouse north and east of the depot supplied steam and electricity.

There were changes over the years. The second-floor restaurant was moved to the inner vestibule on the west side of the building. The ticket office was remodeled and given an open counter facing the waiting room. Meanwhile, the number of passenger trains steadily declined. The Minneapolis & St. Louis and the Omaha ended passenger service in the early 1960s. The Great Western followed in 1965. The Great Northern, Northern Pacific, and Chicago, Burlington & Quincy merged and became the Burlington Northern, and its trains lasted until Amtrak. Following closure of the St. Paul Union Depot, the Great Northern Station became the sole remaining passenger-train station in the Twin Cities, but with at most only four trains a day. Amtrak found it much too expensive and vacated in favor of a smaller facility near University and Cleveland Avenues in the St. Paul Midway. The building was torn down in 1978. The Federal Reserve Bank now occupies the site.

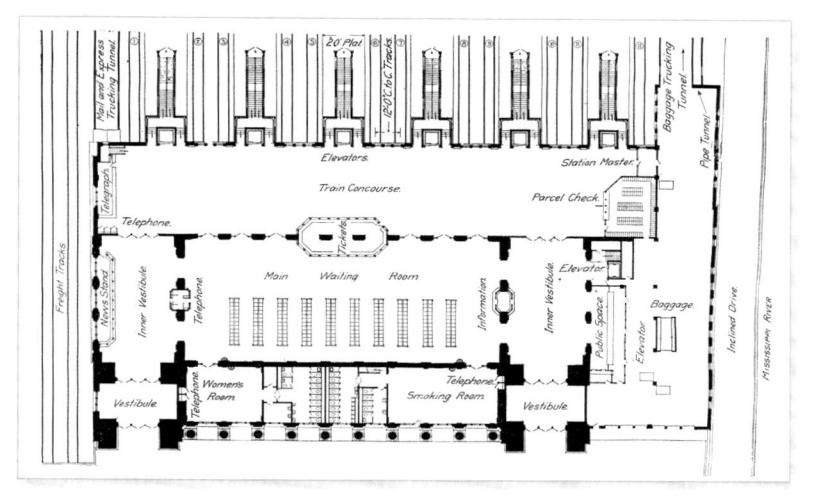

There were two main entrances to the Great Northern Station; both fronted on Hennepin Avenue, where a cabstand and frequent streetcar service were available for local transportation. Inside, both vestibules led to a main waiting room, which was separated from the train arrival and departure concourse by the ticket office. Services adjoining the waiting room included baggage and parcel check, newsstand, and restrooms. There was a station restaurant on the second floor, later relocated to the ground floor near the west vestibule. The upper floors of the building were used for offices. The station was built above the tracks and boarding platforms, which were accessed by stairs and elevators. A Railway Express building was across Hennepin Avenue next to the main downtown post office. Mail and express were moved to the depot platforms on elevated truckways. From *Railway Age Gazette* 56, no. 1.

The floor plan remained largely unchanged, but the depot's waiting room was given a fresh look with new paint and fluorescent lighting in 1950.

Felton represented the Great Western on the St. Paul Union Depot board of directors, and he represented it well. The Great Western was in no position to fund what Felton considered an extravagant project, and he resolutely opposed the more ambitious plans of the other railroads, led by Hill's Great Northern. In 1911 he argued against a proposal to retain William J. Wilgus, chief engineer of the New York Central, as a consultant. Wilgus was a national figure, one of the designers of Grand Central Terminal. Writing to James T. Clark, president of the Chicago, Milwaukee & St. Paul, Felton argued, "The Proposition of Mr. W. J. Wilgus does not appeal to me, and I think it would be a mistake to accept it and that it would result in considerable outlay and expense for which there would be no corresponding result. . . . I do not feel that there is any urgent necessity of our getting any outside and high priced talent. My experience has been that this course is generally unsatisfactory."

By 1914 the engineering committee had selected Charles Sumner Frost as architect for the project, a selection Felton opposed. Frost was a nationally recognized architect of railroad passenger terminals, having designed dozens of stations for the Chicago & North Western and the Milwaukee. The Milwaukee Road and Great Northern stations in Minneapolis were his work. Frost and the engineering committee envisioned a stub and through terminal with elevated tracks constructed on the existing site. It was a plan that would have required relocating the channel of the Mississippi by several hundred feet.

Felton objected, and in an April 1914 letter he challenged the engineering committee: "With reference to my recent letter on the subject of the St. Paul Union Station: I am very strongly opposed to the idea of elevating the tracks in the station because of the expense of that one item and the further expense of the under grade crossing of the freight tracks which are at an acute angle on curves involving the most expensive kind of construction. We have operated, for a great many years, and are operating successfully, tracks on the present surface and I believe they should remain there. . . . I have therefore addressed myself to a plan for utilizing our present facilities. . . . We can certainly postpone it for ten years and within that time the whole situation may be changed and a station midway between Minneapolis and St. Paul may be worked out and the present St. Paul station be merely a way station for St. Paul just as the Minneapolis station is now for Minneapolis. There are so many features connected with this particular station that may cause a change at an early date that it seems to me a crime to enter into any such expenditure as is proposed and I am firmly convinced that the estimates are far out of line. At Kansas City we started out to build a terminal with a maximum estimated cost of $25,000,00 but created a mortgage for $50,000,000. Before the station is in full operation we will have used up the entire $50,000,000. We can figure on the same experience at St. Paul. I very strongly urge that we start out by utilizing only the property we now have and leave a little something to the future and to those who will succeed us in the management of these properties."

Prophetically, Felton liked the idea of a Midway station, a proposal strongly supported by certain commercial interests and pushed by the *Midway News* but opposed by the other railroads and downtown businesses. Felton strongly criticized the cost estimates for the new station and had his chief engineer do an independent analysis, which put the cost at $18,244,711 compared to the $12,887,911 of the engineering committee. Felton was especially concerned about lifting the Great Western's Mississippi River bridge to bring it in line with the elevated trackage that was part of the proposed design and was determined that the Union Depot Company should bear this cost.

The board responded to Felton's charges and directed depot company president Edmund Pennington to secure a second opinion. Pennington hired no less a figure than John F. Wallace, former general manager of the Illinois Central Railway and former chief engineer for the Panama Canal project. A highly respected professional, Wallace came to the Twin Cities on June 2, 1914, to review the proposed plans and inspect the site. He also considered the area between Minneapolis and St. Paul and the possibility and desirability of building a union station in St. Paul's Midway.

In a letter to Pennington dated July 14, 1914, Wallace concurred with Felton's concerns over costs. However, he thought the $18 million figure too high and recommended a budget of $15 million. He also sided with Felton on the matter of the Great Western's bridge, suggesting the Union Depot Company should absorb the cost, citing as precedence similar projects elsewhere. With respect to the depot location he wrote, "It is my best judgment, based on my inspection and study of the situation and the facts and data which have been brought to my attention, and my experience as an engineer and railroad operating official, that the extension and development of the union passenger terminal on the site of the old station will best serve the interests of the railroads using the same, and the City of St. Paul, and is much preferable to any other site that has been considered, or suggested. In conclusion, I would recommend (1) that the site selected be adopted; (2) that the general features of the plan proposed by the Committee of Engineers be approved; and (3) that $15,000,000 be provided for the carrying out and completion of the scheme." Taking his recommendation, the board determined that the Union Depot Company should absorb the cost of raising the lift bridge and voted to proceed over Felton's and the Great Western's objections.

Let the Waters Be Parted

Union Depot Company officials gave St. Paul its first look at the proposed station at a city council meeting in January 1914. It was all about capacity. The plan would grow the terminal property from 17.2 to 54.2 acres, enough room for twenty-six tracks—sixteen of them stub and ten through—compared to the fourteen tracks in the old station. There would be four freight-transfer tracks and a 218-car coach yard provided for the switching and makeup of trains. Total track mileage would go from 9.2 to 24.9.

A three-level station building would rest on the corner of Sibley and Third Streets, with 315 feet fronting on the east side of Sibley and 220 feet fronting on the south side of Third. Sibley Street would continue to the levee, passing beneath the elevated passenger and freight tracks. Third Street would descend to the east with an entrance for baggage, mail, and express in the basement level at Wacouta Street.

The main entrance to the ticket office and waiting room would be on the ground level through a large vestibule at the corner of Third and Sibley. A side hall off the vestibule would lead to eleva-

In 1914 the Union Depot Company revealed plans for a new depot so large that it would have required diverting the channel of the Mississippi River to make room for the head house building, boarding platforms, and yard tracks. This artist's rendering shows architect Charles Frost's conceptual design. The building would have faced Third Street with the main entrance on Sibley Street.

A NEW UNION DEPOT FOR ST. PAUL 101

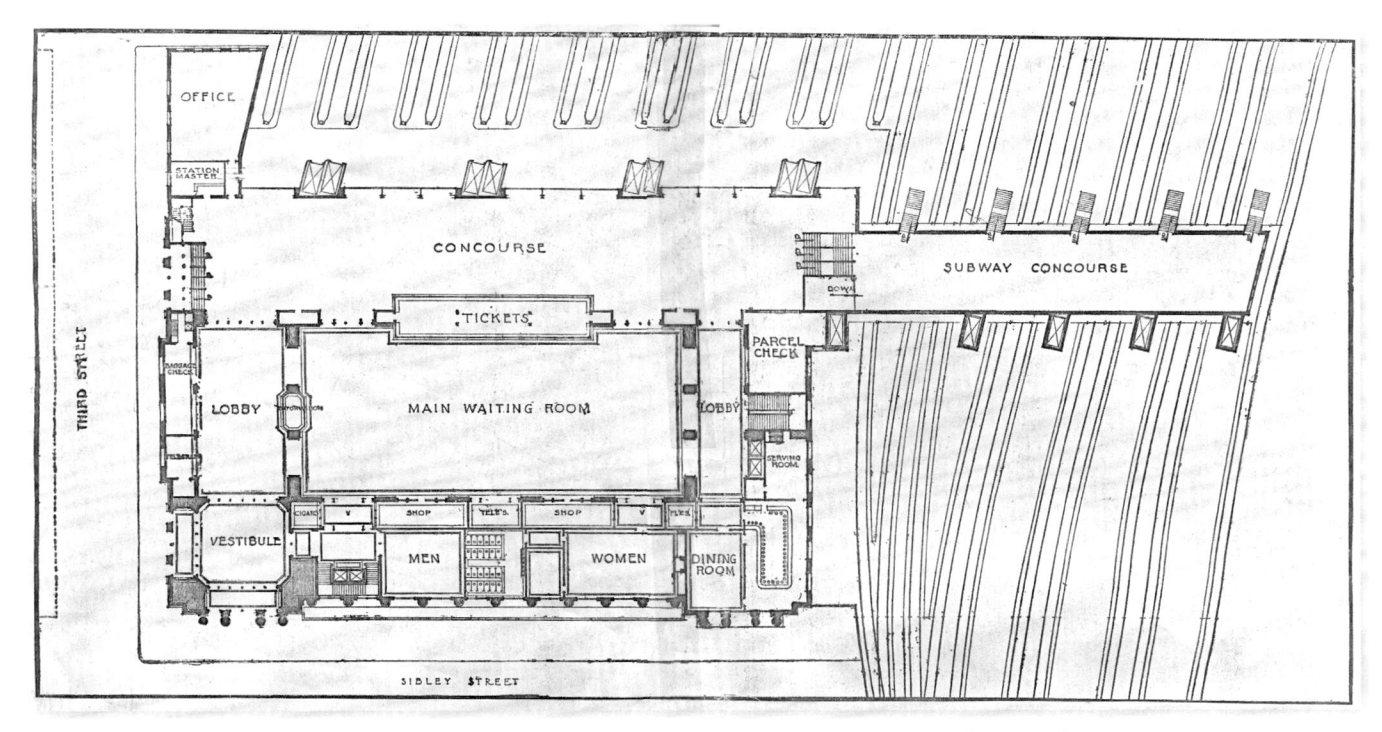

This is the ground floor of the 1914 plan. From the entrance passengers would step through a large vestibule into the lobby, then proceed through the lobby to the main waiting room. The ticket office separated the waiting room from the boarding concourse, which continued as a subway under the tracks. A dining room, lunch counter, parcel check, and shops surrounded the waiting room.

tors and stairs. All of the depot services were to be arranged around the main waiting room, with the ticket office located between the main waiting room and the concourse. The concourse would have a separate entrance to Third Street. The sixteen stub tracks abutted the concourse. A separate subway and concourse would run beneath the through tracks with stairs and elevators leading to the platforms above. A careful study was made of other stations with the goal of providing smooth, easy access to trains from the ticketing and baggage areas. In this design, passengers purchasing tickets and checking baggage would have to walk no more than four hundred feet to their trains.

A twenty-thousand-square-foot baggage room and a forty-thousand-square-foot mailroom would be located in the basement area beneath the tracks. Baggage and mail would be trucked through a subway where it would be raised to track level by one of the twenty-five lifts located at the end of each platform. The second story would have offices and meeting rooms, the kitchen for the main dining room, a small infirmary, and a retiring room for women traveling with small children.

The building would be in the then-popular neoclassical style, the base course of Minnesota granite and the area above in Bedford limestone. Its overall size would be larger than the new Chicago and North Western station in Chicago.

At the time, all of the passenger and freight tracks were at grade and crossed each other at grade. This aggravated congestion in the terminal area was one of the most objectionable features of the old facility. The new plans called for elevating passenger tracks some eighteen feet above the freight tracks, thereby achieving a complete separation. Doing this, however, meant a complete reworking of the approaches to the station along with changes to streets and bridges. At the northern entrance to the depot yards, the existing Third Street viaduct would have to be raised twenty-five feet. Fourth Street, which did not presently cross the tracks, would go under them. The Sixth Street Bridge would have to have several of its piers relocated to accommodate additional tracks. The western approach to the terminal would require even more work. The ten through tracks would cross Sibley Street on a steel viaduct eighteen feet above the street level. From Jackson Street, the tracks of the Omaha and the Milwaukee would begin to descend, passing under the Robert Street Bridge approximately fifteen feet higher than the existing grade. At the Wabasha Street Bridge they would be eleven feet above grade. From that point, the Omaha tracks would descend to grade whereas the Milwaukee's would continue on the viaduct, crossing over Eagle and Chestnut Streets and thereby reducing the approach to the Milwaukee's long grade up and out of the river valley.

More land was needed, and to avoid taking expensive developed property north of Third Street, the plan called for moving the Mississippi River south of its present channel, an alternative that was supported by the St. Paul Association of Commerce. It wanted to increase the amount of developable land adjoining the downtown business district, which then took in some two hundred acres in an area bounded by Wabasha, Tenth Street, Broadway, and the river. Two alternatives were studied. One would divert the course of the river just below Raspberry Island in a new channel over the river flats. Another, more ambitious alternative called for returning the river to an ancient channel from Harriet Island around the West Side bluffs. This plan would have put all of the West Side river flats on the east side of the river, reclaiming six hundred to seven hundred acres of land for commercial and industrial uses. It was estimated it would take fifteen months to complete the work. But Midway business and real estate interests wanted to draw more development to the area between Snelling Avenue and the city limits; they vigorously opposed this proposal.

They were joined by Samuel Felton, who was not persuaded and who continued objecting to the scope and cost of the project. He retained Jarvis Hunt, architect of the recently completed

Kansas City Union Station, to draw up another set of plans that he believed would be less costly. The engineering committee and its chair, Ralph Budd, along with president Earling of the Milwaukee, took strong exception, criticizing the layout of Hunt's design, its lack of room for future expansion, smoke issues, and inadequate space for handling mail and express. However, Felton's concerns found support at the Rock Island, which was then teetering on receivership. In a January 20, 1915, letter, Rock Island president Mudge wrote: "There is a strong feeling on the part of all railway executives and their boards of directors, and, I believe, on the part of the Interstate Commerce Commission that the enormous expenditures for union stations are unwarranted; that the interest upon these expenditures finally becomes a burden upon the people because of the fact that the Commission must eventually allow the roads sufficient rates to pay returns upon the investments. For this reason I think the Board of Directors of the St. Paul Union Depot Company should make every effort to keep the expenditures for that depot at the lowest possible amount consistent with good service to the traveling public. It has seemed to me from the start that the plan of changing the river was an extravagant one, and that some other plan might be adopted that would have capacity to take care of the traffic for a reasonable time, after which the entire geography of the city might be changed and enable a union station at a different location."

Then in April 1915, the Minnesota Legislature declined the railroad's application for a two-and-one-half-cent-per-mile intrastate passenger rate, and everything began unraveling. The Interstate Commerce Commission governed interstate passenger fares, but the U.S. Supreme Court in a 1913 case (Minnesota Rate Case 230 U.S. 352) ruled that states retained regulatory responsibility for trains operating solely within their borders.

An angry Pennington sent a personal note to all members of the board: "Gentlemen: I learn that the Legislature of Minnesota has not granted the two and one-half cent passenger rate. In our arguments that the two-cent rate does not pay, it seems to me that it would be ill advised for us to rush into a fifteen million dollar expenditure for a union depot in St. Paul, and I think that after we get the government's permission to change the river, we had better go slowly, having a meeting of all the roads interested to discuss the matter, and giving out something to the public which will correspond with our showing that a two cent passenger rate does not pay; therefore we cannot go into a much larger expenditure of money for a union station until we can see our way clear to get a return on the money invested. Please think this over, and I will be governed in calling such a meeting by your different answers."

Pennington's strategy was to use the depot issue to leverage support for a rate increase. It drew a mixed response. Samuel Felton of the Great Western returned to some of his old arguments and wrote back: "If we go ahead spending money in this reckless manner and then plead poverty before the legislature and the railroad commissions, I don't think we will make much progress. We are spending nearly fifty million dollars at Kansas City and it made no impression whatever on the legislature of Missouri and wasn't worth a cent as far as argument went for increased passenger fares. The members of the legislature and the public generally just laugh at us and say if we are so foolish as to spend that much money it is our own fault and we are not entitled to ask the public to help us out in order to make good our own lack of business judgment. We can build a station on the present location, with fifty percent more room in it than the old one. Why not do that, especially when you consider that the station I am talking about can be enlarged at any time in the future when the railroads decide it is advisable to change the channel of the river and extend the station facilities?"

There was merit to Felton's arguments and a need for a degree of caution. Passenger revenues were susceptible to a number of forces, not the least being the state of the general economy. Revenues per train mile varied with the volume of traffic, distance traveled, and the rate. At the time, there was more passenger traffic going west than east, reflecting the still ongoing movement of western settlement. Between 1907 and 1917 the Great Northern estimated it carried some 600,000 western settlers and transported 25,000 cars of personal property and household goods. The tour business to the national parks was strong and actively promoted by the railroads. But already there were signs of trouble. In 1914–15 the Great Northern saw a decline in the number of passengers carried and a 13.5 percent drop in its passenger revenue. Some attributed it to general uncertainty following the outbreak of war in Europe, but no one seemed to know for sure. What is known is that costs were rising for all railroads, including the costs of constructing new and expensive passenger terminals.

Responding to this, Ralph Budd, assistant to the president of the Great Northern, took a more moderate approach. He replied, "From the Union Depot Company's standpoint, we feel that this is an opportune time to proceed with the work, and from recent conversation with Chief Engineer Armstrong, I learn he is convinced that it will take five years instead of four to complete the job. It seems likely to [sic] that we will be very much in need of the new facilities five years hence, if a revival of business takes place, and all the work that can be contracted now—to be carried out later—will doubtless show a large saving over what it would cost to contract it in brisk times. From the individual railroad company's standpoint, I do not believe it is possible to influence the State Legislature to any great extent by connecting the Union Depot issue with the increased passenger rate. My conception of the Minnesota passenger rate situation has been that a serious effort should be made with the Legislature now sitting to secure an increase to two and one-half cents, but it was hardly expected that such effort would succeed. It has, however, laid the foundation for an appeal to the Interstate Commerce Commission for permission to increase the rate and plans are being made to that end. I think we must look in that direction for the needed relief and, therefore, believe that we have more to lose than to gain by delaying work longer than necessary on the Union Depot project, which will certainly result in a charge of bad faith and all the retaliation possible on the part of the citizens of St. Paul, with whom the Union Depot dealings must necessarily be had."

The other officers and directors expressed similar views, but theirs was a hollow triumph for good sense, because the War Department ultimately rejected the plans for relocating the channel, forcing the entire project to begin again. There was much complaint, but this time, at least, it was not the railroads' fault.

Starting Over

Starting over meant tearing up the old plans and turning away from the river to a strip of land north of the existing terminal along Third Street, an area then occupied by warehouses, the temporary depot, freight-handling facilities, and team tracks (used to store freight and express cars) owned by the Great Northern. Almost two years would be consumed in planning, arranging financing, acquiring property, and securing the necessary concurrences from the City of St. Paul. The latter involved several ordinances and resolutions permitting the vacating of streets and alleys. Specifically, all streets and alleys south of Third Street and all alleys in the block bounded by Fourth, Sibley, and Wacouta Streets, the future site of the head house, were to be vacated. The Union Depot Company was required to build subways under its elevated tracks at Sibley and Jackson Streets. The public levee along the elevated tracks was to be vacated with the proviso that the Union Depot Company must build a forty-six-foot-wide roadway along the river whenever permission could be secured from the Corps of Engineers.

Providing adequate capacity for moving trains, people, and mail and express was fundamental to the planning. Here, too, it was necessary to start over, and chief engineer Armstrong began with an investigation of track capacity and utilization at the existing depot. St. Paul had most of its trains arriving and departing between 7:00 and 9:00 a.m. and again between 7:00 and 10:00 p.m., with comparatively light traffic in the middle of the day. Moreover, the great majority of these trains were through trains continuing on to Minneapolis and the west, or Chicago and eastern and southern points. Some trains, those to Duluth and a few headed to western points on the Great Northern,

TRAINS USING ST. PAUL UNION DEPOT—SELECTED YEARS

Railroad	1927	1932	1937	1942	1944	1947	1952	1957	1962	1967	1969
Milwaukee	16,379	11,397	12,877	12,741	15,520	13,666	12,406	10,080	7,422	7,300	6,592
Omaha	18,920	15,405	15,310	11,860	10,507	11,457	10,117	6,365	1,460		
Great Northern	16,083	5,399	5,965	5,426	5,918	6,879	6,702	5,761	5,587	5,110	4,212
Soo	11,649	7,674	6,759	6,600	6,612	6,746	6,713	4,394	1,316	164	
Northern Pacific	15,971	5,449	5,323	4,957	5,875	5,295	4,972	5,216	3,506	2,524	1,404
Chicago Great Western	10,372	7,339	6,229	5,742	5,803	5,828	2,886	2,725	1,870		
Burlington	6,172	5,778	7,424	7,347	7,865	7,815	7,484	7,390	5,181	4,997	4,212
Minneapolis & St. Louis	6,880	6,142									
Rock Island	6,026	4,480	5,963	5,956	6,063	5,845	5,945	5,955	4,380	3,156	768
Daily Average											
Arriving	148	93	90	83	88	87	78	67	42	32	24
Departing	149	96	90	83	88	87	78	67	42	32	24
Total	297	189	180	166	176	174	156	134	84	64	48
Passenger tickets	421,194	123,913	145,417	202,846	331,085	239,977	172,418	124,193	93,587	92,948	64,852
Pullman tickets	75,549	33,169	46,232	34,958	35,786	29,010	22,594	10,338	6,783	4,405	
Total tickets sold	496,743	157,082	191,649	237,804	366,871	268,987	195,012	134,531	100,370	97,353	64,852
Pieces of baggage handled	604,160	165,427	345,174	unavailable	1,632,060	1,162,416	847,403	826,622	586,681	407,694	409,413
Pieces of mail	20,164,538	15,584,839	16,454,315	16,570,143	18,966,479	22,325,341	22,624,449	17,942,861	18,963,097	20,798,634	16,155,838

Source: St. Paul Union Depot Company annual reports

originated and terminated at St. Paul. Armstrong calculated that an optimal design, given the available space, would have seven stub tracks and fifteen through tracks. With these the depot could handle 1.1 million passenger cars per year, and if current trends continued, its capacity would not be reached until 1955. (In the final design this was revised slightly to provide for eight stub tracks and thirteen through tracks.)

There were other considerations. In 1916 the depot received and forwarded 1,285,852 pieces of baggage. Approximately 445 tons of mail passed through each day along with the 5 million items of express handled annually. Ticket agents sold 917,220 tickets worth $2,811,659.94. The volume of mail through the station was doubling every seven years, and baggage every ten. The Northwest was growing up and filling in, and everything was passing through St. Paul and its depot. Moreover, at the time there was no expectation that this would change. The depot of 1916 had to be the depot of 1955.

CHARLES SUMNER FROST AND THE FIRM OF FROST AND GRANGER

Charles Sumner Frost was one of the most productive architects of the Gilded Age. Frost, along with his business partner, Alfred H. Granger, and their firm Frost and Granger are credited with some two hundred railroad passenger stations for the Chicago & North Western, Milwaukee, Rock Island, and Great Northern, not to mention dozens of office buildings, schools, and private residences.

Frost, an 1876 graduate of the Massachusetts Institute of Technology, was born in Lewiston, Maine, in 1856. His early career was with the prestigious Boston firm of Peabody and Sterns, whose projects included the Duluth Union Depot and James J. Hill's mansion. In 1881 Frost moved to Chicago and partnered with Henry Ives Cobb in the firm Cobb and Frost. Although a partnership, each of the architects took credit for their respective designs, and Frost enjoyed several important commissions in Chicago, among them the gymnasium and the Durand Art Institute at Lake Forest College, the Union League Club, the Newberry Library, the Chicago Opera House, and the main building of the World's Columbian Exposition. Cobb left the partnership in 1889 and moved to New York, and Frost began turning his attention to the design of railroad terminals.

In 1885 Frost married Mary Hughitt, the daughter of Chicago & North Western president Marvin Hughitt. The Chicago & North Western was then in the process of building new stations throughout its system, and Frost's family connection brought him much of this business. Large notable examples of Frost's designs over the years include the LaSalle Street station and Chicago & North Western terminals in Chicago, the Chicago & North Western station in Milwaukee, the Milwaukee Road and Great Northern stations in Minneapolis, and the St. Paul Union Depot. Frost was responsible for the design of Navy Pier in Chicago in 1914.

Alfred H. Granger partnered with Frost in 1898 after marrying Belle, the other daughter of Marvin Hughitt. Granger, born in Zanesville, Ohio, in 1867, was also a graduate of the Massachusetts Institute of Technology and went on to study at the École des Beaux Arts in Paris. On returning to the United States, he went to work for the Boston firm of Shepley, Ruttan and Coolidge, and in 1891 he was in Chicago supervising construction of the art museum and the public library. He subsequently partnered with Frank Meade in the Cleveland, Ohio, firm of Granger and Meade. Frost and Granger worked together until 1910 when Granger left to establish a separate practice in Philadelphia.

Frost and Granger was a conservative firm, and the work of the partners, both collaboratively and individually, reflected the styles and the tastes of the era. *Architectural Record* for August 1905 noted that their design of buildings "reflected moderation and was praised for its civilized home-like air and gentility and was even more valuable socially than architecturally." It went on to state, "The new building promoted by the American railroads was at last falling into the hands of competent architects with the result that from the comparative standpoint there has been possible greater improvement in this class of buildings than any other." That conservatism, however, did not extend to a slavish adherence to standard railroad design. Their work took its cues from the local surroundings and the standards of the communities the railroads served. Styles used included Beaux-Arts, Romanesque Revival, Renaissance Revival, Arts and Crafts, and Spanish Mission. Stone and brick were the preferred materials. Surviving examples of the partnership's work include depots in Ames, Iowa; Sleepy Eye, Minnesota; Madison, Wausau, Reedsburg, Racine, and Green Bay, Wisconsin; and Lake Forest, Illinois—among others. The Lake Forest depot continues to serve METRA passengers. The others have been converted to business offices, restaurants, or local museums.

Frost continued his work until retirement in 1928. He died on December 11, 1939. Granger retired from his practice in 1936 and died on December 3, 1939.

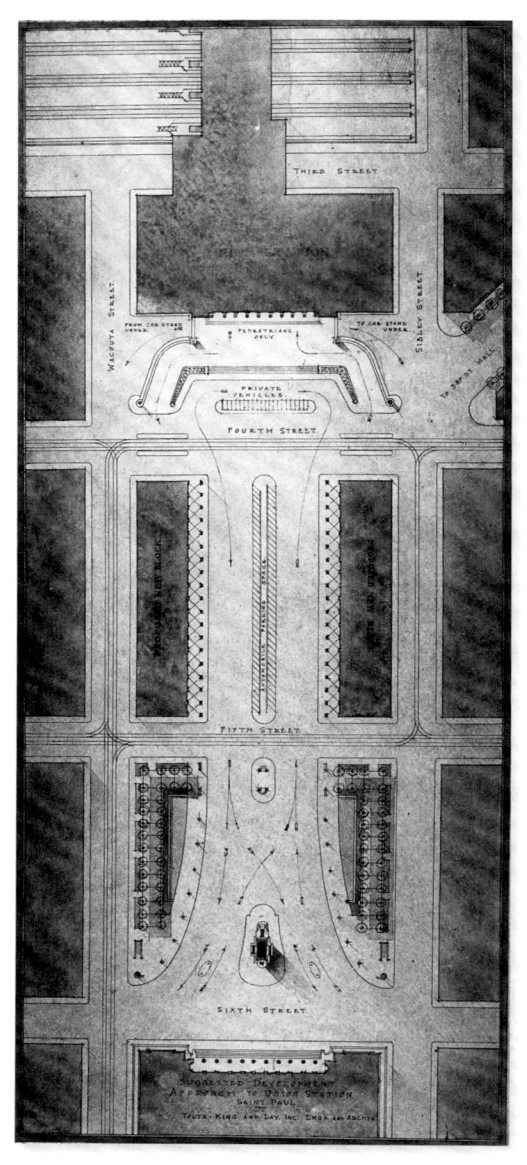

Stretching from Sixth Street all the way to the depot's entrance on Fourth Street, this grand esplanade was proposed by city fathers. When Samuel Felton of the Chicago Great Western suggested the City of St. Paul should pay for it, the matter was dropped.

It also had to be a depot worthy of a capital city, and architect Frost proposed several designs. One sketched shows a grand esplanade, reminiscent of Washington Union Station and the City Beautiful, stretching from Sixth Street to the head house on Fourth Street. It pleased the city fathers, but the railroads had little enthusiasm for such grandeur and expense, and it was never built. The terminal that emerged was less opulent than others of that era and was given mixed praise. *Railway Age* in 1920 called it "a structure of monumental proportions and classic design"; some sixty years later, in its 1974 inventory form, the National Register of Historic Places saw it as a "severe and rather sober example of Neoclassical architecture." Frank Lloyd Wright thought it "a beautifully spacious building, even if they did dog ear the tops of the columns."

There were several components in Frost's design: a head house and business lobby, a concourse leading to a large waiting room, the waiting room itself, platforms, the track structure and approaches, and the undertrack rooms for the handling of mail and express. Work began in 1917 with the demolition of a number of old warehouses along Third Street. In 2011 most of the key features of the buildings remain unchanged from Frost's original plans.

Head House

Built of reinforced concrete and structural steel, the head house building, 300 feet long and 150 feet wide, sits on the north side of Third Street in the block bounded by Third, Wacouta, Fourth, and Sibley Streets. It was designed to face a landscaped plaza, circular drive, and sidewalk. At the top of the steps, three groups of three doors located between Doric columns lead to an outer vestibule, then to the main lobby and an eighteen-window ticket office, along with restrooms, a parcel and baggage check, information desk, drugstore, barber shop, and a dining room and lunch counter.

The head house exterior is finished in gray Bedford limestone with Tennessee marble used for the floor, the walls, wainscoting, counters, and interior columns. Skylights, clerestory windows, and electroliers (chandeliers) provided illumination. A taxi subway-driveway extends beneath the

This is the original floor plan for the depot. The main entrance to the head house building is on Fourth Street. The ticket office, a lunchroom and dining room, shops, restrooms, and a parcel check surround the main lobby, which in turn leads to the concourse and waiting room. Most of these features remain today. From "After the Passenger Gets There," *Railway Age*, May 21, 1920.

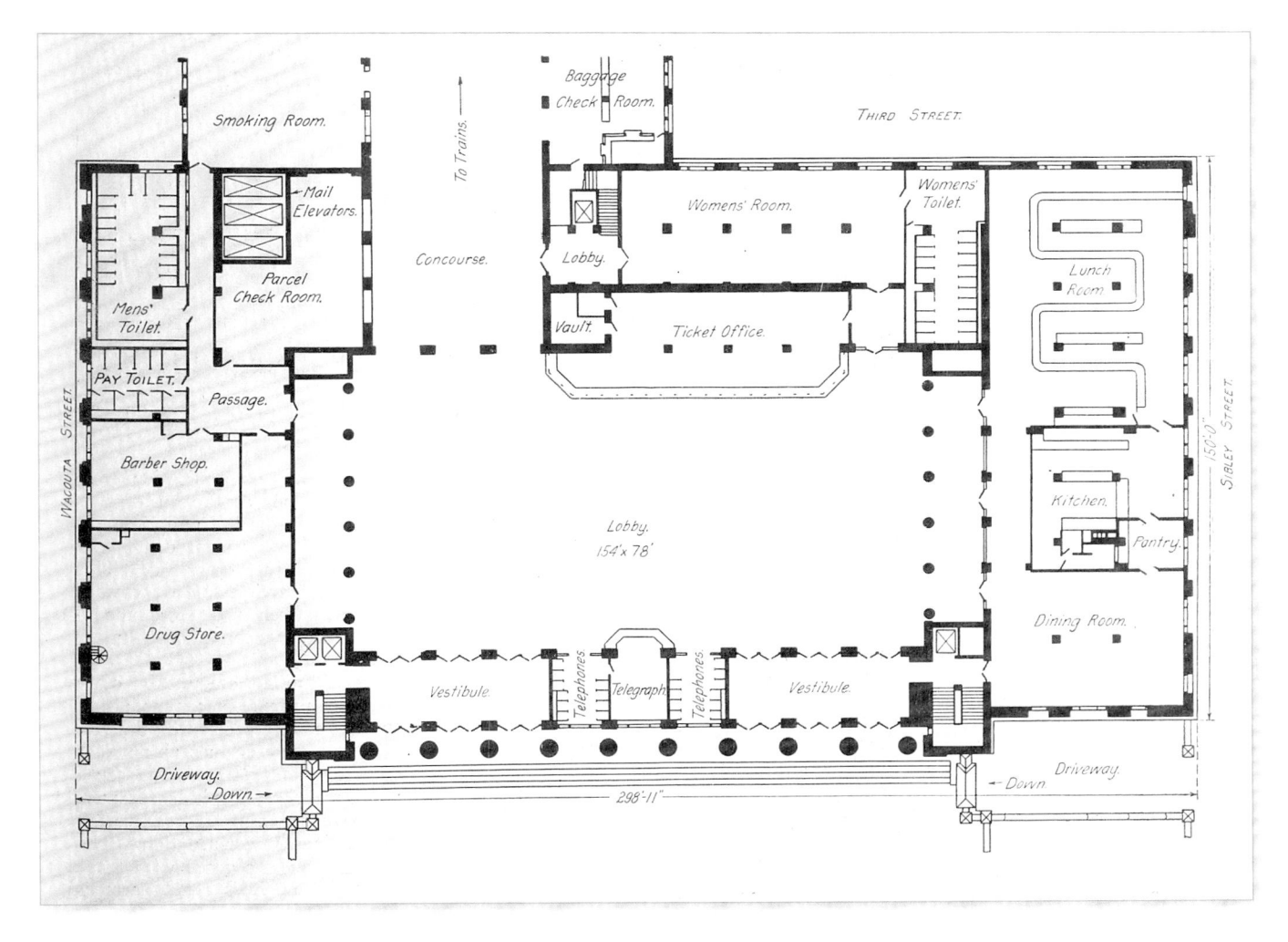

The ticket lobby and entrance are empty, and there are no people lined up at the ticket windows or dashing through the concourse to catch their trains because there is no concourse, just a temporary walkway leading to elevators that took passengers to the old train shed, which would remain in use for two more years. It is April 1920, just a day or two before the head house opens to the public. It will never be this quiet again until April 30, 1971, the day the final trains arrive and depart and the depot closes for good.

entryway steps between Sibley and Wacouta Streets. It was originally intended for VIP passengers wishing to avoid the lobby level.

Two basement levels front on Third Street. A portion of the first was originally used by the U.S. Post Office, and the remainder was taken up by a commissary for the station restaurant and employee locker rooms. The second, or subbasement, level contained mechanical equipment and a large immigrant room with toilet and laundry facilities. Immigration continued in the first decade of the twentieth century, and such accommodations were a part of the depot's original design even though they were never used for that purpose. Two tunnels under Third Street linked this subbasement with an undertrack area beneath the waiting room and concourse. One twenty-foot-wide tunnel was used for the trucking of mail; the other was used for piping and conduits.

Four elevators originally served the head house. Two extended from the subbasement to the third floor, one from the Third Street level to the third floor, and one from the main-floor lobby to the second floor. Three freight elevators, each with a capacity of six thousand pounds, originally operated from the subbasement to the second floor. They were used primarily for moving mail from the subbasement level and the Third Street post office to a large terminal railway post office on the second floor of the concourse. Two steel chutes from Third Street to the basement were used for receiving mail. Another one, from the post office on the Third Street level to the basement, was used to deliver outgoing mail to trains.

The second, or mezzanine, floor of the building was used for depot offices and the regional office of the Pullman Company, as well as an infirmary for passengers and a playroom for children.

Concourse

The station concourse connected the business lobby and the head house with the main waiting room. It was two stories high and extended over Third Street on a series of steel columns located in the middle of the street. A smoking room and baggage check area were located on the first floor. By 1926 WCCO radio had its St. Paul studio in an area next to the smoking room. The second floor of the concourse was originally given to the U.S. Railway Mail Service. Four chutes extended from this area to the mailroom beneath the tracks. The baggage room had a separate chute that also led to the area beneath the tracks.

The main waiting room was seldom this empty. Traffic slowed down considerably during the middle of the day.

Waiting Room

The waiting room was 80 feet wide and 360 feet long and extended over the tracks and platform below. It was a single-story structure except for the seventy-foot section on the north, which was part of the concourse. Originally, the Railway Mail Service terminal post office was located in this second-floor area.

The inside walls are Kittaning brick with terra-cotta above. A decorative frieze, depicting the progress of transportation from the oxcart to the train, wraps around the room. The ceiling is plastered and suspended from steel trusses. Indirect lighting is provided. The space between the ceiling and the roof carries radiators and ventilation ducts. The floor in the waiting room is of two reinforced concrete slabs with an air space in between to accommodate radiators to warm the floor.

Separate doors, arranged in pairs, were provided for tracks 1 through 16. The doors led to a corridor and a stairway to the platforms below. Tracks 17 and 18 share one door. Tracks 19 through 21 were accessed through a passageway at the south end of the waiting room that led to a stairway between tracks 19 and 20. Elevators were provided at each entryway.

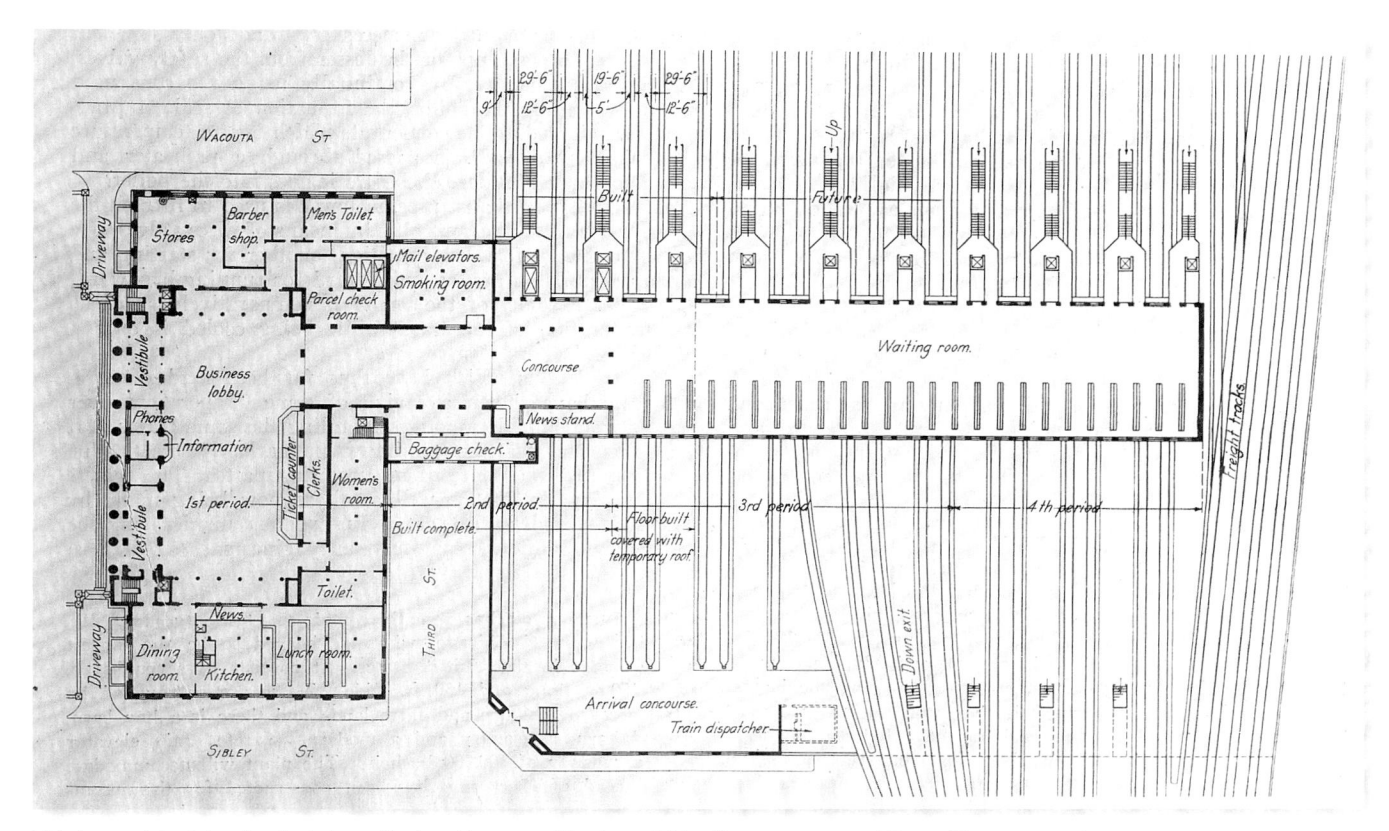

This is an original drawing that shows the head house and business lobby, the concourse and the waiting room, and the order in which they were built. Phase one, beginning in 1917, involved the head house, which was completed and opened to the public in April 1920. Phase two was the concourse, spanning Third Street and the first six elevated tracks. It was completed in October–November 1921. In phase three, completed in 1924, the waiting room was extended from the concourse over the next six elevated tracks, which were built at the same time. The old train shed was also demolished. In phase four the last set of elevated tracks was finished, and the waiting room was extended over them. Finally, on August 21, 1924, all trains were taken off the lower level. The Great Western's Mississippi River bridge was raised in February 1925, and with the exception of finishing work, the project was complete. From "After the Passenger Gets There," *Railway Age*, May 21, 1920.

This ornamental frieze, depicting the history of transportation, encircles the waiting room.

Platforms and Train Sheds

Train boarding platforms were nineteen feet, six inches wide at the entrances to the waiting room stairways. They tapered to eight feet wide at the ends. Butterfly-style train sheds covered the platforms, protecting passengers from rain and inclement weather.

An arrival concourse was located at the end of stub tracks 1 through 8. Doors led directly from the concourse to Third Street. The concourse was intended for arriving and departing commuters not wishing to pass through the station building, but it was rarely used except by occasional VIPs and their entourages who wanted to avoid crowds. By the time the depot opened, the commuter trains were gone.

A telegraph office was located on the arrival concourse with direct telegraph and telephone connections to the dispatchers of the railroads using the depot. All information pertaining to train operations passed through this office, and train crews reported here for their orders.

Track Structure and Undertrack Rooms

The St. Paul Union Depot was a major transfer point for mail and express destined for the Dakotas, Montana, and the Pacific Northwest. Some three hundred thousand square feet were set aside beneath the elevated track structure and boarding platforms.

The elevated track structure was built on a reinforced concrete slab set on pilings driven into swampy ground that was once partly lowland along the river. All of it had been filled. Buildings, since demolished, had once occupied portions of it. During construction, in order to drive these piles, some twenty to fifty feet in length, it was necessary to remove the foundations of these old buildings, many of them set on piles themselves.

In one location, foundations of a long-forgotten building were found with the top about five feet below the surface and the bottom fifteen feet lower. This building was thought to be James J. Hill's original warehouse. The first railroad into St. Paul was built in 1862 over islands and on a pile trestle in the river to where the depot now stands. Parts of this old trestle, which had been abandoned and covered with fill for over fifty years, were found, in good condition.

The Railway Express Agency occupied the Third Street side of the undertrack space with driveways leading to Third Street. Mail, baggage, and milk rooms occupied the Sibley Street side with a tunnel to the post office under Sibley Street for the movement of mail. At this time the railroads were still moving milk in cans in baggage cars.

Elevators, ramps, and chutes made connections between the undertrack rooms and track level.

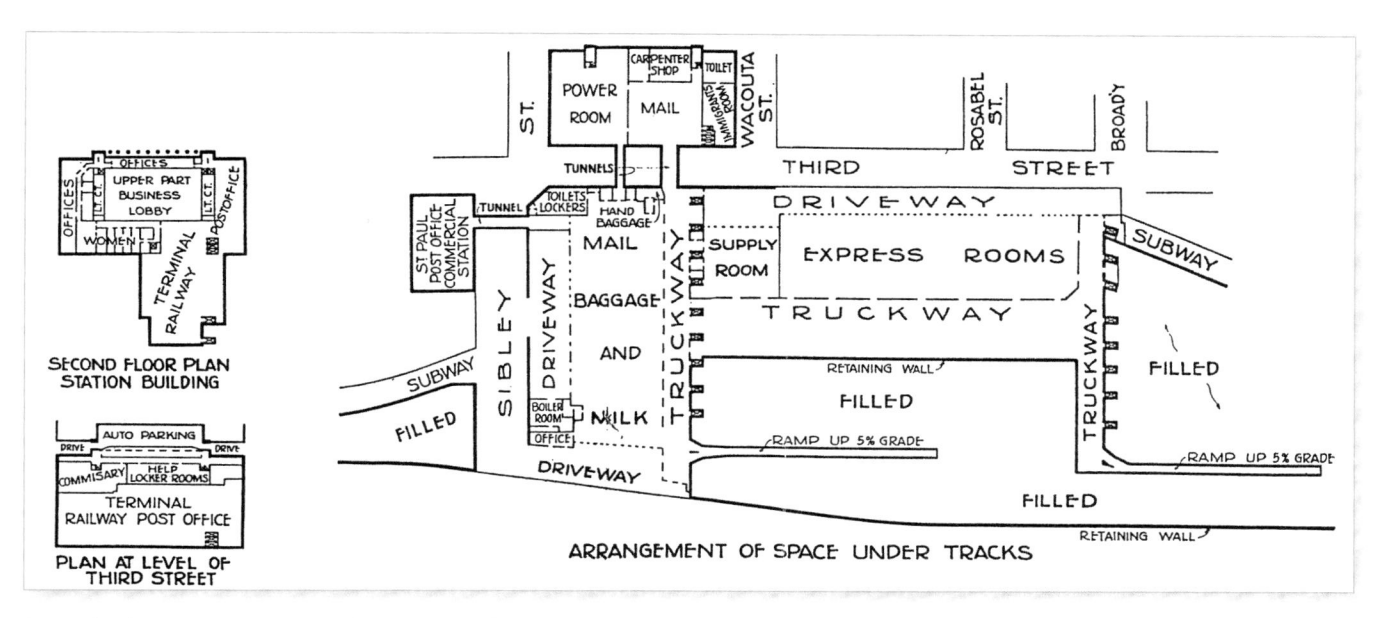

St. Paul Union Depot encompassed 28.97 acres of land. There were twenty-one passenger tracks and two freight tracks and eleven platforms. The main entrance faced Fourth Street. The business lobby, concourse, and waiting room were on one level with stairs and elevators taking passengers from the waiting room to the platforms below. Tracks 1 through 8 were stub tracks and were used by trains originating or terminating in St. Paul. Tracks 9 through 21 were through tracks. Since most trains ran through, these tracks received the heaviest use. It was also more convenient to use them for switching moves when adding or subtracting cars or changing locomotives. An arrival concourse gave passengers access to Third Street without going through the waiting room and business lobby. It was intended for commuter trains, but they were gone by the time the depot opened, and it was seldom used except for VIPs needing a quick getaway. The telegraph office, where train crews received their orders and clearances, was also located on the concourse level. On the east end of track 19 there was a two-story yard office where a yardmaster and train directors controlled train movements in and out of the depot.

Passengers seldom saw the offices above the business lobby or the terminal railway post office, above the concourse, where mail was sorted for local delivery and outgoing trains. It closed with the opening of the new post office building in 1934. A bowling alley and recreation center took its place in 1941.

The Third Street basement was yet another infrequently visited area. A commissary for the depot restaurants, an employee locker room, and additional mail-handling facilities took up most of the space. A power and boiler room, carpenter shop, mail storage, and an immigrant waiting room occupied the subbasement, which was connected by tunnels under Third Street to the large mail and express rooms below the tracks. Driveways provided trucking access for mail, baggage, and express to the train level above. Another set of tunnels ran under Sibley Street to the Lowertown Commercial Post Office.

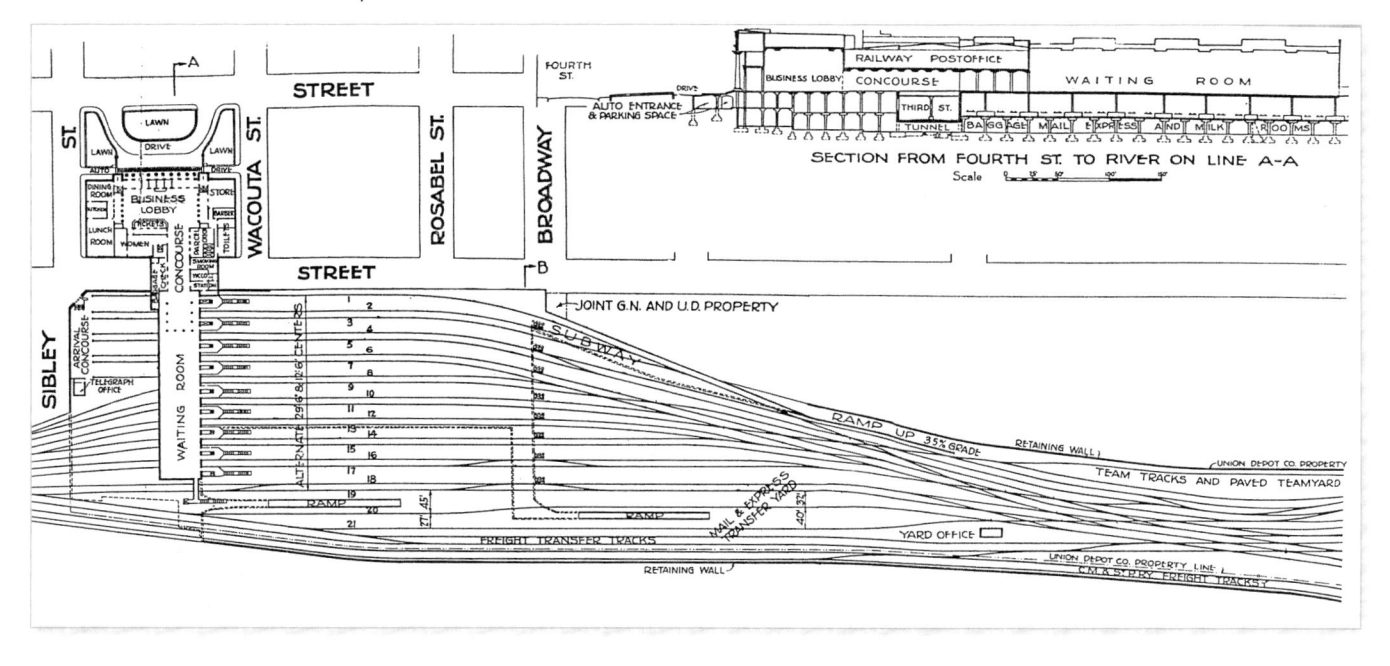

Besides the chutes mentioned earlier, there were three wide chutes between tracks 8 and 9, located just east of the telegraph office. The original intention was to provide only elevators, but after three years of service it was found that elevators were too slow for the volume of business handled, and two ramps were added, one at each end. Tracks 1 through 18 have elevators at each end from the underfloor space to the platforms above.

Track Layout

There were twenty-one station-yard passenger tracks and four freight tracks. All came together at the east end of the yard where two leads branched off. The westbound lead turned north toward Third Street and the Great Northern, Northern Pacific, Soo Line, and Omaha lines; the eastbound lead turned south toward the river valley and the Burlington and Milwaukee main lines. The leads formed a wye with the depot roundhouse in the middle. Westbound tracks of the Milwaukee Road and the Omaha for Minneapolis, Mendota, and southern Minnesota came together with through tracks from the depot just below the Robert Street Bridge. The Chicago Great Western's lead from its Mississippi River bridge diagonally crossed the westbound Milwaukee, Omaha, and depot through tracks. To preclude possible interference due to derailments, tracks were arranged to give several routes from any lead to any track in the yard.

Tracks 17 through 21 were used mainly for the transfer of express and mail and for advance loading of cars. They could accommodate up to ninety eighty-foot baggage cars. Along the north side of the property, east of Broadway, a paved team yard was provided for transferring shipments from baggage and express cars to trucks for local delivery.

Water connections for filling tanks on passenger cars were located about 120 feet apart. Steam connections for heating cars were located at the west end of the stub tracks. Additional connections were provided between each pair of tracks at Broadway and at about 250-foot intervals east of Broadway between tracks 16 and 21.

Train lighting outlets, supplying alternating current at thirty-two and sixty-four volts, were located at the west end of the stub tracks, 1 through 8, between tracks 16 and 19 near Sibley Street, and between tracks 16 and 21 at 180 and 430 feet east of Broadway.

A wood-framed yard office finished with cement stucco was built near the east end of tracks 20 and 21. The first floor provided locker and toilet rooms for switchmen. The second floor was the yardmaster's office. Train directors, who supervised and controlled the movement of all trains through the depot, occupied the third floor. An independent telephone system connected the train directors with each end of each platform, the depot, and the telegraph office. A telautograph (a device that allowed written messages in longhand to be transmitted and reproduced at another location) at the train director's desk was connected to the telegraph office, the ticket office and information desk, the stationmaster's office, and the waiting room. The service was subsequently expanded to other locations.

Construction

St. Paul Union Depot was the largest construction project in downtown St. Paul in the twentieth century, and like today's freeways, it was built while traffic continued to move around the construction. There was nowhere to detour the approximately two hundred trains that called every day, so construction proceeded in four stages, with contractors working around a steady stream of trains, people, and mail and express.

Work on the depot finally got underway in 1917. This crowd couldn't be happier.

There were twelve consulting engineers and construction companies involved in the project. Toltz Engineering Company of St. Paul did the structural engineering work along with Neiler, Rich & Company of Chicago for the mechanical and electrical. George Grant Construction Company and Morris Shepherd & Dougherty as copartners were the general contractors for the first two stages. Foley Brothers Inc. supervised the remainder of the work. Other contractors and companies involved included Frank Eha, Healy Plumbing and Heating Company, and Edward L. Ridler for plumbing and heating; Scribner-Libbey Inc. for roofing; Fulton Asphalt Company for the floors; Commonwealth Electric Company; and Kaestner & Hecht and Otis Elevator Company.

Following the loss of the original station building, temporary facilities were located in two adjoining five-story warehouse buildings on Third Street just east of Sibley Street. One building housed the baggage room and the chief engineer's office on the ground floor; the basement was

The block bounded by Sibley, Fourth, Wacouta, and Third Streets as it appeared before construction. All of these buildings were demolished to make way for the new depot.

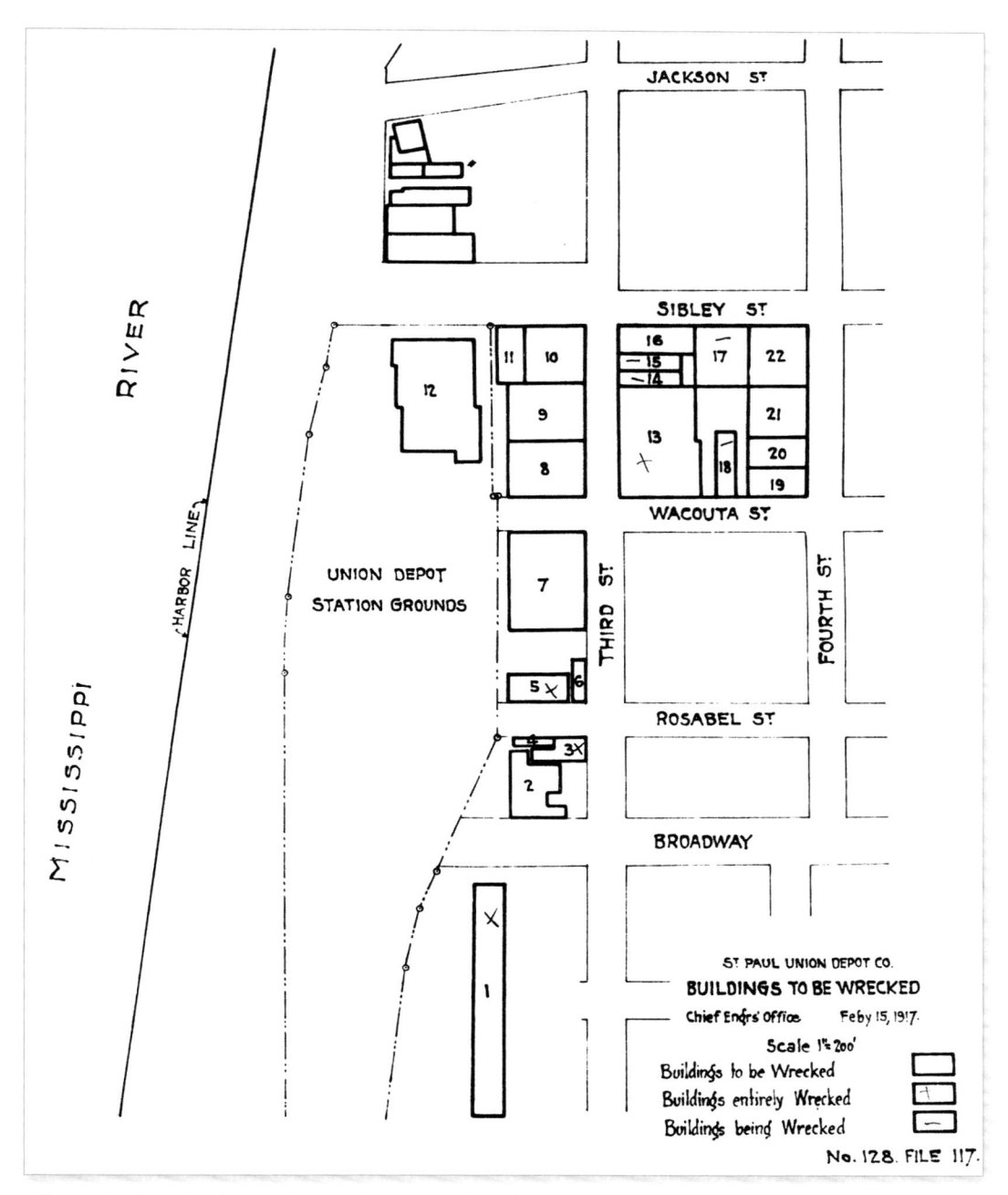

This drawing from the chief engineer's office shows the buildings to be demolished to make way for the new depot: (1) a freight house used by the Chicago, Burlington & Quincy; (2) Great Northern Express Company; (3) saloon; (4) two-story building, vacant; (5) Western Express Company; (6) Adams Express Company; (7) Griggs, Cooper and Company, wholesale grocer; (8) temporary baggage room and express office for Union Depot Company; (9) temporary waiting room and ticket lobby for Union Depot Company; (10) miscellaneous small businesses; (11) restaurant; (12) former Union Depot head house, burned in 1913 and rebuilt as baggage–mail room; (13) Schulze and Company, shoe manufacturer; (14) clothing store; (15) hotel; (16) Banner Clothing Company; (17) restaurant and saloon; (18) Fleischman Distilling Company; (19) St. Paul Clothing Company; (20) L. D. Codden Clothier; (21) Scheffer, Rossum and Company; (22) hotel (demolished in 1921). Work commenced in 1917 and progressed through 1920.

Phase one began in 1917 with construction of the head house building, shown here in a photograph taken at the corner of Third and Sibley Streets, looking northeast.

The head house building in a later view taken at Third and Wacouta Streets, looking northwest.

The head house is well along in this 1919 photograph taken at Fourth and Wacouta Streets.

This view, looking west on Third Street from the southeast corner of Third and Rosabel (now Wall Street), shows early phase two construction. The temporary walkway from the head house to the old train shed is in place, but the concourse is yet to be built across Third Street. Workers are assembling forms for the concrete train deck.

occupied and used by the express companies. The other building had the station waiting room and ticket office on the ground floor and the superintendent's office, Pullman Company office, and an immigrant waiting room on the second floor. A wood-framed concourse built on a viaduct over the tracks led from the temporary station to stairways to the various platforms under the train shed.

Although work got underway in 1917, the First World War and financing issues delayed completion of the new head house until 1920. This first phase also involved construction of a temporary concourse, or passageway, twenty feet wide and extending on an 8 percent grade down the center line of Wacouta Street from the head house to the old concourse and train shed, south of Third Street between Wacouta and Sibley. Once completed, passengers could avail themselves of the services in the new head house and proceed down this passageway to their trains under the old train shed. Arriving passengers had the option of proceeding directly to Sibley Street or returning through the passageway to the head house. During this phase all of the original tracks remained in place and in use for arriving and departing passenger trains. Work was completed on this phase in April 1920, but there was little formal ceremony to mark the occasion. It had been seven years since the fire, and with more work to be done and growing public impatience, the board decided to simply open the building for inspection one day before the start of service. The first train to arrive the next day was Northern Pacific's local from Duluth.

The second phase opened with the demolition of the temporary facilities and adjoining structures and construction of the first six elevated tracks, platforms, and sheds in the area formerly occupied by the temporary station. At the same time, the two-story section of the concourse and waiting room was extended from the new head house over Third Street. A temporary set of elevators and stairs were installed at the south end of the waiting room, taking passengers to the lower-level tracks. This work was completed in October–November 1921. The temporary passageway from the head house to the train shed was removed when the first six elevated tracks went into service.

Phase three began with the construction of another temporary concourse from the southwest corner of the waiting room, diagonally spanning tracks 5 and 6 with four elevators and a stairway to a temporary waiting area on the lower-level tracks south of the limits of the phase three work. The old train shed was then demolished, and construction commenced on the next set of six elevated tracks—four of which were through tracks. All tracks in phases two and three were directly over the mail and express rooms and were supported on a reinforced concrete slab. The waiting room was then extended 210 feet over the second set of six tracks. Phase three work was finished in February 1924.

The 1889 train shed was taken down during phase three.

By August 1920, construction of the first six elevated tracks was well along. The temporary walkway from the head house building to the old train shed is in the foreground.

Another view of phase two shows the platforms and train sheds under construction. The concourse is also under construction and can be seen in the distance.

Here, the concourse is being extended over Third Street.

Phase two is complete, and phase three work has begun. The first six tracks have been elevated and are now in use. The train shed is gone, and pilings are being driven to support the next elevated section. A temporary walkway, seen in the distance, has been built over the construction area to an elevator that takes passengers to the remaining lower-level tracks.

The old and the new pose for the photographer as work progresses on St. Paul Union Depot. Making a special appearance, the *William Crooks* stands on newly elevated tracks while a brand-new 4-8-2 locomotive, named *Marathon*, is in charge of the Oriental Limited. This photograph looks west, upriver. Not visible are the depot and the Robert Street Bridge. The Mississippi River is on the left.

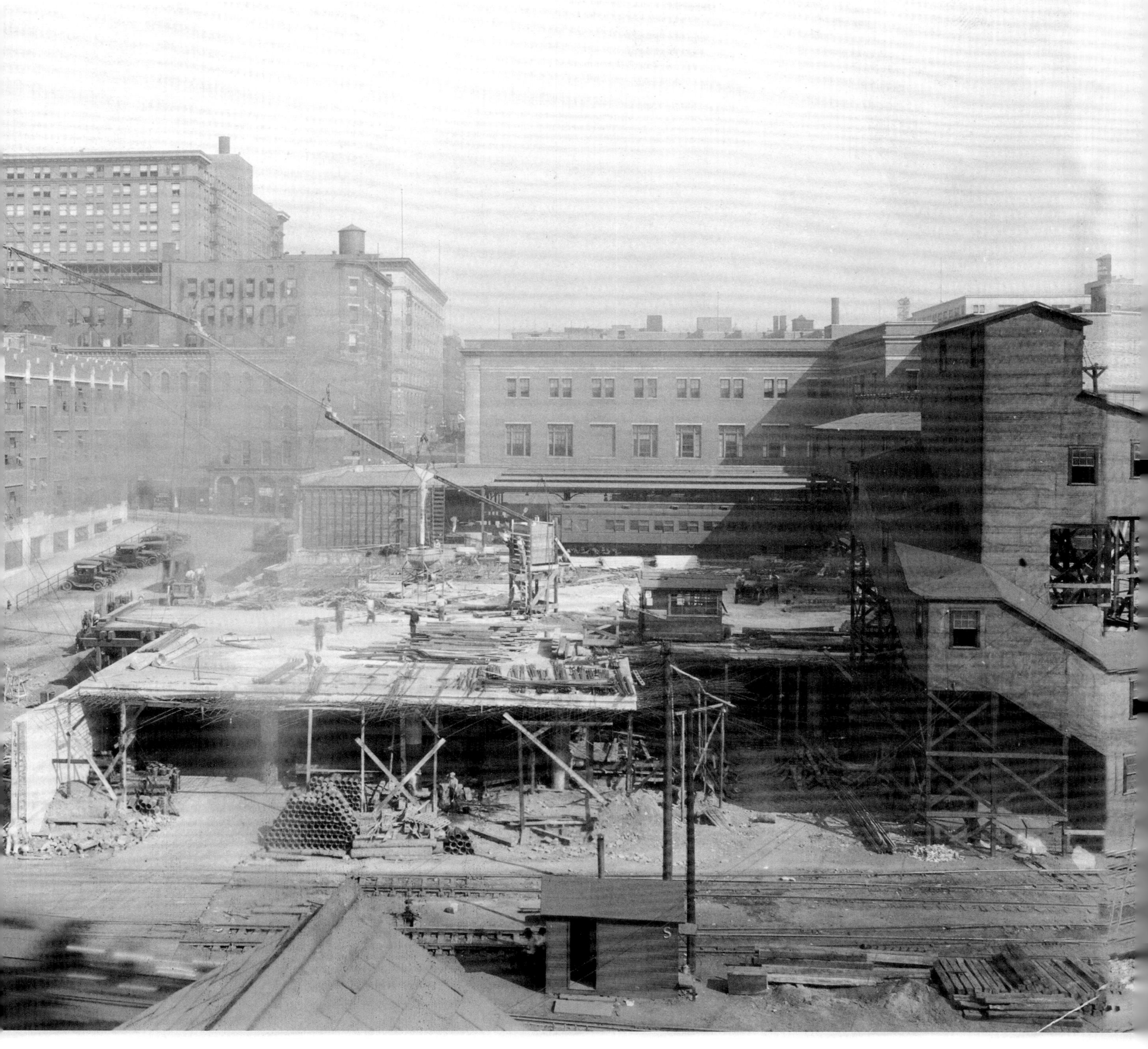

Phase three train-deck construction is well along in this photograph showing the temporary passageway and elevator that took passengers to trains that were still using the lower level. This view looks north toward Fourth Street and the rear of the head house.

Phase four involved construction of four more elevated tracks and completion of the waiting room. For this work another temporary concourse was built at the end of phase three from the southeast corner of the waiting room extending approximately 150 feet to the south with elevators and stairways leading to a temporary waiting room on the remaining lower-level tracks. On August 21, 1924, all passenger trains were removed from the lower level, forcing Chicago Great Western trains to execute a back-up move via the east throat until its Mississippi River bridge was raised in February 1925. That date marked the completion of all elevated trackage and, with the exception of miscellaneous finishing work that continued into 1926, was the final day of construction. At last, it was done. Now would come the challenge of making it work.

It is winter early in 1924, and this photograph, looking east from the Robert Street Bridge, shows phase four in its early stages. On August 21, 1924, the train deck and waiting room were completed and all trains moved to the-upper level tracks.

In this early 1925 photograph looking west, upriver, the Chicago Great Western bridge is on the left, and work on the train platforms nears completion. Demolition of the old Robert Street Bridge is underway. It is missing its center span. The Wabasha Street Bridge can be seen upriver in the distance; it would be replaced in the late 1990s.

It's noon, and the depot tracks are empty, awaiting the late afternoon rush of arriving and departing passenger trains. Few if any of these automobiles belonged to depot passengers, but the Lower Levee, after its 1938 WPA reconstruction, must have been a convenient downtown parking lot. Jackson Street passes under the elevated tracks in the foreground with Sibley Street crossing below the tracks and passing the front of the Milwaukee freight house on the right. Today, Shepard Road has obliterated all of what is seen here.

Locomotive headlights wash the platforms, and the depot waiting room and concourse are aglow in this 1929 nighttime view from the roof of the Merchant Bank Building. The lights are on in the Lowertown post office at Third and Sibley Streets where mail is being sorted for morning delivery. By 1935 a new First National Bank will take the place of the Merchant Bank Building, and a new downtown post office will occupy the site of the Lowertown post office.

4
Arrivals and Departures

An Operating Agreement

On December 18, 1916, the nine stock-holding tenants of the St. Paul Union Depot Company signed an operating agreement for use of the new union passenger station. The depot would cost some $15 million and the agreement bound the railroad companies to guarantee the bonds for its construction. If any of the owning roads defaulted on the mortgage bonds, its share would become an obligation of the others and would be divided proportionately. They could recover separately by filing suit against the defaulting railroad, but the liability was still theirs. It also defined the rights and responsibilities of the owning roads, guaranteed nondiscriminatory use and access to the property for ninety-nine years, and provided for apportionment of operating expenses along with assignment of liability in the event of accidents. An arbitration process was provided for settling disputes.

The railroads agreed that this would be their principal passenger terminal in St. Paul and that they would use it exclusively for all regular passenger services, except for certain commuter stations that were still in use at the time of the agreement. The Great Northern Railway was guaranteed exclusive use of the first three tracks in the depot and preferential use of the next four, which was a carryover from the 1879 agreement and in consideration of additional property made available by the Great Northern for the new facility.

The agreement was short-lived. Barely had the notaries affixed their seals when a dispute arose over the allocation and sharing of operating expenses. Once again, the complaining party was the president of the Chicago Great Western, Samuel Felton.

The Great Western ran some fine trains, but it was hit hard by the financial difficulties of the Depression, and it was never able to afford the new streamlined cars and locomotives of its competitors. Here, in 1946, its *Mill Cities Limited* from Kansas City ascends Westminster Hill for Minneapolis. Its cars and locomotive date from World War I.

The Great Western was a smaller passenger player. Its trains reached Chicago, Kansas City, and Omaha, but they faced stiff competition from the Burlington, the Omaha, the Rock Island, and the Milwaukee, all of them fielding multiple trains over shorter routes serving more populous intermediate stations.

The Great Western ran some fine trains. Its *Great Western Limited* between Chicago and the Twin Cities was outfitted with the latest and best Pullman sleeping and observation cars, an elegant diner, and a buffet car. The Great Western was an innovator. In the 1920s it introduced a combined rail–air service between the Twin Cities, St. Louis, and Cleveland. It was the first railroad to purchase a gasoline-electric motorcar, forerunner of the diesel locomotive, from the Electro-Motive Engineering Corporation, the future Electro-Motive Division of General Motors. The Great Western offered the only direct route from the Twin Cities to the emerging medical center at Rochester, Minnesota, serving it with a through Chicago passenger train, the *Legionnaire*, and two nonstop locals—one of them was the three-car *Blue Bird* powered by a gas-electric motorcar, the forerunner of all streamlined passenger trains in America.

The 1916 agreement allocated operating expenses solely on the basis of the number of passenger cars using the depot. Passenger cars on trains traveling 25 miles or less were counted as one car, those traveling 25 miles but less than 150 miles were counted as two cars, and on trains traveling over 150 miles each passenger car was counted as three cars. Baggage cars, mail, express, and freight cars were counted as one car regardless of the distance traveled. All expenses, including those associated with the handling of mail, baggage, and express; ticket sales; passenger services; and facility maintenance, among others, were prorated and divided by the number of cars each railroad brought to the depot.

Samuel Felton argued this arrangement was inequitable because a railroad with fewer trains, like the Great Western, was in effect subsidizing other railroads that used depot services more intensively. The depot company's board of directors assigned the matter to an executive committee for further analysis. A number of alternatives were presented to the Great Western, but none of them were found to be acceptable. Finally, the Great Western called for arbitration, and the matter was brought before a panel of three referees, one appointed by the depot company, one appointed by the Great Western, and a third neutral referee.

The resulting 1923 arbitration award divided the depot property into six zones with all fixed charges and operating expenses divided among them. Another arbitration in 1940 amended parts of the award, but its basic outline and the zone system remained in effect until the depot closed in 1971.

Zone 1: Head House and Concourse

Zone 1 expenses included personnel costs associated with the sale of tickets and the maintenance and operation of the head house, passenger concourse, and elevators leading to the track platforms. Personnel included gate men, train callers, information clerks, telephone operators, janitors, and other personnel assigned to this zone. Revenues credited included the rental of concessions and the rental of space used by the U.S. Post Office. Expenses were apportioned to each railroad according to the number of tickets, including sleeping and parlor car tickets, sold at the depot ticket office, the St. Paul city ticket offices, and the offices of the various railroad companies.

Gatemen's wages were in zone 1. Here, two of them check the telautograph for the status of arriving trains.

Zone 2: Undertrack Structures

Zone 2 comprised the area under the passenger boarding platforms used for the handling of baggage, mail, and express. It included all the ramps and the elevators used to transfer baggage, mail, and express to the track-level platforms. Expenses, including personnel, maintenance, and other operating costs associated with the handling of baggage, mail, and express, were charged to zone 2. Revenues credited included those from the rental of space to express companies and the U.S. Post Office and the storage and handling of baggage.

Expenses were apportioned among the railroad companies according to the actual number of pieces handled; all items were counted twice, once in and once out. To determine the number of sacks of mail handled, an actual count was made during the first seven days in April and October of each year; a monthly total was obtained by multiplying the average daily count of these seven days by the number of days in the month.

Mail and express were charged to zone 2. A depot employee stands by as railway mail clerks load a railway post office car.

Railroads were charged for using the depot's tracks to interchange freight cars with another railroad. A Milwaukee Road freight passes the depot on its way to Minneapolis in the early 1940s.

Zone 3: Freight Transfer Tracks

Two freight transfer (interchange) tracks crossed the depot property linking the Great Western, Milwaukee, and Omaha tracks coming from the south and west (Minneapolis) with the Great Northern, Northern Pacific, Burlington, Omaha, and Soo Line tracks on the east side of the depot property. All costs associated with the maintenance of these tracks, together with a percentage of the value of the labor of depot personnel involved in the operation of freight movements, were charged to this zone, with the expenses allocated to the tenant railroads according to the number of cars and locomotives of each railroad that used them.

Zone 4: Passenger Tracks

Passenger train tracks, turnouts, and train platforms and sheds composed this zone with all maintenance and operating costs and the costs of personnel associated with the movement of passenger trains (switchmen, yardmasters, train directors, etc.) assigned to it. Expenses were allocated to the railroads according to the number of passenger cars arriving and departing from the depot with each car counted twice, once upon arrival and once upon departure. Locomotives and tenders were counted as two cars. Each three cars arriving and departing in commuter trains traveling less than twenty-six miles were counted as one car.

Passenger train movements composed zone 4, with railroads charged according to the number of cars and locomotives in arriving and departing trains. Here, a switchman inspects the *Afternoon Hiawatha* as it arrives from Minneapolis.

Zone 5: Team Tracks

The depot's team tracks were used to store freight and express cars for loading or unloading. There were two of them, running parallel with Third Street and connected to, and served by, the Great Northern's passenger main line. The term "team" derived from the early use of horse-drawn wagons to haul cargo. After trucks arrived, the term stuck. Besides freight and express cars, they were occasionally used to store passenger cars for large special events, such as touring theatrical companies and circuses. The railroads occasionally used them to exhibit new trains or locomotives.

St. Paul Union Depot's team tracks paralleled Third Street. They were considered part of zone 5, but were seldom used for unloading freight. More often they stored passenger cars or were used for special events, such as this 1934 exhibition of the Union Pacific's M-10000, one of the country's first streamlined trains.

Expenses allocated to them included maintenance of the tracks together with personnel that might, from time to time, be assigned, such as clerks or watchmen. Expenses were apportioned according to the number of cars handled with revenues credited for mail, express, freight, or other business.

Zone 6: Engine Terminal

This zone included the engine house, machine shop, turntable, coaling station, water tank, and ancillary servicing facilities. In later years, when diesels came into use, the water and coaling facilities were removed, and diesel storage tanks and fueling facilities were added. The Great Northern began storing and fueling its diesel locomotives at the depot engine house following closure of its Jackson Street roundhouse.

Charges assigned to this zone included expenses for facility maintenance, locomotive repairs, and depreciation; time of enginemen, conductors, and brakemen; master mechanic, roundhouse foreman, engine house employees; 15 percent of the wages of switch tenders; 15 percent of the pro-

Before diesels took over, the Great Northern used its Jackson Street roundhouse for servicing steam locomotives. Because diesel power did not require the same level of maintenance between runs, only fueling and inspections and light repairs, the Great Northern and the Burlington moved to the depot's engine house, which was much closer to the depot. A locomotive coming in on one passenger train might get serviced and go out again on another run in just a few hours.

portion of yard telephone operators and yardmasters; along with the cost of fuel, lubricants, parts, and supplies.

Revenues credited included switching services for other than the tenant lines; the sale of water, coal, and oil (later diesel); and charges for use of the turntable. Net expenses were apportioned by dividing the total number of hours of engine service by the number of hours of engine service provided for each tenant line.

More Distractions and Disputes

It took an arbitration to settle the terms and language of the operating agreement, but there were other disputes and arbitrations over charges and revenues. Each of the tenant lines and the depot company zealously guarded their interests and in protecting them took a strongly adversarial approach. It was said by one lawyer that opposing counsels would not be satisfied until they brought tears to their opponents' eyes.

None of this brought additional passengers or revenues to the depot company or the railroads, at a time when more and more people were buying automobiles or turning to buses and airplanes for transportation. For decades, the railroads continued to behave like monopolies, warring over a market that was no longer exclusively theirs. These disputes were a distraction at a time when the railroads and the depot company should have been working together to reduce expenses, share revenues, and promote rail passenger travel. But the culture was all about competition: winning and losing and making your competitor pay. Rather than collaboration, they chose to fight over the scraps.

One dispute in 1925 involved Great Northern's trains 27 and 28. Although sometimes carrying a coach or two for local business, westbound train 27 and eastbound train 28 were primarily mail and express trains between St. Paul, Seattle, and intermediate points. Next to the *Oriental Limited*, they were the hottest schedules on the railroad, often running more than twenty cars of mail, express, perishables, and high-value commodities, such as silk, destined for Eastern markets. Train 28 usually returned from the coast with several empty cars. It was logical, the railroad reasoned, to drop these empties at its Mississippi Street coach yards rather than dragging them all the way to the depot, only to pull them back to the coach yard once the rest of the train was unloaded or its cars forwarded to connecting lines. The Great Northern asserted that these cars were nonrevenue: they carried no business, and the railroad had no reason to bring them to the depot and pay the depot tolls and assessments plus whatever switching costs it might incur returning them to the coach yards.

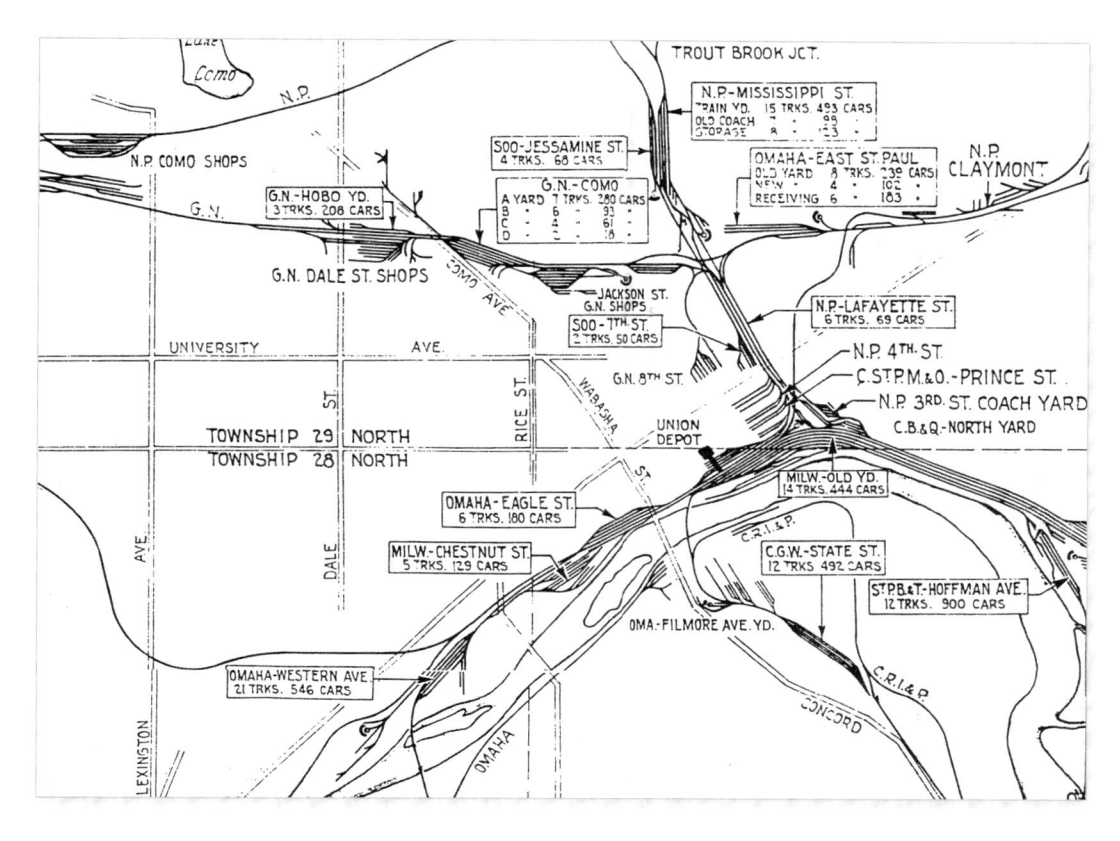

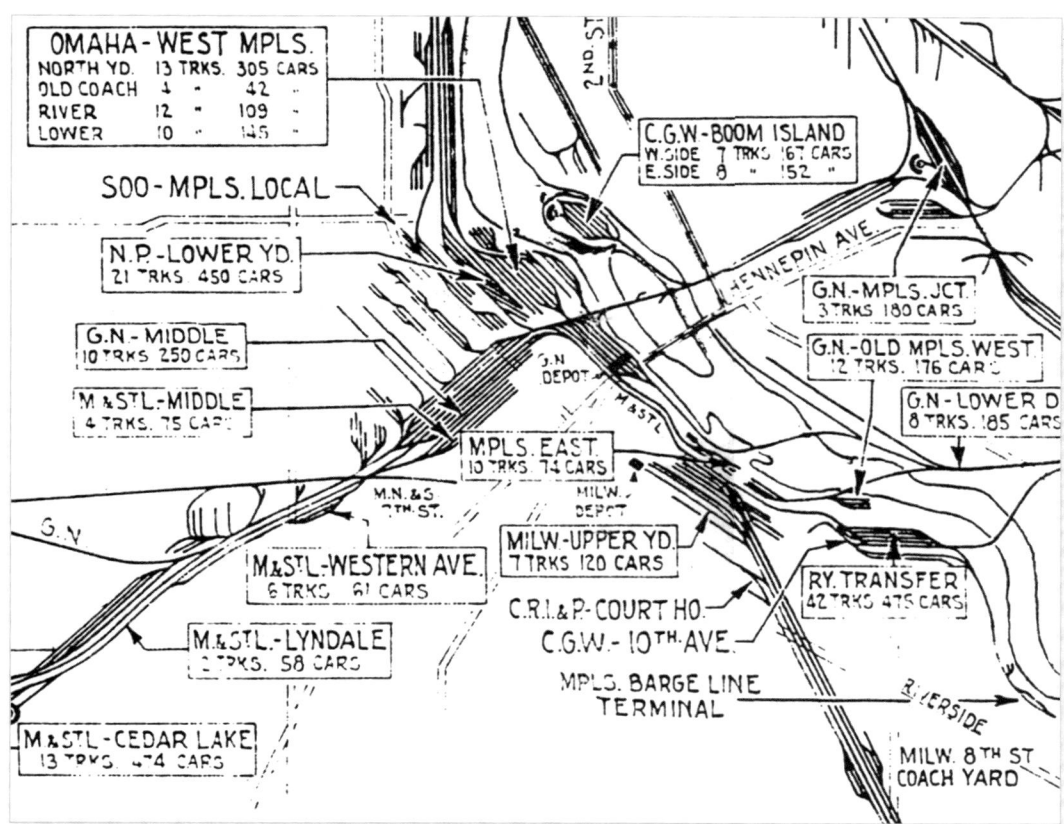

These 1937 maps show the Twin Cities railroad lines and their relationships to the principal freight yards, freight and passenger terminals, and shops. The St. Paul Union Depot is shown, along with the connecting rail lines and passenger-car and locomotive servicing facilities that included the Northern Pacific's coach yards at Third Street and its Como Shops, which performed heavy repairs on passenger equipment. Also shown are Great Northern's passenger car repair shop at Jackson Street and its Dale Street locomotive shops.

In Minneapolis the Great Northern Station handled Great Northern, Northern Pacific, Burlington, Omaha, and Chicago Great Western passenger trains. Burlington trains were serviced at a small yard north of the Great Northern Station. Chicago Great Western trains used yard and shop facilities on Boom Island. The Omaha had its passenger yard and roundhouse just north of Broadway.

The Rock Island, Milwaukee, and Soo Line used the Short Line between St. Paul and Minneapolis. Their trains arrived and departed from the Milwaukee depot at Washington and Third Avenues. Milwaukee passenger trains were serviced at a coach yard near Eighth Street and Franklin Avenue. The Rock Island had a small yard not far from the Milwaukee's. Most Soo Line passenger trains originated in St. Paul and were serviced by the Northern Pacific at its Third Street coach yards. The Soo Line's Shoreham Shops in Northeast Minneapolis handled all heavy passenger-car and locomotive work. *Source:* 1937 study by Minnesota Transfer Railway Company.

Not surprisingly, the Union Depot Company disagreed, citing sections in the operating agreement that required roads using the depot to bring all their trains to the depot and that said trains and all of their cars shall be subject to all depot fees and assessments. Setting out cars for operating convenience did not relieve the railroad from its obligations as a user of the depot. All cars in a train should be counted.

The dispute wound its way to arbitration for the usual arguing and hairsplitting. On the surface, it seemed the railroad had the better argument. Why pay for something that wasn't needed and, in fact, cost the railroad money? Logic, however, didn't always prevail in railroad arbitrations. Two of the three arbitrators found for the depot company, comparing the operating agreement to a real estate lease, reasoning that even though a property wasn't used or occupied 100 percent of the time, the tenant was still obligated to pay rent. The railroad ended up paying for something it couldn't use and actually cost it money.

A ruling in a 1935 dispute on a similar issue had a different outcome. Prior to August 1932, the Chicago, St. Paul, Minneapolis & Omaha ran all its special excursion trains through St. Paul Union Depot and paid the required depot charges. These were mainly weekend outings to destinations in

ARRIVALS AND DEPARTURES   141

western Wisconsin. Then in 1932 and 1933, presumably to avoid the depot charges and save money, it switched them to its East St. Paul station, which until a few years before had hosted locals and commuter trains to and from Stillwater and points in western Wisconsin. Tickets were sold at the railroad's general offices in downtown St. Paul, at the East St. Paul station, and aboard the excursion trains. The railroad held that it wasn't obligated to report ticket sales or pay depot charges for trains that didn't use St. Paul Union Depot facilities.

The Union Depot Company claimed the operating agreement required the tenant railroads to use St. Paul Union Depot for all of their passenger trains and that ticket sales and revenues from all St. Paul outlets had to be reported on the depot account and included in depot charges.

The arbitrator disagreed and based the finding on specific language in the operating agreement that referred to St. Paul Union Depot as the "principal" station, noting also that all "regular," presumably scheduled, trains were required to use the depot but not necessarily extras or special trains. The arbitrator went further, chiding the depot company for presuming the agreement reached beyond the depot to include an operation in which the depot company was in no way involved.

It is unclear why this even came to arbitration except that other roads were using the depot for

Railroads encouraged excursion trips because they were usually low mileage and used otherwise inactive passenger equipment. They also built goodwill for the railroad and helped sell their regular passenger trains. This happy group is on a Chicago, St. Paul, Minneapolis & Omaha fan trip sponsored by the Minnesota Railfans Association, July 24, 1949. Tickets were usually sold by the sponsoring organization or by the railroad at its local office. Nevertheless, St. Paul Union Depot, pointing to the operating agreement, demanded a percentage of the revenue from the sale of tickets. Arbitration was required to sort things out.

their special excursion trains and paying depot charges, and they were furious the Omaha was getting away free, leaving them to shoulder a larger share of depot expense. The Omaha's excursion trains were popular. The eight trains carried over three thousand people, and all the ticket revenue went to the railroad, which only added to the general perturbation. The other roads could have followed the Omaha's example or worked out a separate agreement among themselves and the depot company, but instead they reflexively decided to pick a fight. It took five more years, but in 1940 they finally agreed on a formula for allocating charges for excursion trains.

Another issue involved the Pullman Company and the sale of sleeping-car space. For over forty years Pullman tickets had been charged and billed against the issuing railroad, not the Pullman Company. A few of the tenant roads, again the Chicago Great Western among them, sold fewer Pull-

In another dispute, the Union Depot Company's legal counsel went after the Pullman Company demanding a share of Pullman's revenue from the sale of sleeping-car tickets. Pullman sleeping cars, as this photo shows, were extremely popular for overnight travel. Under the terms of the Pullman contract, Pullman supplied the cars and the railroads sold the tickets, with a portion of the revenue going to Pullman. Pullman rejected the Union Depot Company's demands and threatened to withdraw from the depot. The Union Depot Company eventually backed down.

man tickets than the others and were convinced Pullman was not paying its full share of operating expenses even though the railroads selling Pullman tickets were acting as agents for Pullman and absorbing the costs of selling its space. In 1925 these tenants succeeded in getting depot counsel to issue an opinion that the Pullman Company should be billed directly. Pullman, then a mighty player in the passenger business, announced it had no intention of paying any part of station expense and would withdraw its tickets from sale at the depot. The ensuing controversy pitted the president of the depot company, who opposed separate billing, against the depot company's legal counsel. Responding to an embarrassing public outcry over inconvenience to passengers, the Great Northern, Northern Pacific, and Omaha made separate arrangements with Pullman. The dispute dragged on for several weeks but was finally put to rest, and the whole matter was dropped at a special board meeting.

In 1968, with passenger service waning and Amtrak just three years away, the Union Depot Company and the railroads still found something to quibble about. At issue was the sale of tickets at the Minneapolis depots and ticket offices for trains boarded at St. Paul Union Depot. Should they be included in the St. Paul city count? The Great Northern argued they should not and cited past practice and an agreement that had been in force since the mid-1930s. Depot counsel and comptroller disagreed and polled the other lines for their opinion on the issue. But so few people were riding that it made little difference, and the five railroads still running the handful of trains that were left fell in line and agreed to include the tickets in the count. Of greater importance, and by then the looming issue, was what to do with a huge facility that was rapidly running out of time.

Personnel and Organization

Railroad passenger terminals were expensive, labor-intensive operations, requiring large numbers of employees to tend to the needs of the thousands of people and tons of mail, baggage, and express that passed through them every day. Approximately 140 people worked at the St. Paul Union Depot in 1895. By 1925 there were over 600. The new terminal was over twice the size of the old and had become a city unto itself. Besides the terminal employees who sold the tickets, switched the cars, loaded and unloaded baggage and mail, and saw to the needs and comfort of passengers, there were 200 more who were employees of express companies and taxicab operators; concessionaires such as the Union News Company, which operated the drugstore, newsstand, and restaurant and coffee shop; and the Pullman Company, which maintained a regional office in the depot. In addition, the tenant railroads had office space for passenger agents and supervisors in the head house and space under the tracks for the storage of materials and locker rooms for car maintenance employees. The

The depot was a busy place in summer 1949, so busy that switchboard operator and information clerk Hattie Trauning almost needed an extra pair of hands but still managed a smile for the photographer while trying to keep up with the calls that were coming her way during the Fourth of July weekend. Callers wanted to know about arrivals and departures, especially whether a train was on time. For that she would turn to a train status board maintained by the stationmaster, who received regular updates by telautograph from train directors in the yard tower. Still others might want to check with the baggage room about luggage or a special package, or inquire about a Pullman reservation at the ticket office. The *St. Paul Pioneer Press* reported that the travel rush that began that Friday broke all St. Paul railroad travel records. H. P. Congdon, vice president and general manager of the depot, was quoted: "The rush was so great and sustained there has been no quiet period during the movement of trains. The jam became so heavy that the temperature, even with many windows open, went up 10 degrees on two of the year's hottest days."

Redcaps, or station porters, assisted passengers with their luggage, arranged for taxicabs, answered questions, directed passengers to trains, helped the blind, infirm, and those in wheelchairs, watched out for small children traveling alone, and in dozens of other ways worked to ensure the safety and comfort of arriving and departing travelers. Redcaps were mostly African Americans. This group photo was taken at the depot in 1952. Charles Rideaux held the senior position and is seen kneeling in this photograph *(right front)*. He was a redcap for thirty-two years and a prominent member of St. Paul's African American community.

ARRIVALS AND DEPARTURES

depot was also the headquarters for the Tenth Division of the U.S. Railway Mail Service, which operated a large mail-processing facility on the second floor above the concourse.

Like the railroads of that era, whose organizational structures were patterned after the military, the St. Paul Union Depot Company was a top-down affair with a series of departments reporting to a general manager, a president, and a board of directors, which consisted of one representative from each of the tenant railroads that owned the Union Depot Company. This structure would remain in effect and in place until the operating departments of the depot company were merged with those of the Minnesota Transfer Railway just prior to World War II.

The president of one of the owning railroads served as president of the depot company. The office had a fixed term and was rotated among the various railroad companies. A general manager reported to the president and was the chief operating officer. Below the general manager was a general superintendent who gave direction to all of the departments and managed day-to-day operations. The executive department was also home to the chief engineer who maintained all fixed facilities and was in charge of communications, legal counsel, and the comptroller.

The stationmaster had charge of operations, which was the largest single department, and the largest number of employees in the depot company including ticket clerks, gatemen, elevator operators, matrons (who cared for the needs of traveling women and children), porters (redcaps), information clerks, and telephone operators.

The trainmaster was responsible for the direction, control, and safe operation of all train movements on the property. Reporting to the trainmaster were the train directors. They saw to it that incoming and outgoing trains were routed to the appropriate tracks and gave direction to switchmen and switch tenders to line the routes appropriately, a job not unlike that of today's air traffic controllers. A yardmaster oversaw the work of a switch foreman, the switchmen, and switch tenders who were assigned to a specific switch or group of switches at the entrance to the depot or within its yard limits. Train crews of all the various

The stationmaster checks the telautograph for track assignments of incoming trains before making an announcement on the station PA system.

The trainmaster talks with the train director on a platform phone. Phones like this were part of the depot's communications system and were used by supervisors and train crews to contact the tower. Conductors called in when a train was ready to depart to confirm the route out of the depot was lined and locked.

railroads were under the supervision of the trainmaster and were subject to St. Paul Union Depot rules when operating within the yard limits of the depot company.

The job of the roadmaster was to keep all tracks, switches, and signals in good repair and to supervise snow and ice removal during the winter months. Reporting to the roadmaster was a track foreman who supervised the work of the track maintenance crews.

The mail and baggage foreman supervised all personnel responsible for the handling of mail, baggage, and express as well as the operation of the parcel room.

All locomotive engineers, locomotive firemen, and mechanical personnel took direction from the master mechanic, whose office was in the depot roundhouse.

The building superintendent had responsibility for the maintenance of the depot building and other structures and reported to the general superintendent but worked closely with the chief engineer. The building superintendent supervised a force of electricians, plumbers, carpenters, painters, and other personnel as well as the engineers responsible for operating and maintaining the building's boilers and steam heating system.

Daily Operations

On the cusp of the Great Depression, some three years after construction was completed, the August 4, 1929, timetable issued by the St. Paul Union Depot Company showed 120 trains using the depot, 33 fewer than in 1917, the year construction began. By 1929 the Burlington had discontinued its commuter runs to St. Paul Park, and other roads had dropped a number of their locals, all in response to automobile and bus competition. That year the Omaha was the busiest, with 28 trains, followed closely by the Milwaukee with 22.

The 8:00–9:00 a.m. hour saw the most activity, with twenty-one trains. The middle of the day was much quieter, with only two trains between 11:00 a.m. and noon and thirteen between noon and 4:00 p.m. Things picked up from 5:00 p.m. through 1:00 a.m., with fifty-seven trains. This pattern of morning and early evening peaks would continue, although in greatly diminished numbers, until the depot closed its doors. Even in 1929, the number of trains calling on the depot was far below its designed capacity and declined still more during the Great Depression. It revived, briefly, during World War II, only to resume its postwar slide all the way to Amtrak in May 1971.

St. Paul Union Depot was primarily a run-through operation. Arrivals from the east and south continued west to Minneapolis, terminating at either the Milwaukee or Great Northern stations. Others went on to points in the Pacific Northwest. Trains originating in Minneapolis passed through St. Paul Union Depot and headed east and south to places like Chicago, St. Louis, Omaha, and Kansas City. Those originating at St. Paul Union Depot on the Great Northern, Northern Pacific, Minneapolis & St. Louis, Milwaukee, and the Soo Line went west through Minneapolis to destinations in Minnesota, the Dakotas, or Canada.

Navigating train and engine movements through the twelve miles of track, forty-two slip switches, and eighty-two turnouts within the depot yard limits was the responsibility of train directors and a yardmaster located in a two-story building at the east end of track 19. From here directors had a sweeping view of the yard and the approaches off the Great Northern, Northern Pacific, and Burlington main lines. Unlike other large depots, St. Paul Union Depot did not have an interlocking plant, where train directors and levermen controlled switches and signals that routed trains in and out of the depot. One was considered several times but never built because of the cost and the belief of depot officials that there wasn't enough activity to justify the expense. Instead, St. Paul used a force of some forty switchmen who were each responsible for all switches within a certain territory. Train directors communicated with and gave direction to switchmen over a PA system and a series of speakers and horns located throughout the yard. There was also a telephone at the end of each platform with a direct connection to the yard office.

In addition to direct private telephone lines to the stationmaster's office, telegraph office, and ticket office and information desk, train directors used a device called the telautograph to report information on the status of arriving and departing trains. The telautograph was a machine that electromechanically transferred a handwritten message to multiple receiving devices. A pen at the receiver transcribed the message in the writer's handwriting to a long roll of paper, which could be read by the recipient. Sending and receiving telautographs were located in the yard office and the telegraph office. Receiving telautographs were located at the Third Street switch tender, ticket office and information desk, stationmaster's office, telegraph office, waiting room (for gatemen), mail foreman's office, baggage room, and the chief porter's desk.

It's quiet now, but during busy morning and evening hours train directors scrambled to route incoming and outgoing trains. Switchmen received their orders from the train director over a loudspeaker system and set all the depot's switches manually. The toggle switches in the box on the train director's desk selected a speaker or groups of speakers. The telephones are direct lines to the interlocking towers at Westminster, Chestnut Street, Division Street, Dayton's Bluff, and Newport. Operators at these towers controlled signals and switches that routed trains as they approached the depot. They also advised the train director when a train passed their location so depot forces would have time to prepare for its arrival. The telautograph, in the middle of the train director's desk, transmitted written information on train status to depot personnel. The binoculars came in handy, too.

This building, at the east end of track 19, is where train directors and the yard master controlled and routed all of the trains arriving and departing St. Paul Union Depot. It was a tower, not unlike an airport control tower, with an excellent 360-degree view of the depot's yard and platforms. Train directors could observe arriving and departing trains and confirm that switches were properly lined for the intended route.

This close-up view of a telautograph shows the train director using a special stylus to write out a message that will be printed at another location in the depot. The telautograph was used to send train arrival and departure information and track assignments to gatemen in the waiting room, the ticket office and information desk, and the trainmaster's office.

The depot's telegraph office was its link to train dispatchers at all the railroads using the depot. Train conductors reported here to pick up their orders and special instructions. It was staffed twenty-four hours a day, seven days a week. Here, a novice telegrapher tries his hand at the key.

If the yard tower was the epicenter of depot operations, the telegraph office was its principal link with the railroads and the train dispatchers who were responsible for train movements outside the depot limits. The telegraph office was located on the train deck just east of the arrival concourse. It had both Morse and direct telephone connections to the dispatchers at each of the tenant railroads. They kept the depot advised of the status of all trains, especially if there were exceptions to scheduled operations, delays, consist or power changes, or other special needs that needed attention by depot personnel. It was here that departing conductors checked in and received their clearances and train orders.

Each night the third-shift operator polled the dispatchers of each of the railroads for information on incoming trains, noting their expected arrival times and consists, specifically, the order and

President Harry Truman on a 1948 campaign visit to the Twin Cities.

car numbers of each of the mail and express cars, Pullman sleepers, coaches, diners, and lounge cars in the consist as well as the assigned locomotive. This information was handed off to the other departments who needed it, along with the daily work order, to plan for the coming day.

The daily work order was the basis for station activities on any given day. Trains were listed in sequence by scheduled arrival and departure times along with expected actual times, the anticipated track number that would be assigned, and any exceptions to the normal or scheduled routine for that particular train—and there were plenty of exceptions.

There might be a group aboard an incoming train in an extra or private car that required special attention. Tour groups to Glacier and Yellowstone Park were very common during the warm weather months, along with conventions and traveling theater companies. Scheduled trains often had extra cars to accommodate large tourist movements. Sometimes extra cars had to be added or others taken off. St. Paul was the corporate headquarters for the Great Northern, Northern Pacific, and Omaha railroads; their executives used private business cars that traveled in scheduled trains, and these cars had to be switched. Occasionally, the Great Northern or Northern Pacific had a car that was deadheading home to the shops. During World War II there were troop trains carrying military personnel and their equipment.

Then there were the VIPs, celebrities, and politicians, among them the Duke and Duchess of Windsor, Presidents Coolidge, Roosevelt, Truman, and Eisenhower, and vice president-to-be Richard Nixon. They traveled in private business cars or, in the case of the presidents, on special trains with Secret Service protection.

The Duke and Duchess of Windsor preferred discretion and were driven away in a limousine from the seldom-used arrival concourse on Kellogg Boulevard. The presidents, always people friendly, enjoyed the crowds and preferred to walk through the waiting room and concourse, smiling and waving as they made their way to the waiting motorcade at the entrance. President Roosevelt was an exception. During the war he made a secret tour of defense plants, New Brighton's among them. His special train passed by the depot late at night on its way to the Twin Cities Army Ammunition Plant for a 1:00 a.m. appearance.

At peak times, when there were too many cars for a scheduled train, it would be divided into sections, one section following the other, three to five minutes apart. The first section might have all the baggage, mail, and express cars and coaches along with a diner and lounge car; the second section would bring up the Pullman sleeping cars, another diner and lounge car, and possibly an observation or parlor car for passengers traveling first class. As late as the 1960s, such moves were

Depot workers, railroad officials, and the press crowd the platform of the business car that brought the Duke and Duchess of Windsor to St. Paul on a 1941 visit.

All spit and polish, a Pullman porter looks on as the Pullman conductor checks his manifest. It is 1955, and the *Empire Builder* will soon be on its way to Seattle and Portland.

still fairly common. Declining patronage had forced the Great Northern to combine its *Western Star* transcontinental passenger train with the *Fast Mail* trains 27 and 28, but the 1962 Seattle World's Fair generated enough additional business to warrant a separate section between St. Paul and Seattle, and the *Western Star* briefly returned to its former glory as a full passenger train with coaches, a diner and a lounge car, sleepers, and a full observation car.

In the winter months, when through transcontinental trains from Seattle and Portland destined for Chicago were running late due to bad weather, a make-up train would be assembled in Minneapolis and depart on time to accommodate Twin Cities riders and local passengers between the Twin Cities and Chicago. This became a standard procedure in the 1960s as ridership declined and the railroads combined trains between the Twin Cities and Chicago to reduce expenses. The Milwaukee's *Morning Hiawatha* was combined with its transcontinental *Olympian Hiawatha* from the coast, and the Great Northern's *Empire Builder* and the Northern Pacific's *North Coast Limited* were merged with the Burlington's *Morning Zephyr*. If the train from the west was extremely late, the *Hiawatha* and the *Zephyr* departed separately, guaranteeing Twin Cities passengers an on-time connection at Chicago for the *Broadway*, the *General*, the *Commodore Vanderbilt*, and the *20th Century Limited* for New York City and other East Coast points.

Depot personnel faced special challenges when winter snows and cold moved in. Switches had to be kept clear, along with boarding platforms, sidewalks, steps, and the main driveway at the front of the head house. Shovels, switch brooms, and even picks were put to good use. The depot owned a snow-melting machine that ran on diesel fuel. Whenever six or more inches of snow fell, it was brought out and pushed through the yard by a locomotive to clear all the switches and turnouts.

ARRIVALS AND DEPARTURES   155

This snow-melting machine cleared depot tracks and switches after a heavy snowfall. With dozens of switches and multiple tracks and platforms, snow removal was a high priority for depot forces. Extra workers were sometimes hired to hand-shovel and deice switches and platforms.

Severe storms brought every available employee to the yard to keep things moving. Propane switch heaters were installed in 1956, which helped considerably with the work. Ice presented an even bigger problem during extreme cold. Passenger cars were steam heated, and condensate from leaking steam lines quickly turned to ice that built up on the tracks and in the flangeway next to the rail, creating a derailment hazard. Removing it was a difficult but necessary job.

Ticketing and Reservations

A ticket was required for train travel, and buying one meant a trip to the depot or one of the downtown ticket offices. Patience was sometimes required. Coach travel involved a simple cash transaction—no bank credit cards or checks—but if a reserved seat or Pullman space was needed or the trip involved more than one railroad, then the railroad reservation bureaus had to be contacted, and the space had to be reserved and confirmed before a ticket could be issued. All of this took time. There were no computers or Internet services; the agent had to call or wire the reservation bureau for confirmation. Most knowledgeable travelers arranged things in advance because the railroads were

Whether it was business or pleasure, a train trip began at the Union Depot ticket counter. For these gentlemen, it was likely business. Suit and tie and polished shoes were de rigueur for train travel.

Passengers fill the waiting room, and a crowd queues up at track 9 waiting to board the Omaha's *North American*, due out at 12:10 for Shakopee, Le Sueur, St. Peter, Mankato, St. James, Windom, Worthington, Sibley, Sheldon, Alton, LeMars, Sioux City, Council Bluffs, and Omaha. The trip would consume eight and one-half hours and 378 miles at an average speed of slightly less than forty-five miles per hour. The train was discontinued in 1959.

in no hurry. They had their protocols, and if you wanted to ride their trains you played by their rules. You didn't show up just before departure and demand a bedroom on the *North Coast Limited* and expect to get one, because you wouldn't.

Tickets came in several varieties. The simplest was a blank form on which the agent wrote the destination, the applicable tariff, the railroad(s) providing the transportation, and then stamped it with the ticket validator. The validator imprinted the date, the name of the railroad issuing the ticket, and the station of origin. Another ticket, the simplex ticket, was preprinted with all the stations on the line. The agent would cut the ticket in such a way that all of the stations printed on the ticket were mutilated except the destination. Still another ticket type was the one-point card ticket with a preprinted destination. These were most often used for transportation to frequently traveled stations. The selling agent simply stamped it with the ticket validator. There were specialized tickets for special events and excursions, party tickets for large groups such as theatrical or vaudeville troupes, tickets for clergy and drovers, and even tickets for corpses, which were handled as checked baggage. Commutation tickets were sold in book form for suburban services.

Interline tickets, those involving several carriers and multiple routes, presented a higher level of complexity, and most sensible travelers purchased them in advance at a downtown ticket office, not at the depot just before the train was due. But occasionally someone would show up at the last minute, forcing the agent to scramble. Before the book-style ticket was introduced, interline tickets consisted of a series of coupons, one for each railroad. Each coupon required a separate endorsement by the selling agent, creating the mile-long ticket of vaudeville comedy fame. Prepar-

A depot ticket clerk pulls a preprinted ticket from the ticket rack at St. Paul Union Depot. The preprinted ticket saved time at the ticket window but required separate tickets for dozens of destinations. Large racks like this were a feature of every railroad ticket office. By the 1960s ticket machines had come into use. Clerks entered a code, and the machine printed the proper ticket.

ing an interline ticket meant inquiring of the traveler where they wanted to go and, often, by which route. For example, a passenger wishing to travel from St. Paul to Omaha could originate on either the Omaha or the Chicago Great Western and travel direct to Omaha, or they could take the Rock Island out of St. Paul and change trains in Des Moines, Iowa. The agent typically consulted the *Official Guide* to determine the best connections for the traveler, asked the passenger which route they preferred, and then assembled the ticket, taking care to locate the proper tariffs for each coupon for each railroad, and endorse and date each coupon. Reserved space required a call or wire to the reservation bureaus of the respective railroads—unless the ticket happened to control space on the desired train. If an agent lacked the proper coupons, a skeleton ticket could be used. A skeleton ticket was a blank form that the agent completed by filling in the destination, route, and the railroads, together with the tariffs and any special conditions. Most railroads discouraged the use of

A standard book ticket form. These came into general use in the 1950s.

skeleton tickets, and some refused to honor them out of concern for security and the possibility that they could be forged. A skeleton ticket was a blank check.

Tickets were treated as carefully as if they were cash. All of the forms were numbered, inventoried monthly (sometimes more frequently), and subject to periodic audit. They were kept in a locked ticket case. The agent kept a record of all sales and created a monthly report. Agents were held personally accountable for the ticket inventory and were responsible for shortages.

In St. Paul, Minneapolis, and most major cities, the railroads maintained large downtown ticket offices that not only sold transportation but also functioned as travel bureaus that planned trips for individuals or groups, booked hotel accommodations, reserved rental cars, arranged for baggage pickups—anything the traveler might need. They were comfortable places with couches and overstuffed chairs where customers could relax and consult travel brochures and timetables, or wait and read a newspaper while the agent made the necessary arrangements, confirmed reservations, made up the tickets, and prepared an itinerary.

Every railroad that offered reserved coach, parlor car, or Pullman accommodations operated a reservation bureau. The bureaus performed two functions: to manage and assign space in a particular car, or line, from one destination to another; and to provide information to other passenger departments (such as operations or dining car) on the number of passengers expected on a particular train on a certain date, so they could plan accordingly. On smaller roads with limited passenger service, the reservation bureau might have no more than one or two people working in the operating department at headquarters, and the staff at a city ticket office might handle reservations in addition to their other responsibilities. On major eastern carriers such as the New York Central or the Pennsylvania, the bureaus were huge, employing dozens of people at multiple locations. In addition to the reservation bureaus, certain busy stations held reserved space on lines that either originated at that station or were on trains that served the station. For example, the Milwaukee's reservation bureau was in Chicago Union Station, but the Milwaukee depot ticket office in Milwaukee, Wisconsin, controlled a certain number of sleeping and parlor car spaces on lines that served the Milwaukee depot. A ticket agent at St. Paul Union Depot would have to call Milwaukee to see if reserved space was available for a passenger boarding at St. Paul and traveling to Milwaukee.

For each train with reserved space, the reservation bureaus prepared a master diagram showing the occupancy of reserved seats, parlor and Pullman accommodations, and where passengers would be boarding and deboarding. The master diagram and related paperwork were forwarded to the initial terminal and picked up by the train and Pullman conductors at the start of their run. On most

In 1915 the Chicago & North Western downtown ticket office was in the Ryan Hotel at Third and Robert Streets. Downtown offices were usually more convenient for travelers, especially business people. The offices were hospitable places to make arrangements for long trips or vacations.

long-distance or overnight trains, passengers could expect to arrive at the train gate about forty-five minutes before departure and find the train and Pullman conductors at a check-in desk ready to greet them and collect their tickets. After comparing the tickets with the master diagram, the train conductor would collect the ticket for the rail transportation, and the Pullman conductor would take the ticket, or coupon, for the reserved accommodations. The two tickets went in separate pouches or envelopes, and the passenger was given a check or receipt. Mistakes were rare, although sometimes there was a duplicate sale, and the passenger would have to be given alternate space from among the open (unsold) accommodations on the master diagram. A few accommodations were usually set aside or held open just in case of such duplicate sales. On departure, if a passenger didn't show, the conductor made a notation on the master diagram and arranged to wire ticket offices along the route and the reservation bureau, notifying them of the available space so it could be released for possible sale. All tickets were retained by the conductor and, if necessary, passed through to relief conductors until the train reached its final terminal where they were turned in along with other reports and forwarded to the passenger accounting departments of the respective railroads.

In this day of online reservations and ticketing, it is difficult to imagine how the railroads managed the thousands of reservations on the hundreds of trains they operated every day, particularly during the crush of World War II. It was a highly labor-intensive operation that employed hundreds of clerks. It worked, but by today's standards it was slow and cumbersome. In 1950 the railroads lost $508.5 million on passenger service. Include the costs of reservations, ticket collection, accounting protocols and the associated paperwork, and the employees involved and the total represented a substantial contribution to the passenger deficit. Consider a 1951 story in *Railway Age* praising Union Pacific for replacing 550 individual interline ticket forms with a standard book-type ticket. That was progress, but multiply 550 times the seventy-one railroads then offering passenger service and the resulting 39,000 separate forms show the magnitude of the industry's paper problem. The railroads were reluctant to accept any form of industry standardization, and while the passenger traffic associations were able to effect some cooperation, including eventual adoption of the book-style ticket form—a major improvement—individuality persisted. There was even talk of a national railroad reservation bureau owned by and serving all the carriers, but such talk went nowhere.

Most of the barriers were technological. Computerization was in its infancy, and the Internet was decades away. There were important differences among the railroads, and local needs and circumstances affected ticketing policies and procedures as well. There were also concerns about security and the possibility of fraud. In the mid-1960s, the Great Northern, never a big passenger player but in a rather farsighted effort to reduce its costs, worked with Control Data Corporation to implement a computerized optical scanning system involving a new ticket form, a ticket imprinter, and sets of imprinter plates for each station. St. Paul Union Depot adopted a ticket printing system that did away with much of the paper shuffling.

These ticket boys are at work in the Northern Pacific auditor's office in St. Paul. Their job was to sort the tickets collected by train conductors and match them with stubs and receipts from the various ticket offices where they were sold.

Yards

Both the Great Northern and Northern Pacific had their coach and engine servicing facilities near the depot. The Great Northern's coach yard was at Mississippi Street, about a mile west on its main line from Minneapolis. Its steam and later its diesel locomotives were serviced at the Jackson Street roundhouse, next to the coach yard. The Northern Pacific's coach yard and commissary adjoined the Burlington's main line just east of the depot wye. Engine servicing was performed at its Mississippi Street roundhouse.

The Northern Pacific's coach yard and commissary were located east of the depot, viewed here from the Third Street viaduct looking toward Dayton's Bluff and the Mississippi River. Coaches and sleeping cars were cleaned and inspected and dining and club cars were stocked. The commissary stored supplies and foodstuffs for the dining car department and had its own bakery and butcher shop. Many of the menu items that were served aboard the trains were prepared here by commissary bakers and chefs.

The Great Northern's coach yard was at Mississippi Street, seen here looking east as the *Gopher*, the afternoon train for Duluth, goes by.

Passenger trains on the Milwaukee Road, Omaha, Chicago Great Western, and Rock Island originated in Minneapolis, and all of their coach and locomotive facilities were in that city, as were the Soo Line's, except that its westbound trains to Winnipeg and Vancouver, which started in St. Paul, had their engines and passenger cars serviced in St. Paul by the Northern Pacific. The Minneapolis & St. Louis had a similar arrangement with the Northern Pacific.

Work performed in these yards was confined largely to inspections, cleaning, light running repairs, and the stocking of dining and lounge cars. Occasionally an air conditioning unit or a wheel set might have to be changed out, but scheduled consists were seldom broken up unless there was a serious problem requiring a trip to the Jackson Street Shops on the Great Northern or Como Shops on the Northern Pacific. The Great Northern and Northern Pacific's transcontinental trains ran through from Chicago to Seattle. All dining and lounge cars were routinely exchanged in St. Paul as were any cars requiring maintenance. Engines and switching crews from the respective railroads usually handled such station work. They would move in, break up a train, and add or set out cars. They would also bring in an entire consist from the coach yard prior to loading and departure and return one to the yard following its arrival. The depot's switch engine and crews did some of this, but they were more often engaged in shuffling mail and express cars.

The depot's five-stall engine house handled maintenance on the depot's own switch engines,

The *Afternoon Zephyr* for Chicago passes a Great Northern switch engine bringing a string of cars from the Mississippi Street coach yards to the depot. The railroads moved passenger equipment between the coach yards and the depot several times a day.

but occasionally work was done for one of the owning roads as well. The Great Northern closed its Jackson Street Shops in the 1950s and moved its locomotive fueling and servicing to the depot roundhouse once it completed conversion from steam to diesel power. The Burlington and the Soo Line subsequently joined it there. The depot completed the changeover from steam to diesel in 1956 with the retirement of its remaining steam engine, which by then was called on only when the diesel switcher was in the shop or for snow-melting duties during the winter months. All coaling and watering facilities for steam locomotives were subsequently removed.

Services and Amenities

For waiting passengers and those at the depot waiting to greet arrivals, a restaurant, coffee shop, drugstore, newsstand, and even a barbershop, model railroad display, and a bowling alley were available to take care of their needs and help pass the time. Train and people watching were popular recreations, and visitors came down to the depot just for the experience. While there, they might pick up a railroad timetable or a travel brochure and dream about a trip to places like Yellowstone and Glacier National Parks.

The depot's restaurant had a wonderful reputation and a regular clientele. There were always hungry passengers who wanted to avoid high-priced dining cars, and they would show up and grab a quick breakfast or a sandwich before their train departed. Hundreds of downtown workers stopped by for lunch or supper, and on Thanksgiving, turkey dinners with all the trimmings brought families by streetcar to the depot from all over St. Paul.

When the head house opened in 1920, a concession contract was awarded to the Union News Company of New York for operation of the drugstore, barbershop, newsstands, and restaurants, including an employee lunchroom on the Third Street level. The Fred Harvey Company also made a proposal. Harvey provided all dining car service on the Santa Fe Railway and owned and operated hotels and

The depot restaurant and coffee shop was a great place for breakfast and was much less expensive than the dining car. These ladies are just finishing their coffee and dividing up the check. Everyone wore hats.

The depot restaurant and coffee shop had regular clientele. It was a popular place for family Sunday dinners, as this 1962 crowd shows. More often it served travelers, depot personnel, and workers in nearby offices. As the trains disappeared, so did the customers. It eventually closed down for lack of business. In 1971 you could get still get a cup of coffee at the depot, but it came from a vending machine.

station lunchrooms throughout the West. Its offer asked for a greater percentage of the revenue split and was rejected for that reason. Under the terms of the agreement, the Union Depot Company owned and provided all fixtures and furnishings. The Union News Company staffed and stocked the concessions and paid a percentage of its sales to the depot company.

Business fell off during the Depression. The drugstore closed, and hours were reduced at the newsstands and the restaurant. In 1939 the Union News Company left and the Union

Mother and daughter look for something to read at the depot's newsstand.

The Twin City Model Railroad club moved to the depot in 1940. Enthusiastic depot officials helped the club construct its layout and viewing stand. For over thirty years it was a destination for visiting families and school groups. When the depot closed, the club moved its layout to Bandana Square, the former Northern Pacific Como Shops in St. Paul.

Depot Company took over, farming out some concessions to other operators. The drugstore reopened under different management, but the depot company vacated the lunchroom, leaving the dining room as the main food service area.

The Twin City Model Railroad Club moved into the vacated space in 1940. It was a wonderful public relations move for the depot company. The display and operation brought hundreds of people to the depot over the next thirty years and proved an important tool for educating the public, especially young people, on the importance of railroads and passenger trains. The display was open two evenings per week. School groups could watch as depot employees operated the layout as part of the tour.

When St. Paul's new downtown post office opened in 1934, the U.S. Post Office closed its mail-sorting operation above the concourse and moved it across Sibley Street to the new building, leaving the depot with hundreds of square feet of empty space, which saw little use until a twelve-lane bowling alley was installed in 1941.

A woman makes an inquiry at the Travelers' Aid desk. Travelers' Aid was founded in the 1850s in St. Louis to help travelers going west. It is a volunteer organization and is there to assist people with travel questions or issues. It was a busy place in the 1930s, 1940s, and 1950s.

Train Time in the 1950s

Their numbers had thinned, and those remaining had fewer riders, but dozens of trains, enough to fill the arrival and departure board, still called on the depot well into the 1950s. The locals were gone, but the Great Northern, Northern Pacific, Milwaukee, Omaha, Soo Line, Burlington, Chicago Great Western, and the Rock Island still fielded multiple trains to Chicago, Kansas City, St. Louis, Canada, the Pacific Northwest, and assorted intermediate points in the Dakotas, Montana, Wisconsin,

The business lobby is a busy place on this 1952 morning. Passengers wait for trains while others line up to buy tickets. A few servicemen try their luck on the pinball machines. Baggage stacks up at the cabstand.

and Iowa. Train time was a busy time, and from the lunch counter to the yard office everyone had to be on their toes.

The ticket office baggage and parcel check room and information desk opened at 5:00 a.m. By 6:00 a.m., cabs were queuing up and dropping passengers at the front steps, the lunch room was serving breakfast, passengers were buying newspapers and magazines at the newsstand, there were lines at the ticket windows, and people were drifting into the waiting room to greet arriving passengers or wait to board their train.

The train directors and switchmen had already handled their first arrival and departure: the Milwaukee's *Fast Mail*, train 57 from Chicago and Milwaukee, in at 5:10 a.m. The *Fast Mail* carried no passengers, but its eighteen to twenty cars were loaded with mail and express—including two railway post office cars that were used for sorting mail en route. Cars destined for the Twin Cities were set out. Other cars would be moved later that morning to the Great Northern's train 27, the *Fast Mail*, to the Pacific Northwest.

Depot tracks 19, 20, and 21 were the principal mail tracks, and cars off the *Fast Mail* had already been moved to these tracks and were being unloaded by depot mail handling forces. Sacks for local delivery were put on a conveyor that ran through a tunnel under Sibley Street to the main post office. Sacks that needed to be reloaded onto other trains or trucks were routed to the mail sorting area under the train deck.

Next at 5:55 a.m. came the Northern Pacific's overnight local from Duluth. It carried a sleeping car and coaches, but it was mainly a mail train with a railway post office car and several storage mail cars. These were set out for similar handling. The train and the passenger cars went on to Minneapolis.

Things got serious between 7:00 and 8:30 a.m. The yard office was a hectic place as the trainmaster and train director, working off the daily work order, routed incoming and departing trains to and from their assigned tracks. As incoming trains passed various interlocking towers on their way to the depot, operators reported the train and the time to the train directors. For example, the Milwaukee's westbound *Pioneer Limited* headed for St. Paul Union Depot would be reported as it passed St. Croix Tower near Hastings, at Inver Grove, at Hoffman Avenue on Dayton's Bluff, and finally at Division Street where it would be cleared to enter the depot yard limits. Eastbound trains from Minneapolis for St. Paul were reported when they departed the Milwaukee or Great Northern stations and passed St. Anthony and Westminster Towers.

It was a twenty-minute run between the two cities, giving train directors time to make plans.

ST. PAUL UNION DEPOT ARRIVALS AND DEPARTURES—JUNE 1941

Time (A.M.)	Train	From	To
5:55	NP 65	Duluth	Minneapolis
6:30	GN 28, Fast Mail	Willmar, Spokane	St. Paul
6:50	RI 18	Kansas City	Minneapolis
7:00	RI 562, Zephyr-Rocket	St. Louis	Minneapolis
7:00	CGW 21, Twin City Ltd	Omaha, Oelwein	Minneapolis
7:15	CBQ 47, Blackhawk	Rock Island, Chicago	Minneapolis
7:15	SL/CNW 4, Soo-Dominion	Minot, Vancouver	St. Paul
7:20	SL 5	Owen, Wis., Chicago	Minneapolis
7:25	CNW 210, Mondamin	Sioux Falls, Omaha	Minneapolis
7:25	MILW 1, Pioneer Ltd	Chicago	Minneapolis
7:30	NP 12, Int'l Falls Exp	International Falls	St. Paul
7:35	SL 105	St. Paul	Enderlin, N.D.
7:35	CNW 202, Nightingale	Omaha, Los Angeles	Minneapolis
7:38	SL 7	Sault Sainte Marie, Montreal	Minneapolis
7:45	CNW 515, Victory	Madison, Manitowoc, Chicago	Minneapolis
7:45	GN 4	Wilmar, Williston	St. Paul
7:45	NP 4, Alaskan	Seattle, Tacoma	St. Paul
7:55	SL 110, Winnipeger	Winnipeg	St. Paul
7:55	CNW 405, North Western Ltd	Milwaukee, Chicago	Minneapolis
8:00	GN 8, Winnipeg Ltd	St. Cloud, Winnipeg, Grand Forks, Vancouver	St. Paul
8:00	GN 11, Alexandrian	St. Paul	St. Cloud, Grand Forks
8:10	CNW 62, Namekagon	St. Paul	Ashland, Wis.
8:10	CGW 23, Minnesotan/Mill Cities Ltd	Oelwein, Kansas City, Chicago	Minneapolis
8:15	CBQ 51, North Coast Ltd	Chicago	St. Paul
8:15	NP 62	Minneapolis	Duluth
8:20	CGW 44	Minneapolis	Rochester
8:20	SL 2	Minneapolis	Chicago
8:25	CGQ 22, Morning Zephyr	Minneapolis	Chicago
8:30	CBQ 49, Empire Builder	Chicago	St. Paul
8:35	NP 1, North Coast Ltd	St. Paul	Winnipeg, Cody, Red Lodge, Gardner, Spokane, Portland, Tacoma, Seattle
8:35	MILW 6, Morning Hiawatha	Minneapolis	Chicago
8:40	MILW 15, Olympian	Chicago	Seattle, Tacoma
8:45	CNW 502, Viking	Madison, Chicago	Minneapolis
8:45	CGW 22	Minneapolis	Omaha
8:45	GN 27, Fast Mail	St. Paul	Wilmar, Spokane

Time	Train	From	To
9:00	CBQ 52	Minneapolis	Chicago
9:00	GN 20, Gopher	St. Paul	Duluth
9:15	MILW 118, MN Marquette	Minneapolis	Calmar Iowa, Madison, Chicago
9:40	CNW 203, North American	Minneapolis	Omaha
10:30	MILW 103, MN Marquette	Chicago, Madison, Calmar	Minneapolis
11:00	MILW 58	Minneapolis	Chicago
11:59	MILW 55	Chicago	Minneapolis
(P.M.)			
12:30	NP 61	Duluth	Minneapolis
12:40	GN 23, Badger	Duluth	St. Paul
12:50	RI 507, Kansas City Rocket	Minneapolis	Kansas City
1:00	MILW 100, Aftn Hiawatha	Minneapolis	Chicago
1:55	RI 16, Short Line Express	Kansas City	Minneapolis
1:56	SL 62	Minneapolis	Duluth
3:00	CNW 400, The 400	Minneapolis	Milwaukee, Chicago
3:00	CBQ 21, Morning Zephyr	Chicago	Minneapolis
3:30	CGW 24, Mill Cities Ltd	Minneapolis	Rochester, Oelwein, Kansas City
4:00	SL 1	Minneapolis	Chicago
4:30	CGQ 24, Aftn Zephyr	Minneapolis	Chicago
4:30	GN 24, Badger	St. Paul	Duluth
5:05	MILW 5, Morning Hiawatha	Milwaukee, Chicago	Minneapolis
5:19	SL 63	Duluth	Minneapolis
5:30	RI 561, Zephyr-Rocket	Minneapolis	St. Louis
5:50	SL 6	Minneapolis	Owen, Wis.
5:50	SL 106	Enderlin, N.D.	St. Paul
5:55	RI 15, Short Line Exp	Minneapolis	Kansas City
6:20	MILW 122	Minneapolis	Calmar, Iowa
6:30	CGW 43	Rochester	Minneapolis
7:00	MILW 121	Calmar, Iowa	Minneapolis
7:15	CNW 204, North American	Omaha	Minneapolis
7:20	CNW 510, Viking	Madison, Chicago	Minneapolis
7:20	RI 508, Minneapolis Rocket	Kansas City	Minneapolis
7:30	CGW 25	Oelwein, Kansas City, Omaha	Minneapolis
7:45	SL 109, Winnipeger	St. Paul	Winnipeg
8:00	GN 19, Gopher	Duluth	St. Paul
8:05	CNW 514, Victory	Minneapolis	Madison, Manitowoc, Chicago
8:25	SL 8	Minneapolis	Sault Sainte Marie, Montreal
8:30	GN 7, Winnipeg Ltd	St. Paul	Grand Forks, Winnipeg, Vancouver

Time	Train	From	To
8:35	CNW 63, Namekagon	Ashland	St. Paul
8:45	CNW 201, Nightingale	Minneapolis	Omaha, Los Angeles
8:45	CGW 26, Minnesotan	Minneapolis	Oelwein, Chicago, Omaha
9:00	CBQ 45	Chicago	Minneapolis
9:00	CNW 503, Soo-Dominion	Madison, Chicago	St. Paul
9:05	GN 12, Alexandrian	St. Cloud, Grand Forks	St. Paul
9:15	CNW 401, The 400	Milwaukee, Chicago	Minneapolis
9:20	MILW 56, Fast Mail	Minneapolis	Chicago
9:35	GN 3	St. Paul	Williston
9:40	NP 11, Int'l Falls Exp	St. Paul	International Falls
9:45	CBQ 45, Aftn Zephyr	Chicago	Minneapolis
10:00	SL 3, Soo-Dominion	St. Paul	Minot, Vancouver
10:15	CNW 209, Mondamin	Minneapolis	Sioux Falls, Omaha
10:15	NP 3, Alaskan	St. Paul	Seattle, Tacoma
10:20	CBQ 48, Blackhawk	Minneapolis	Rock Island, Chicago
10:30	GN 2, Empire Builder	Seattle, Tacoma, Portland, Great Falls	St. Paul
10:45	NP 2, North Coast Ltd	Seattle, Tacoma, Portland, Gardner, Red Lodge, Cody, Winnipeg	St. Paul
10:55	CBQ 44, Empire Builder	St. Paul	Chicago
11:00	CBQ 50, North Coast Ltd	St. Paul	Chicago
11:00	MILW 16, Olympian	Seattle, Tacoma	Chicago
11:00	RI 17	Minneapolis	Kansas City
11:20	CNW 406, North Western Ltd	Minneapolis	Milwaukee, Chicago
11:25	CNW 506, Chicago Ltd	Minneapolis	Madison, Chicago
11:30	MILW 4, Pioneer Ltd	Minneapolis	Chicago
11:59	NP 66	Minneapolis	Duluth

Six months before World War II began, there were 170 train movements in and out of St. Paul Union Depot each day. Passenger trains struck out from St. Paul for every major city in the Midwest, the Dakotas, Montana, the Pacific Northwest, and Texas and Winnipeg, Montreal, and Vancouver in Canada. Through Pullman cars and coaches made connections in Omaha and Kansas City with trains for California and the Southwest. At Chicago, travelers could board trains for East Coast points. The June 1941 edition of the *Official Guide* showed St. Paul Union Depot to be a very busy place.

Milwaukee Road, Soo Line, and Rock Island eastbounds, descending the Short Line Hill, were routed to one of the through tracks. Because time was short and only ten minutes were normally allowed for a St. Paul stop, gatemen had already sent passengers streaming down from the waiting room to the platform so they were ready when the train came to a halt. People, baggage, and mail aboard, the conductor gave a quick look for stragglers, called the yard tower from the plat-

The Division Street tower controlled access to the depot yard from the Burlington's main line.

form phone to advise the train director, and highballed the engineer. As porters and trainmen pulled up step stools and slammed Dutch doors, the engineer turned on the engine bell and headlight, and the train eased slowly away from the train shed toward one of the lead tracks, its route guided by switchmen's hand signals.

Chicago-bound Great Northern, Burlington, and Northern Pacific arrivals traced a more circuitous route, pulling by the depot roundhouse and then backing in on the east leg of the wye. The Burlington *Zephyr* seldom dawdled, taking no more than ten minutes to load and go. However, Great Northern and Northern Pacific

On orders from the dispatcher, the Division Street operator aligns the switches and signals to set up a route for an approaching train.

ARRIVALS AND DEPARTURES

The operator at Division Street was in contact with and received orders from the Burlington dispatcher by telephone and telegraph. There was also a direct telephone line to the train director in the tower at St. Paul Union Depot.

A brakeman hangs the rear marker lights on a departing train.

trains needed more time for station work. Both the *Empire Builder* and the *North Coast Limited* received fresh dining and lounge cars at St. Paul. There were sleepers, coaches, and mail cars that had to be switched out and a Burlington road engine exchanged for Great Northern and Northern Pacific power. In later years, the *Morning Zephyr* was combined with the *Empire Builder* and the *North Coast Limited* for Chicago, and there ensued a furious switching operation as three trains became one.

There were other arrivals and departures, and depot forces handled them expeditiously.

Viewed from the train director's tower, the depot's switch engine moves around the yard on a snowy winter night in 1952.

On the Great Northern, the *Badger*, the morning train for Duluth, departed at 8:10 a.m. followed by Northern Pacific train 62 for the same destination at 8:45. Great Northern's *Fast Mail* for Seattle departed at 9:30 a.m., preceded by the *Western Star* at 8:30, which was closely followed by the *Mainstreeter* for Seattle at 8:40 a.m. On the Omaha, the *North Western Limited* arrived from Chicago along with the *Nightingale* from Omaha. Still more activity kept things hopping until midmorning, when the pace slackened, only to resume as late afternoon and evening approached.

Just before midnight the ticket office and information desk, and the baggage desk, closed as the last train of the day, Northern Pacific local 66, departed for Duluth–Superior. By then the res-

ARRIVALS AND DEPARTURES   □ □ □   **177**

It's almost midnight, and the depot is winding down. A few passengers buy tickets for early morning trains.

taurant and newsstand were dark and the depot was empty except for a lone custodian pushing a broom along the concourse. The depot was at rest, or so it seemed, but below the train deck dozens of workers sorted mail and express while others on the platform loaded waiting mail cars for their morning departures. In the yard office the train director was busy routing a freight transfer around a switch engine pulling a string of cars back to the coach yards while the night yardmaster and trainmaster conferred over plans for a new day.

On a moonlit night, the mail crane, iconic symbol of the Railway Mail Service, awaits the westbound St. Paul–Miles City RPO at St. Cloud's Northern Pacific depot. Soon there will be a whistle and a dinging of crossing bells, then a headlight, and a railway mail clerk, peering into the darkness, will extend the catching arm and grab the pouch as the train hurtles by at sixty miles per hour.

5

Mail and Express

Railway Mail

Out on the train platforms, beneath the train deck, in the subbasement, and in a huge room above the concourse, dozens of employees could be found twenty-four hours a day and seven days a week, moving, sorting, loading, and unloading the carloads of mail, baggage, and express that moved through St. Paul Union Depot. The U.S. Railway Mail Service had fifteen geographic divisions. The Tenth Division was headquartered at St. Paul, and St. Paul Union Depot was its hub.

In the early 1920s, 91 percent of personal and business communication between cities was by letter and moved by railway. The long-distance telephone was an expensive novelty, and telegrams were reserved for the most urgent news. Mail service on the railroad from St. Paul to Chicago began in 1869, and by 1920, the year the head house opened, the Railway Mail Service was already sixty years old. That year there were some 2,300 railway post office runs between U.S. cities, and 4,100 trains each day carried railway post office cars (RPOs) staffed with over thirteen thousand clerks who sorted the mail en route. These were mostly scheduled passenger runs that carried RPOs and storage mail and express cars, but there were also high-priority mail and express trains with no passengers yet traveling at passenger-train speeds. In St. Paul, as in other major U.S. cities, the main post office conveniently adjoined the railroad station. Each day thousands of packages and pouches filled with sorted and unsorted mail were taken off and put aboard mail cars on arriving and departing trains.

A railway postal clerk watches and waits as his car, loaded with mail for Williston, North Dakota, and intermediate points, is about to be switched into Great Northern's *Empire Builder*, scheduled to depart St. Paul Union Depot in twenty minutes.

RPOs were one of several specialized car types used for the transport of mail and express. They were owned by the railroads but constructed and outfitted according to U.S. Post Office Department specification. There were also storage mail cars and, in later years, piggyback trailers. Railway Express used its own specialized cars for the movement of fresh fish and seafood, refrigerator cars for high-value perishables, and even horse cars for transporting racehorses to and from stables and racetracks. All of these were moved in mail and passenger trains.

RPOs typically came with a sixty-, thirty-, or fifteen-foot mail-sorting apartment. Those with sixty-foot apartments used the extra space in the car for the storage of mail. Some, with thirty- or

MAIL AND EXPRESS   □ □ □   181

fifteen-foot apartments, used the rest of the car for a small passenger section and an area for the storage of mail, baggage, and express. These were combination cars, or combines, and were found on local or branch-line trains. Self-propelled gas-electric cars came into common use in the 1920s and 1930s, replacing steam-powered passenger trains on branch and secondary lines. Most of them had a fifteen-foot RPO apartment, a separate baggage and express room, and seating for thirty to forty passengers in the coach section. A few had larger RPO apartments with the remaining space set aside for storage mail and express. These typically towed one or two coaches for passengers.

Inside the typical sixty-foot RPO there was a small closet for employee belongings, a lavatory,

Railroads began using self-propelled gasoline-electric cars to reduce costs on low-volume branch lines. These cars came with smaller, often one-person, railway mail compartments. This Northern Pacific train is probably working the Staples, Minnesota–Oakes, North Dakota, branch.

A railway post office crew sorts the mail aboard Milwaukee train 56, the *Fast Mail*, headed for Chicago.

and a watercooler. Mail pouches were loaded aboard through sliding doors and stored in bins until they were opened and dumped on tray tables for sorting. There were dozens of letter cases with slots (pigeonholes) labeled for post offices or connecting RPO routes. Racks held open pouches that would be filled with sorted mail as the run progressed.

The size of the RPO assigned to a particular train, or run, was based on the volume of business and determined by the U.S. Post Office. Mail and express trains on busy routes between major cities often carried two RPOs interspersed with one or two storage cars that were worked en route. First-class mail carried and sorted in RPOs included letters and flats and some small parcels as well as registered and certified mail and second-class mail—periodicals and newspapers. RPOs often carried money and valuables, and for that reason they were locked and secured throughout the run, and the clerks carried firearms.

A sixty-foot RPO typically had a crew of six clerks. One of them was a car foreman. A thirty-foot car had a crew of three, and a fifteen-foot car, on branch lines, one. These were U.S. Post Office employees, and they stayed with the car through the length of its run. They would report for work two or three hours ahead of departure and begin sorting mail for near stations and post offices. The sorting continued while the train was under way. Trains didn't stop just to pick up or drop off mail. Clerks picked up mail pouches "on the fly" at station mail cranes, dumped them, and then sorted and repouched the contents. Sometimes mail picked up at one station would be sorted, repouched, and thrown off at the next station down the line. At the end of the run, sorted mail was delivered to the destination post office or handed over to a transfer clerk at the opposite terminal and dispatched on another RPO.

Closed-pouch mail, including third class (bulk mail) and fourth class (parcel post) was presorted at the post office and delivered to the railroad terminal—in this case St. Paul Union Depot—for loading on the proper train. Closed-pouch mail could be carried in the RPO, if space was available, but more often it was sent in separate storage mail cars. They were loaded or unloaded en route at scheduled stops or at the destination station or terminal. Some closed-pouch mail moved in sealed cars that were filled with mail destined for a specific station. They might be set out en route, go all the way to the destination terminal for unloading, or be forwarded to their destinations on other trains.

The railroads were paid according to the number of pouches and the corresponding amount of space they used. At St. Paul Union Depot and other major mail terminals, the U.S. Post Office assigned transfer clerks to monitor loading and confirm that counts were correct.

Storage mail cars carried presorted sacked mail and packages. Some cars were sealed and not opened until reaching their destination. Others, like this one, were worked en route. Mail sacks and packages were grouped and arranged in the car according to the town or city where they would come off.

St. Paul Union Depot was the hub for the Tenth Division of the U.S. Railway Mail Service and a terminal railway post office. Mail was sorted and resorted from incoming to outgoing trains in a large area on the second floor of the concourse. This work moved to the new post office when it opened in 1934. The depot company subsequently leased the space to a concessionaire, who installed a bowling alley in 1941.

Passenger trains weren't scheduled to stop at every town, and when they didn't, mail was picked up on the fly. Here, the postmaster at Brook Park, Minnesota, attaches a mail sack to the mail crane.

In 1959 railroads received 8.74 cents per mile for moving three feet of storage mail, the equivalent of 49 pouches. To this they added terminal charges for the loading and unloading of cars, which was done by railroad personnel, or in the case of St. Paul Union Depot, depot personnel.

Schedules

Schedules prepared by the U.S. Post Office for each of the fifteen Railway Mail Service divisions were the basis for moving the mail between every community in the United States. The railroads built their operating plans and assembled equipment and personnel around these schedules as did Railway Express, whose shipments often moved in cars in the same trains. Most traffic flowed westward from major cities along the eastern seaboard and Chicago to the far west and the Pacific Coast. The schedules were designed such that any two city pairs or post offices were served directly or through connecting trains at one of the major hubs, including St. Paul. In rural areas mail was transferred from trains to trucks or, in the early days, horse-drawn wagons, for delivery to local post offices.

The *Badger*, Great Northern's morning train from St. Paul to Duluth, approaches the pickup point at seventy-five miles per hour.

The railway mail clerk aboard the St. Paul–Duluth RPO studies the approaching mail crane and gets ready to deploy the hook and snag the mail sack.

Catch complete. The mail sack is pulled into the car. Its contents are dumped on a sorting table, and clerks begin going through the pile, looking especially for letters going to stations farther down the line. These will have to be sorted quickly and repouched so they can be thrown off the train as it goes by.

All RPO routes were named beginning with the eastern or northern city and ending with the southern or western city. Thus, in Minnesota, among other routes, there was the St. Paul–Miles City, St. Paul–Minot, and the Duluth–St. Paul.

Every train in the country that carried a railway post office car or closed-pouch mail was listed in these schedules along with departure and arrival times at endpoints and impor-

Trains 56 and 57, the Milwaukee's *Fast Mail* between the Twin Cities and Chicago, were among the busiest mail trains in the country. Train 56, here running in the lighter direction, often ran with over twenty cars of mail and express and was the principal conduit for mail headed for the Pacific Northwest from Chicago, New York, and East Coast points. At St. Paul, much of it was handed over to the Great Northern or Northern Pacific for relay to the coast. Here, train 57, running in the lighter direction but still carrying two back-to-back RPOs, waits to depart St. Paul Union Depot.

tant mail route junctions. They also showed the number of linear feet that the post office leased in cars on each train.

RPO clerks were expected to know these schedules by heart along with routings to individual post offices. The latter were called schemes. To sort mail, a clerk had to know from memory the path that every piece of mail had to follow to reach its destination post office. There were hundreds of possible routings and combinations of routings. Accuracy was essential, and with thousands of pieces of mail to sort, there was no time on a seventy-mile-per-hour mail or passenger train to consult a printed schedule. Clerks were examined regularly to test their proficiency. Test scores of 99 percent were the acceptable norm.

The Busy Tenth

St. Paul and Minneapolis were gateways for mail moving to the West, the Pacific Northwest, the western Canadian provinces, Alaska, and the Orient. They were one of the busiest railway mail

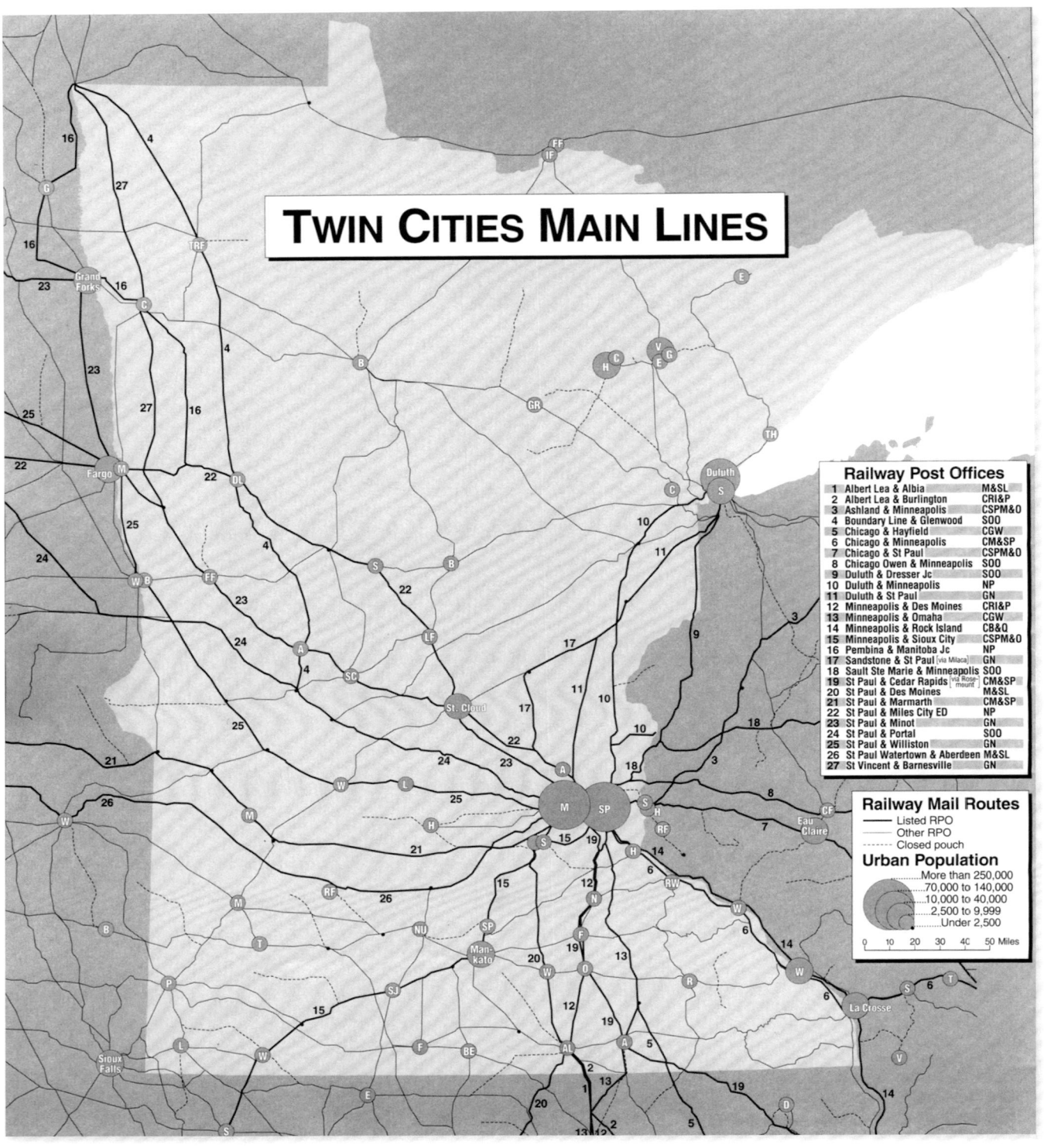

Twin Cities Main Lines

Railway Post Offices

1	Albert Lea & Albia	M&SL
2	Albert Lea & Burlington	CRI&P
3	Ashland & Minneapolis	CSPM&O
4	Boundary Line & Glenwood	SOO
5	Chicago & Hayfield	CGW
6	Chicago & Minneapolis	CM&SP
7	Chicago & St Paul	CSPM&O
8	Chicago Owen & Minneapolis	SOO
9	Duluth & Dresser Jc	SOO
10	Duluth & Minneapolis	NP
11	Duluth & St Paul	GN
12	Minneapolis & Des Moines	CRI&P
13	Minneapolis & Omaha	CGW
14	Minneapolis & Rock Island	CB&Q
15	Minneapolis & Sioux City	CSPM&O
16	Pembina & Manitoba Jc	NP
17	Sandstone & St Paul [via Milaca]	GN
18	Sault Ste Marie & Minneapolis	SOO
19	St Paul & Cedar Rapids [via Rosemount]	CM&SP
20	St Paul & Des Moines	M&SL
21	St Paul & Marmarth	CM&SP
22	St Paul & Miles City ED	NP
23	St Paul & Minot	GN
24	St Paul & Portal	SOO
25	St Paul & Williston	GN
26	St Paul Watertown & Aberdeen	M&SL
27	St Vincent & Barnesville	GN

Railway Mail Routes
— Listed RPO
— Other RPO
--- Closed pouch

Urban Population
- More than 250,000
- 70,000 to 140,000
- 10,000 to 40,000
- 2,500 to 9,999
- Under 2,500

0 10 20 30 40 50 Miles

Nineteen of Minnesota's twenty-seven main RPO routes originated in the Twin Cities and distributed mail to other routes at connecting stations and post offices throughout the state. Most of the main-line routes had more than one train daily in each direction. Bold lines correspond to the RPO routes listed by number at the side of the map. Other routes on secondary, or branch, lines are shown with lighter lines. Dotted lines are closed-pouch routes that carried presorted mail, often from a connecting RPO, to post offices in smaller communities. By the 1950s most presorted, closed-pouch mail was carried by truck. By then the local passenger trains were gone. All of these routes had scheduled connections, and clerks were expected to know them from memory. The letters in circles are abbreviations for towns served by RPOs, for example, NU for New Ulm.

The Milwaukee led all Minnesota railroads, hauling 30 percent of the total amount of mail, mainly because of its Chicago connection on trains 56 and 57. The Great Northern followed at 20 percent, and the Northern Pacific at 18 percent, with the Chicago & North Western (Omaha), Soo Line, Rock Island, Chicago Great Western, Minneaplis & St. Louis, and Burlington, in descending order, handling the rest.

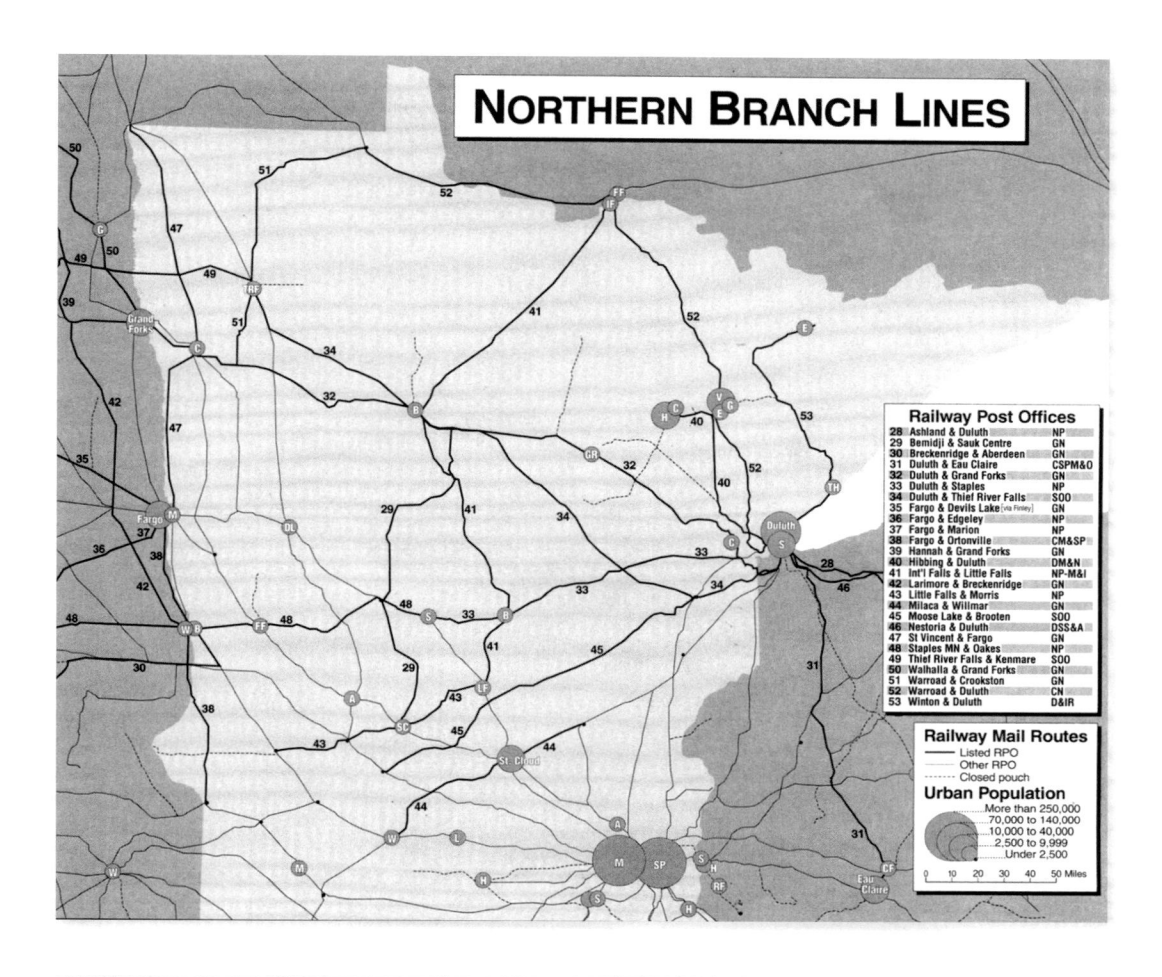

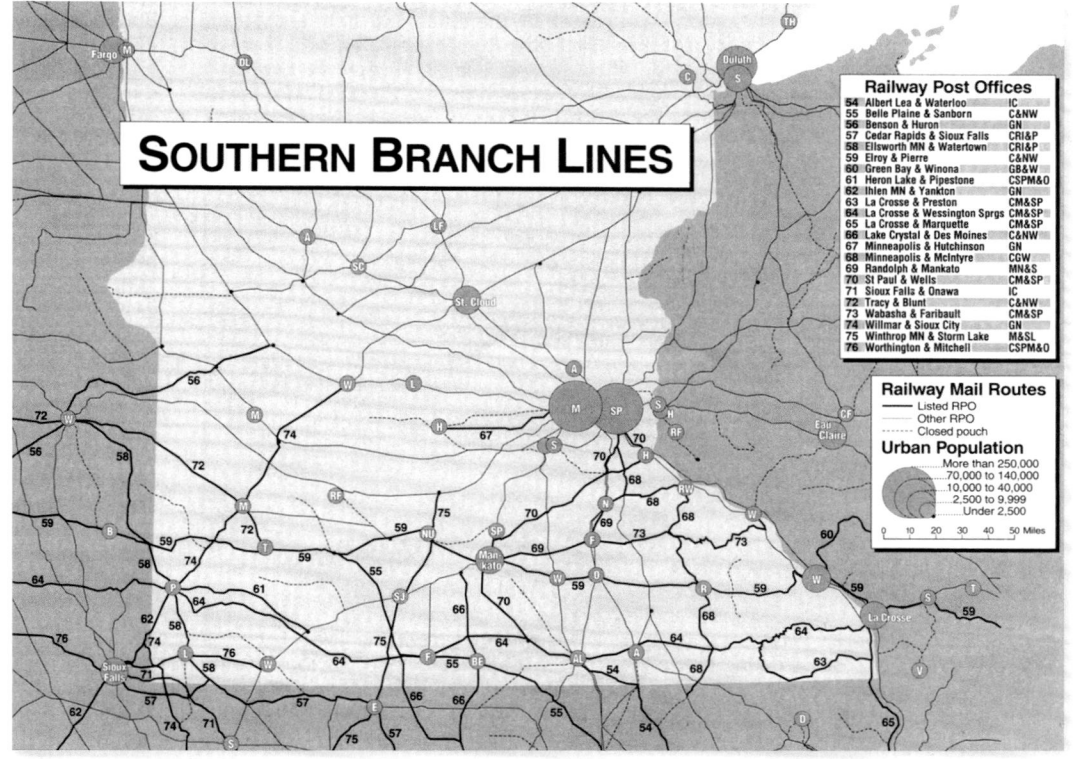

Northern Branch Lines

Railway Post Offices

28	Ashland & Duluth	NP
29	Bemidji & Sauk Centre	GN
30	Breckenridge & Aberdeen	GN
31	Duluth & Eau Claire	CSPM&O
32	Duluth & Grand Forks	GN
33	Duluth & Staples	NP
34	Duluth & Thief River Falls	SOO
35	Fargo & Devils Lake [via Finley]	GN
36	Fargo & Edgeley	NP
37	Fargo & Marion	NP
38	Fargo & Ortonville	CM&SP
39	Hannah & Grand Forks	GN
40	Hibbing & Duluth	DM&N
41	Int'l Falls & Little Falls	NP-M&I
42	Larimore & Breckenridge	GN
43	Little Falls & Morris	NP
44	Milaca & Willmar	GN
45	Moose Lake & Brooten	SOO
46	Nestoria & Duluth	DSS&A
47	St Vincent & Fargo	GN
48	Staples MN & Oakes	NP
49	Thief River Falls & Kenmare	SOO
50	Waihalla & Grand Forks	GN
51	Warroad & Crookston	GN
52	Warroad & Duluth	CN
53	Winton & Duluth	D&IR

Railway Mail Routes
— Listed RPO
— Other RPO
----- Closed pouch

Urban Population
- More than 250,000
- 70,000 to 140,000
- 10,000 to 40,000
- 2,500 to 9,999
- Under 2,500

0 10 20 30 40 50 Miles

Southern Branch Lines

Railway Post Offices

54	Albert Lea & Waterloo	IC
55	Belle Plaine & Sanborn	C&NW
56	Benson & Huron	GN
57	Cedar Rapids & Sioux Falls	CRI&P
58	Ellsworth MN & Watertown	CRI&P
59	Elroy & Pierre	C&NW
60	Green Bay & Winona	GB&W
61	Heron Lake & Pipestone	CSPM&O
62	Ihlen MN & Yankton	GN
63	La Crosse & Preston	CM&SP
64	La Crosse & Wessington Sprgs	CM&SP
65	La Crosse & Marquette	CM&SP
66	Lake Crystal & Des Moines	C&NW
67	Minneapolis & Hutchinson	GN
68	Minneapolis & McIntyre	CGW
69	Randolph & Mankato	MN&S
70	St Paul & Wells	CM&SP
71	Sioux Falls & Onawa	IC
72	Tracy & Blunt	C&NW
73	Wabasha & Faribault	CM&SP
74	Willmar & Sioux City	GN
75	Winthrop MN & Storm Lake	M&SL
76	Worthington & Mitchell	CSPM&O

Railway Mail Routes
— Listed RPO
— Other RPO
----- Closed pouch

Urban Population
- More than 250,000
- 70,000 to 140,000
- 10,000 to 40,000
- 2,500 to 9,999
- Under 2,500

0 10 20 30 40 50 Miles

RPO routes in northern and southern Minnesota that operated with, or connected to, the Twin Cities main lines are shown in bold and correspond to the numbers at the side of the maps. Other routes are shown as lighter lines. Dotted lines are closed-pouch routes. Many of the routes in northern Minnesota are branches of main lines from the Twin Cities that were focused on Duluth. In southern Minnesota several routes are also branches of Twin Cities' main lines. Others have connections with Chicago RPO routes reaching into South Dakota and Iowa.

centers in the country, with the Tenth Division leading the nation in the number and miles of RPO routes.

The Chicago–Twin Cities route was at the top with eight daily RPO runs on three railroads. Of these, the Milwaukee's overnight mail trains 57 westbound and 56 eastbound took the lead with two RPOs and as many as twenty storage mail and express cars. Some of these were destined for the Twin Cities while others were handed over at St. Paul Union Depot to the Great Northern for relay on its *Fast Mail* to western points.

The Chicago & Minneapolis RPO on trains 56 and 57 was the fifth-heaviest run in the United States, bested only by the New York Central's New York & Chicago, the Pennsylvania's New York & Pittsburgh and New York & Washington, and the New Haven's Boston & New York. Besides its RPOs, westbound train 57's storage cars were loaded with parcel post from the big mail-order houses as well as magazines, catalogs, telephone directories, and advertising from eastern printers and trans-Atlantic mail from the port of New York. Eastbound train 56 ran lighter than its westbound counterpart, reflecting the general concentration of business and industry in the eastern half of the United States. In 1918 it is estimated that the Chicago & Minneapolis RPO earned $1.1 million for the Milwaukee Road, employed 1.3 percent of the nation's mail clerks, and carried 1.7 percent of all railway mail in the United States—all of it handled through St. Paul.

The Chicago and North Western's Chicago & St. Paul route was the second major run in the Chicago corridor, carrying mail from Madison and other southern Wisconsin points and Wausau, Green Bay, and the Fox River Valley from connecting trains. Westbound it carried mail for southern Minnesota, South Dakota, and the Black Hills through a connecting train at Elroy, Wisconsin.

Going west, the St. Paul & Williston RPO on the Great Northern's *Fast Mail* via Willmar and the St. Paul & Minot RPO via St. Cloud and Fergus Falls ferried transcontinental mail to the Pacific Northwest, Alaska, and the Orient. The *Alaskan*, Northern Pacific's secondary passenger train to Seattle, carried the St. Paul & Miles City RPO and long strings of storage mail cars.

The principal link to California and Pacific ports via the Union Pacific and Southern Pacific was the Chicago Great Western's Minneapolis & Omaha RPO, the heaviest RPO line on the entire Great Western system.

The Soo Line's St. Paul & Portal RPO took mail to the Canadian border and Portal, North Dakota; from there it continued on to Moose Jaw, Saskatchewan, and Vancouver, British Columbia. The Duluth corridor hosted six passenger trains with RPOs each way plus two closed-pouch runs and a local RPO between St. Paul and Taylors Falls. The St. Paul & Cedar Rapids on the Milwaukee

Road, the Minneapolis & Des Moines on the Rock Island, and the Minneapolis & Rock Island RPO on the Burlington forwarded mail to Iowa and points south. Three important RPO lines ran north into Wisconsin and upper Michigan with connections at Sault Ste. Marie for Toronto, Ottawa, and Montreal.

Of Books and Canaries

The U.S. Post Office was fussy about parcel post, but Railway Express would take anything from a box of books to a crate of canaries. And everywhere the mail went, Railway Express would go. Parcel post service was first offered by the U.S. Post Office in 1913 as an alternative to what was perceived as predatory pricing by the four express companies of the time: Adams Express, Wells Fargo, American Express, and Southern Express. There was much protest on their part about government competition for the small-package business, but parcel post would take only shipments of eleven pounds or less, leaving the rest to the express companies. The weight limit increased to seventy

Northern Pacific and the Burlington heavily promoted their railway express business. Burlington handled express between St. Paul and Chicago, Northern Pacific from St. Paul to Tacoma, Washington.

pounds in 1931, but postal regulations restricted the range of items that could be shipped by U.S. mail, in effect creating two distinct markets, one served by the post office and the other by Railway Express. The latter consisted of oversize items, live animals, perishables, gold, stocks and bonds, and other high-value goods. The U.S. Post Office and the express companies shared depot and terminal facilities and moved their shipments in the same passenger and mail trains.

When World War I came along, the U.S. government created the U.S. Railway Administration, which took over management of the nation's railroads on January 1, 1918. In June of that year the four express companies were merged under government supervision, becoming the American Railway Express Company. Eleven years later, the railroads, dissatisfied with the compensation they were receiving, purchased American Railway Express for $30 million and formed the Railway Express Agency. Its familiar red and green color scheme and diamond logo would be associated with express shipments for the next fifty years. At its peak just after World War II, Railway Express had twenty-three thousand offices employing eighty thousand people and owned more trucks than any other company in the country.

Railway Express was a premium service with five-day delivery guaranteed, something the U.S. Post Office would not do. Customers could bring their shipment to the Railway Express office, usu-

For expedited delivery, Railway Express began coordinating its services and schedules with the airlines. In 1933 a Rock Island train transfers shipments to a Northwest Airlines Trimotor at Holman Field across the river from St. Paul Union Depot.

Railway Express shipped anything—even man's best friend. Here's a happy reunion at the Litchfield, Minnesota, depot.

ally at the railroad station, or call for one of its green trucks to come by and pick it up. Railway Express published a set of routing guides and loading diagrams for all of its car lines, along with schedules, much like the Railway Mail Service did for its RPOs. Once at the station, the shipment was sorted according to the routing guide and put on board an express car for movement in the next available train.

At other times reunions were sad. A flag-draped coffin is unloaded at St. Paul Union Depot.

Shipments moved in sealed cars that could be opened en route for loading and unloading, or they might go directly to their destination—or the nearest destination town or city—where they were sorted again before being sent on their way. Some cars carried express messengers who handled en route sorting and helped with the loading and unloading of shipments. They were also responsible for the care of special cargo and the guarding of valuables and money. Small items such as diamonds and jewelry were kept in a safe aboard the car, but there was also cash moving between banks and the Federal Reserve, stocks and bonds, and negotiated checks. Much of this was kept in sealed strongboxes that were under constant armed guard. In the late 1940s and 1950s, during the Cold War, the company contracted with the U.S. Atomic Energy Commission to ship classified material in special lead-lined express cars.

Carload shipments included time-sensitive perishables in refrigerator cars, auto parts, machine tools, clothing, weekly newsmagazines—just about anything that had to get to its destination quickly and reliably. At St. Paul, carload shipments were loaded and unloaded at one of the Union Depot's team tracks or switched to nearby freight houses.

It's Showtime

More pieces of mail moved through the St. Paul Union Depot in its ninety-year history than people, and the depot company earned more revenue from mail than from the sale of railroad tickets. It also committed more employees and resources to mail handling, and near the end of the passenger train era, it was the grubby mail and express cars, not the elegant Pullmans, that kept the doors open.

The importance of mail and express gave it considerable standing in the depot's organization. With a workforce of over four hundred people involved in the loading, unloading, and sorting of mail, the general baggage and mail agent oversaw the largest department in the depot company and reported directly to the general manager. There were also dozens of employees who worked for Railway Express and were responsible for express shipments.

The railroads and the St. Paul Union Depot Company operated under a contract with the U.S. Post Office, which assigned a force of transfer clerks to every shift to oversee the loading and unloading of mail. The transfer clerks wielded considerable power. Not only did they validate the count of mail pouches and space used in every car, which determined what the depot company and the railroad were paid, but they could also stop, or hold, a train in the event of a delay in loading mail. Transfer clerks closely monitored overall work performance and efficiency. A bad report meant fines.

Railway Express and the Railway Mail Service frequently transferred sums of money and checks between banks and the Federal Reserve. Security was tight. RPOs and Railway Express cars were locked and the clerks armed.

Time was critical and delays were unacceptable, especially on through trains, which were only allowed a fixed amount of time for station work. Not only passengers but mail, baggage, and express had to be loaded and unloaded. Sometimes a car had to be added or taken off—all done in as little as five minutes and under the close scrutiny of depot and railroad officials.

Practically every train arriving and departing St. Paul Union Depot had multiple cars of mail and express. The railroads sent train consists—including the number of storage, express, and RPO cars and the respective car numbers—each day, and with this information, a general foreman prepared a work plan and schedule and made sure equipment and employees were in place and at the ready. Mornings saw the heaviest volume of incoming mail and express and were the most hectic given the number of trains arriving and departing in a short span of time. Among them was the Milwaukee's train 57 loaded with mail from Milwaukee, Chicago, and points east. There was the Omaha's *Nightingale* and the Great Western's train 14 with mail from Omaha and their important connections with Union Pacific trains from California and the Pacific coast. More rolled in on the Rock Island from Kansas City and St. Louis, on the Soo Line from Winnipeg and Sault Sainte Marie and eastern Canada, and on the Great Northern and Northern Pacific.

A long mail train, possibly train 57 from Chicago, departs St. Paul Union Depot for Minneapolis.

The Drill

In the 1940s and 1950s, some forty to fifty thousand mail bags per day, along with thousands of parcel post packages and Railway Express, moved through the depot, and that volume held steady well into the 1960s. Even milk and cream moved by rail. Before the introduction of refrigerated trucks and bulk shipping, hundreds of milk and cream cans were picked up at rural stations, kept under ice in baggage and express cars, and delivered to the depot for transfer to local dairies.

Baggage statistics were similarly impressive. In 1935 depot forces handled 335,274 pieces of baggage, 142,046 bundles of newspapers, 1,204 corpses, and 341,954 ten-gallon cans of cream.

With such volume, crews had to be at the ready as the trains pulled in. Mail and baggage carts were hooked together and pre-positioned on the station platforms ready to receive mail pouches, Railway Express, and baggage once the train came to a halt. Time was short, and the operation was well organized. The RPOs got top priority. Sorted mail for connecting RPOs came off and was stacked on one set of carts, mail for local delivery on another. Meanwhile a switch engine might couple up to set out storage cars of mail and express to be forwarded on other trains or switched to tracks 20 and 21 for unloading. Often arriving mail and express trains such as the Milwaukee's train 57 or Great Northern's train 28 had carload shipments that had to be taken to one of the railroad freight houses or moved to the depot team tracks for unloading.

Once loaded, the mail, baggage, and express carts were tied together and pulled by a small gas-powered tractor to freight elevators at the end of the platforms or to one of the two ramps—the east ramp or the west ramp—near track 20 that led to the undertrack and subbasement sorting area. Driveway crossings at each of the tracks allowed tractor drivers to reach all of the station platforms. The undertrack mailroom occupied approximately 120,000 square feet and was divided into sections where groups of mail handlers sorted mail bag by bag. Carts with mail for local delivery were taken through a tunnel under Sibley Street to the St. Paul Post Office. Mail destined for other trains was sorted, then loaded on carts and trucked back to the platforms. Unsorted mail went under Third Street in another tunnel to the subbasement and was put aboard freight elevators for the second-floor terminal post office where it was sorted, then returned to the station platforms for loading on outbound trains. Mail was sorted for approximately 130 outbound destinations, and these destinations in turn had additional sorts before final delivery. About one-third of the mail had to be reworked at the terminal post office.

Railway Express shipments were sent to the Third Street loading dock for customer pickup or put on Railway Express delivery trucks. Others were resorted for placement on outbound trains.

Hundreds of mail sacks are stacked and await loading on outbound trains in the mail-handling area beneath the elevated track platforms at St. Paul Union Depot.

Railway Express occupied an area of approximately 75,000 square feet. During World War II Railway Express employed approximately five hundred people at the depot and loaded and unloaded some five hundred truckloads of express every eighteen hours, some one million packages per month.

Outbound mail, baggage, and express arrived at the depot throughout the day. Sorted and unsorted mailbags and packages came over from the post office to be sorted by mail handlers for loading aboard the proper train. Train baggage came down in elevators from the depot baggage room, and express arrived from the Railway Express area. Once the morning rush was over, mail and express dribbled in all day from connecting trains and RPOs; the pace picked up again in late afternoon as trains began arriving in greater numbers.

Mail foremen worked each shift and took charge of loading departing cars. All sacks loaded aboard RPOs and storage cars were recorded and verified by U.S. Post Office transfer clerks to be sure the railroad and the depot received correct payment. RPOs and storage mail and express cars for outbound trains were stored and loaded on tracks 19, 20, and 21. As cutoff times approached, these cars were picked up by a switch engine and put into position for placement in the departing train. Often loading would go on right up to scheduled departure time. Once loading was completed, storage cars were locked, and the transfer clerk placed a colored placard in a slot on the side of the car. A white placard with the car's destination indicated it would be worked en route. Blue placards went on cars that were not to be opened until they reached their destination, and salmon-colored cards were placed on destination relay cars that were only to be opened and worked at certain designated points. The clerk then handed over the transfer slips, which were similar to waybills, to the train's conductor. The train was then ready for departure.

Mail handling was physically demanding work and was unassisted by automation until 1949. That year the depot company installed a mail conveyor belt from track 21 to the mail-sorting rooms below. Track 21 was the principal track for the loading and unloading of mail. The belt system was expanded in 1953, further reducing labor costs. Ten years later, in 1959, the depot company installed the first automated mail-sorting system in the United States. It was the wonder of its day.

Mail came into the sorting area from four sources: by conveyor from the trains, by hand truck from the trains; by hand truck from the loading dock for motor trucks, and by conveyor belts from the post office for loading on outbound trains and trucks. In 1957 the bags of inbound mail were handled as follows: train conveyor, 12,360; by hand trucks from trains, 10,296; and by hand trucks from motor trucks, 3,315. Outbound mail averaged 27,044 bags per day via train, and 3,500 bags per

A worker closes the door on a loaded storage mail car. He will affix a colored placard showing the car's destination and its contents. The car will then be ready for switching into an outbound train.

day by truck, for a total daily average of 56,489 bags of mail, all of it separated manually for 140 destinations.

With the automated system, all mail bags and packages were placed on a system of conveyor belts that went by three reading stations where employees read the tag on the bag or the address on the package and entered a destination code. When the item reached its separation point, it was pushed off the conveyor to a chute leading to a mail cart. From there it was taken to track level for loading on a departing train or to the loading dock for a waiting truck.

The system cost approximately $1 million, but the speedier sorting allowed the depot company to close down mail operations between midnight and five in the morning, saving some $450,000 annually in labor costs. In another effort, the depot company and the U.S. Post Office, along with Railway Express and the Great Northern, introduced collapsible containers for handling storage mail and express. These welded-mesh containers came with a pallet-type base. They could be stacked on top of each other and loaded and unloaded by one employee with a forklift truck.

The automated sorting system installed in the depot in 1959 speeded up sorting of letters and parcel post shipments. A worker could read the tag on a mail pouch or the address on a parcel post shipment and punch a code that would send it on a conveyor to the proper location for loading on a departing train or truck, or to the post office for resorting or local delivery.

From RPOs to 707s

These improvements brought down labor costs and improved productivity, and the railroads and depot companies spent large sums installing them at busy terminals around the country. But as costs continued to rise, the railroads began to question the overall profitability of the mail business and disputes arose with the U.S. Post Office over compensation for moving the mail.

Since 1916 the railroads had been required by statute to transport all mail offered them by the U.S. Post Office on any passenger train in conformance with postal regulations. As part of the mail-handling service, they were required to construct RPOs and storage mail cars according to U.S. Post Office specifications and to provide station space for handling mail and office space for postal transfer clerks. In addition, they were responsible for safeguarding the mail while it was in their custody and for providing space in RPOs for sorting and distribution of mail, including that received from connecting carriers. The regulations also required they provide free transportation to any postal employee or official traveling on U.S. Post Office business on any train they operated. Sufficient personnel and transfer facilities had to be provided to handle whatever mail was offered, even though there often was considerable idle time for employees and equipment between trains. This included dock space and parking for loading and unloading trucks.

Nationally, mail volumes increased during World War II, from 26 billion pieces in 1939 to 36 billion in 1945. More rolling stock, larger facilities, and additional employees were needed to handle the volume. At the same time, inflation pushed up costs. The railroads went to the Interstate Commerce Commission (ICC) in 1947 seeking a 95 percent rate increase. They were granted a 25 percent increase while the ICC held hearings and studied the matter. The railroads told the ICC that labor costs had gone up 144 percent and terminal costs 111 percent since 1928 when the last pay rate was set. During these hearings the railroads also took note of the disparity between mail rates paid to the railroads and those paid to the airlines. Harry Murphy, president of the Burlington, commented before the ICC that the railroads in fiscal year 1949 carried 94 percent of the intercity first-class mail and received $27 million for the service, whereas the airlines received $55.5 million for the remaining 6 percent.

The railroads were granted a 19 percent increase on top of the 25 percent increase on January 1, 1951. The ICC also ordered a change in the basis of compensation from weight to volume. Tests were conducted to determine how many pouches could be stored per linear foot, and the railroads were to be compensated accordingly.

This was a setback for the railroads, and the situation didn't improve: the U.S. Post Office began a gradual shift of first-class mail to the airlines and second-, third-, and fourth-class mail to trucks. In fiscal year 1953 the airlines moved 1.5 billion pieces of first-class mail by air. The railroads protested because much of this was regular first-class mail carrying a three-cent stamp, not premium airmail at six cents. By the end of 1954, some 14 million ton-miles of first-class mail had been switched from rail to air. While overall mail volumes were up, it was clear by the late 1950s that, with the introduction of jet aircraft, all long-distance first-class mail would eventually move by air and local first-class mail would move by truck—a shift that was accelerated by the railroads' aggressive discontinuance of local and then long-distance passenger trains.

By 1960 the railroads had determined there was no future in the intercity passenger business,

By the 1960s more mail and express shipments were moving in piggyback trailers, and the depot purchased a portable loader to speed the loading and unloading of shipments.

and the U.S. Post Office was phasing out the RPO. That year the U.S. Post Office reorganized, dissolving the national postal transportation organization, along with the Railway Mail Service districts, in favor of a regional system. 1963 brought the biggest change to date with the introduction of the zip code and a switch to large sectional sorting facilities. Mail would move between the centers and the local post offices that were linked to each center. The centers were located near freeways and airports, not railroad terminals. By 1964 the number of RPO routes was down to 219.

In 1966 the Great Northern hired the firm of Wyer, Dick and Company to study its remaining passenger business and make recommendations. The report noted that some 25 percent of Great Northern's mail revenues came from RPO cars and found that revenue "highly vulnerable." It was a prophetic statement. The following year the U.S. Post Office ended its contract with the railroads. They now had to compete with each other and bid for the business. Non-first-class mail continued to move on the remaining passenger trains, but where a passenger train wasn't available, a freight train had to do. Service suffered, and the U.S. Post Office pressured the railroads into moving mail in expedited freight service, made easier by the introduction of piggyback (trailer on flatcar) and flexi-van service. Sorted, zip-coded mail could be loaded aboard a truck trailer at a sectional center and then put aboard a flatcar. On arrival at the destination city, it could be driven directly to the post office for distribution.

During September and October 1967, RPOs on 162 trains were discontinued, leaving Minnesota and St. Paul Union Depot with the St. Paul–Williston, St. Paul–Miles City, and the St. Paul–Duluth routes. The St. Paul–Duluth route disappeared in 1968, and the rest would go before Amtrak Day on May 1, 1971. Nationally, there were forty transfer offices still in operation on January 1, 1970, St. Paul Union Depot among them, and four hundred trains still carried storage mail.

Railway Express had similar troubles but didn't fare as well. Under the 1929 operating-ownership agreement, the railroads agreed to supply rolling stock and terminal space and handle express traffic in their trains. In turn, Railway Express would pay operating expenses and remit any balance to the rails according to the volume of express traffic handled by each owning railroad. In the 1940s and early 1950s, it was still moving thousands of express cars along 190,000 miles of rail line in 10,000 trains each day and employing 91,000 people. Hundreds of its green delivery trucks with Camel cigarette ads crowded city streets. Railway Express's contribution to the railroads was slightly higher in 1952 and 1953 than in 1944, while during the same interval total passenger revenues fell by almost 50 percent. However, this increase in revenue for express concealed a rather alarming drop in volume from 231 million individual shipments in 1946 to 87 million in 1950. The

As passenger trains were discontinued, more mail began moving by truck, and the depot became a major rail–truck transfer point.

decline in volume had been offset by an increase in charges from an average of $1.69 a shipment to $3.18 in the same time frame. There were growing concerns among the railroads that express-related expenses were increasing faster than the contributions they received from Railway Express, and in 1954, when the contracts came up for renewal, only sixty railroads signed up.

As passenger train discontinuances multiplied, Railway Express revised its railroad operating agreements. In 1958, it secured flexibility to move shipments by any mode of its choice. It had been in the air express business since the 1930s, holding contracts with some twenty-four airlines for the joint handling of express. It also sought ICC authority to begin using trucks on routes that no longer had rail passenger service. The ICC agreed, but in response to pressure from the motor carrier industry, Railway Express was allowed to use trucks only for shipments that moved at least part of the way by rail. This turned out to be a crippling blow since it excluded Railway Express from a large share of the market.

What followed was a death spiral. The Chicago & North Western, citing diversions to other modes and a loss of $500,000 on the business, dropped its express contract. It then used the loss as justification for discontinuing more of its passenger trains. It argued before the ICC, "We are unable to see any sign of adverse impact in the communities to which railroad passenger service has been reduced or eliminated. In fact, substitute mail and express service has in many cases been superior to the service previously provided by the railroad at tremendous loss." New York Central's president Alfred Perlman offered similar sentiments in 1960 when it withdrew from the corporation. "The old method of collecting parcels at gathering points and then loading them into passenger cars is obsolete." The Southern Railway felt similarly, and in 1964 it quit the express business. In 1962 the Burlington noted express volume was down by 6.8 percent followed by a 7 percent drop in 1963 and another 5 percent drop in 1965. This was significant for St. Paul Union Depot because it was an important terminal for the Burlington's business. Railway Express adopted an acronym, calling itself REA Express in 1960, but that didn't help.

In 1959 Lehman Brothers and U.S. Freight Company offered to buy Railway Express, but the financing fell through. Greyhound, already in the package express business, showed an interest in 1964, but a number of the railroads were dissatisfied with the offer, and it too fell apart. Finally, tired of the losses and declining business, the railroads sold Railway Express in 1969 for $2.5 million to an investor group led by Spencer D. Mosley. The new owners made the name REA Express permanent on June 1, 1970, and with it adopted a new logo. By then REA had closed its operations and withdrawn from St. Paul Union Depot. What was left of its business moved on trucks or via air.

REA suffered as passenger trains shriveled. In the end, it was never able to compete with the rising fortunes of UPS and Federal Express. The company entered bankruptcy in 1975 and was liquidated in July of that year.

Depot mail business was strong right up to the commencement of Amtrak. RPOs were gone by 1971, but storage and bulk mail traffic kept growing, although much of it was shifting to trucks. Two portable conveyors were purchased in 1968 to facilitate the transfer of storage mail to and from trucks and trains.

The U.S. Post Office wanted all of its terminal operations handled by mail messenger contracts that included a facility, the sorting of mail bags and parcels to outbound destinations, and the furnishing of a shuttle service between the contract facility and the railroads. It was a perfect opportunity for the depot company but would have required an expenditure of $1.9 million for facility modifications and improvements. For that, the depot company wanted a forty-four-month agreement from the U.S. Post Office and various other assurances in the event of contract cancellation. The U.S. Post Office would not agree to these terms, and at its November 18, 1969, meeting, the St. Paul Union Depot Company board of directors voted unanimously to proceed no further. Seventeen months later the depot saw its last passenger trains, and the attention of the board turned elsewhere.

Three silent sentinels guard the platforms with names for trains that will soon be gone.

6

Last Call

Gathering Gloom

James J. Hill was no great friend of the passenger train, and among western railroads his Great Northern was no great player in the passenger business. But Hill demanded that whatever bore his brand had to be the best. And so it was that his son and successor, Louis Hill, and Great Northern president Ralph Budd came to the St. Paul Union Depot on June 10, 1929, to dedicate the *Empire Builder*, a train that would carry James J. Hill's brand into the twenty-first century. From its oil-fired 4-8-2 Mountain-type locomotive to its luxuriously appointed Pullman sleeping cars, diner, and eighty-three-foot Sun Parlor observation car with buffet lounge, barber and beauty shop, and valet and lady's maid, the *Empire Builder* epitomized the finest in rail transportation and was an elegant companion to the *Oriental Limited,* the Great Northern's second offering in the Chicago–Twin Cities–Seattle trade.

Rival Milwaukee Road had already upgraded its Chicago–Seattle *Olympian* with new Pullman cars in 1927, and Hill's old nemesis, the Northern Pacific, would reequip its *North Coast Limited* in 1930. Optimism prevailed in the passenger departments of the nation's railroads, and while there were early signs of trouble, few believed that the great trains would ever make their last calls. But the market crash on October 24, 1929, and the Great Depression that followed underscored the economic weaknesses of the passenger train. Fewer trains, and fewer people, came to call on St. Paul Union Depot. The passenger numbers of the 1920s would never return, and by the end of the 1930s, five of the railroads that owned St. Paul Union Depot would be in bankruptcy.

On June 10, 1929, Great Northern's *Empire Builder* poses for its inaugural portrait at the St. Paul Union Depot. Following ceremonies, the engineer on Mountain locomotive 2517 will turn on its headlight and engine bell, open the throttle, and ease the train away from the platform on its 1,800-mile journey to the coast.

The *Empire Builder* of 1929 came with an enclosed solarium observation car with a lounge serving fine cocktails—once Prohibition was over—a valet, and a lady's maid, along with a barbershop and shower bath. Of course, only first-class Pullman passengers need apply. This was an era before shorts, sweatpants, jeans, cell phones, and loud, misbehaving children ruined the atmosphere of rail travel. The train is seen arriving at the Great Northern Station in Minneapolis.

The *Oriental Limited* was Great Northern's secondary train on the Chicago–Seattle run, but it was never second-best. It was withdrawn during the Depression but returned after World War II, and it was reequipped and renamed the *Western Star* in 1951.

First-class travel meant thick carpets, heavy chairs, and dark wood. In 1929, the *Oriental Limited* took forty-eight hours to reach Seattle from St. Paul, but in these surroundings time wasn't important for travelers who could afford and enjoy the very best. Formal attire required.

A split nail was never a problem for first-class passengers on the *Oriental Limited*. A lady's maid could always be summoned to treat such emergencies.

Weakness was evident as early as 1924, when revenue passenger train miles declined 4 percent compared to 1923, a decline made more disappointing when compared to a report by the Bureau of Railway Economics that revenue miles had increased slightly between 1922 and 1923. There were fewer passengers, and they were traveling longer distances. On the Great Northern the average distance traveled in 1920 was 80 miles, by 1924 it was 107 miles, and by 1931 it had nearly doubled to 202 miles. Fewer local passengers meant fewer passengers per mile, leading to less revenue and lots of empty seats on trains traveling short distances, such as the Burlington's St. Paul–Newport local runs, discontinued in 1924. St. Paul Union Depot sold 508,000 tickets in 1904 and 302,000 in 1929, the difference largely attributable to a decline in local passenger trips.

This travel-weary lady was enjoying a shower aboard the 1929 *Empire Builder*. Such comforts were available to first-class Pullman passengers.

The *Wall Street Journal* intoned in its February 18, 1926, edition: "Short haul business is gone as far as railroads are concerned and cannot be regained by them. The only thing to do is to adapt operations to new conditions. Local business on the Northern Pacific fell off 50% from 1920 to 1924, while long haul passenger business increased only slightly. In 1925, 150,000 persons visited Yellowstone National Park. Automobiles brought 100,000 of them. From 1914 to 1924 there was a falling off of 60% in all passenger business. Sooner or later railroads will be compelled to cut down on the cost of local passenger service and the sooner the better."

Great Northern president Ralph Budd offered similar sentiments in a letter to ICC commissioner E. I. Lewis in June 1926: "I am greatly in favor of economizing in passenger service and have considered it an alarming thing for the railways of Minnesota that with a decrease of more than 60 per cent in traffic since 1920 there has been very little decrease in passenger train miles."

The situation was much worse among short-line electric interurban railways, built to link smaller rural communities with larger cities and towns. Nationally, gross revenues peaked in 1918–

Here's the Great Northern's competition. The Northern Pacific's *North Coast Limited* meets a local on the siding at Homestake Pass, Montana, just east of Butte.

Coach passengers could enjoy lunch at their seats on the *North Coast Limited*.

19, followed by a sharp decline. The St. Paul & Southern, opened in 1914 between St. Paul and Hastings, fell into receivership in 1919 and was abandoned in 1928. On the Iron Range, the Mesaba Electric Railway was placed in receivership in 1924 and abandoned in 1927. Others, the Minneapolis, Anoka & Cuyuna Range, the Minneapolis, Northfield & Southern (Dan Patch Line), and the Electric Short Line Railway—the latter two powered by gasoline-electric motorcars—sustained heavy financial losses. The Minneapolis, Anoka & Cuyuna Range ended its passenger service in 1939, the Minneapolis, Northfield & Southern

COMPARISON OF PASSENGER TRAIN MILES AND PASSENGERS CARRIED ON GREAT NORTHERN

Year	Passenger Train Miles	Passengers Carried
1920	14,667,330	18,360,678
1921	14,558,131	13,372,072
1922	14,139,612	11,148,295
1923	14,460,723	10,434,122
1924	13,835,789	7,130,571

Passenger train miles declined only slightly between 1920 and 1924, but the number of passengers traveling fell by over 50 percent. These were mostly local passengers who had switched to automobiles. By 1924 the railroads had lost the local business for good, and they began aggressively discontinuing branch line, or local, trains and substituting mixed-freight and passenger trains, or even buses. *Source:* Ralph Budd, president of Great Northern, June 1926 letter to E. I. Lewis, ICC commissioner.

in 1942. Only the Minneapolis to Hutchinson Electric Short Line Railway survived World War II, discontinuing its last train in 1946.

Street railway ridership was similarly affected. The Twin City Rapid Transit Company had its all-time peak year in 1920, carrying 238 million riders. By 1932 it was down to 113 million. That year it abandoned its two suburban lines to Lake Minnetonka and Stillwater.

The culprit in all this was the automobile. A rich man's toy at the turn of the century, by 1921, with the passage of the Federal Aid Highway Act and the expansion of improved roads, the automobile became the dominant mode of local and eventually intercity transportation. By 1923 per capita automobile ownership in Minnesota exceeded the national average. In 1929 4.5 million automobiles came off the assembly lines, and 23.1 million were registered nationally.

To attract business, the railroads responded by cutting fares and offering special round-trip discounts on the weekends, a practice that continued well into the 1960s. Travelers responded in greater numbers, but not enough to cover the loss of revenue.

When there wasn't enough business to justify a separate passenger train, especially on branch lines, the railroads substituted mixed-train service—a train with freight and typically a single passenger car, which often was a combination car, or combine, with a passenger compartment, baggage section, and a small, fifteen-foot RPO. Schedules were slower because of the frequent need to set out and pick up freight cars, but it kept some level of service as well as mail contracts, which

Gas-electric cars came into use on branch lines and on railroads with limited passenger traffic. This car ran on the Minneapolis, Northfield & Southern between Minneapolis and Northfield. It's 1942, and despite additional wartime business, the railroad concluded it was a lost cause and applied to the Railroad and Warehouse Commission to discontinue the service. The regulators concurred, and the car would soon make its last run.

Great Northern president Ralph Budd thought buses were the answer for local passenger traffic and convinced his board that it should acquire a number of fledgling companies and merge them, creating Northland Transportation Company, whose buses are seen here in 1925 at the Minneapolis depot at Seventh Street and First Avenue North.

by then provided more revenue than passenger fares on local trains. The railroads also turned to self-propelled, gasoline-electric or diesel-electric motorcars. They were cheaper to operate than a locomotive-hauled train and often preserved a local service that might otherwise have had to be discontinued. Since communities fought discontinuance, even when no one was riding and the railroad was taking huge losses, and regulators weren't always sympathetic to the railroad's arguments and sometimes ordered continued operation for months, even years, discontinuance came as a last resort, especially if it was the last train on a line. Between 1920 and 1934 railroads in Minnesota filed eighty-one petitions to completely discontinue passenger service on various lines. Not one of them was approved.

Buses were strong competitors, especially on local runs. By 1923 there were thirty-three intercity bus lines competing with Great Northern passenger trains on parallel highway routes. Other railroads faced similar competition. Great Northern president Ralph Budd decided to take a "if you can't lick 'em, join 'em" approach, and once the necessary regulatory authority was in place, Great Northern's board gave Budd approval to acquire a number of small bus companies and merge them into Northland Transportation Company, a Great Northern subsidiary.

Where local passenger trains proved unsustainable, Great Northern moved to discontinue them and substitute Northland buses. Rail and bus services were coordinated to offer the best service at the lowest possible cost. It was a successful business venture, but Great Northern's board, believing it not to be a part of the railroad's core business, was not sufficiently impressed and unwisely sold it to Greyhound in 1929.

Service consolidation between common destinations was also pursued in an effort to reduce train miles and expense. The Great Northern, Northern Pacific, and the Soo Line each operated several separate trains on different routes between the Twin Cities and Duluth–Superior. A service pool allowed the railroads to coordinate schedules and share revenues; passengers enjoyed the convenience of interchangeable tickets with a choice of trains and departure times. Great Northern had had great success in reducing passenger-train mileage in the Seattle–Portland corridor in a pooling arrangement with the Union Pacific and the Northern Pacific. But in Minnesota, Great Northern president Budd was in no hurry to cut deals with his rivals. Between the Twin Cities and Duluth–Superior, the Great Northern had a better route, a shorter time, and a larger chunk of the passenger business than either Northern Pacific or Soo Line. He was also concerned about the attitude of the ICC and Minnesota politicians toward agreements that might appear collusive or anticompetitive. He preferred that the other two roads test the waters first.

In 1924 the Northern Pacific and the Soo Line proposed a joint service that would allow the Northern Pacific to drop one of its day trains and the Soo Line to drop its overnight run. The Soo's general passenger agent, H. M. Lewis, smoothed the way with a statement in the *Minneapolis Journal* on June 4, 1924: "The private automobile and the motorbus have made heavy inroads on the Duluth–Twin City business. When the paved road is completed the competition to rail service will be increased between these two points. We believe in this pooling plan that both railroads will profit."

The ICC gave its blessing, and the *St. Paul Daily News* rejoiced on February 10, 1926: "Economy in operations is the prayer of every railroad official. One answer to that prayer was given by the Interstate Commerce Commission Tuesday when it authorized the Northern Pacific and the Soo Line to pool their interests in passenger service from the Twin Cities to Duluth. This means an annual savings of $115,000. Although a trifle when compared to the millions invested, it is another step of the railroads to reduce the cost of operations. The public welcomes such a program of efficiency launched by the carriers, for it is the public which pays, whether operating costs are high or low. The Northern Pacific and the Soo Line are to be congratulated in their efforts to cut down operating expenses without injury to the service."

That good press was enough for Budd—especially since it was benefiting his competitors and not the Great Northern. He directed vice president Kenney to begin talks with the Northern Pacific and the Soo Line. Agreement came on July 27, 1927. The ICC signed off on November 12, and the pool started November 27, 1927. The term was for two years, and it was subject to renewal.

	Northern Pacific (%)	**Great Northern (%)**	**Soo (%)**
Mail	67.5883	27.1955	5.2163
Carload express	44.0734	34.6853	21.2413
Less-than-carload express	44.0813	41.03255	14.8862
Newspapers	54.7164	45.2836	–
Milk	16.8010	83.1990	–

Total nonpassenger revenues were fairly evenly divided between Northern Pacific and Great Northern, with the Soo Line getting less under the terms of the pooling agreement. This revenue lost importance as highways improved and trucks took traffic away from the rails.

SCHEDULES PRIOR TO POOLING

Train number	20	62	60	62	64	24	60	66	18
Railroad	GN	NP	Soo	Soo	NP	GN	NP	NP	GN
Depart Minneapolis	9:35A	8:10	10:00	1:20P	1:30	4:30	5:10	11:20	11:59
Depart St. Paul	9:00	8:50	10:45	1:50	2:00	4:00	5:40	11:59	11:20
Arrive Duluth	2:25	2:10	5:20	5:50	6:30	8:30	5:50	6:30	6:30

Train number	23	61	61	63	63	19	59	65	17
Railroad	GN	Soo	NP	Soo	NP	GN	NP	NP	GN
Depart Duluth	8:25A	7:50	8:35	1:30	2:00	4:00	5:00	11:30	11:30
Arrive St. Paul	1:45P	2:10	1:45	5:00	6:25	8:30	8:55	6:20	6:30
Arrive Minneapolis	1:12	3:00	2:25	6:00	7:00	8:00	9:30	7:00	5:55

SCHEDULES AFTER POOLING

Train number	20	62	60	62	64	24	66
Railroad	GN	NP	Soo	Soo	NP	GN	NP
Depart Minneapolis	9:35A	8:10	10:00	1:20	1:30	4:30	11:20
Depart St. Paul	9:00	8:50	10:45	1:50	2:00	4:00	11:59
Arrive Duluth	2:25	2:10	5:20	5:50	7:00	8:30	6:30

Train number	23	61	61	63	63	19	65
Railroad	GN	Soo	NP	Soo	NP	GN	NP
Depart Duluth	8:25A	7:50	8:35	1:30	2:00	4:00	11:30
Arrive St. Paul	1:45P	2:10	1:45	5:30	6:55	8:30	6:20
Arrive Minneapolis	1:12	3:00	2:25	6:00	7:30	8:00	7:00

The 1927 pooling agreement allowed Northern Pacific and Great Northern to each drop one daily round-trip between the Twin Cities and Duluth, a considerable savings in train miles with only a slight loss in revenues. The Soo Line kept both of its trains. Further discontinuances would follow in the 1930s. When Amtrak came along in 1971, there was only one daily round-trip on the former Great Northern route, which the state of Minnesota subsidized for a few years until a budget crisis ended the subsidy and, with it, the service.

The agreement between the three roads called for the Northern Pacific and the Great Northern to each get 40 percent of all passenger fares and parlor car and baggage revenues with 20 percent going to the Soo Line. The division of revenues from express, newspapers, and milk were specified as well.

The divisions were based on pre-1927 revenues and train mileage. The agreement applied to revenues and not expenses. Only through business between the Twin Cities and Duluth came under the agreement; intermediate points were not included, nor were dining car or Pullman revenues. The Great Northern agreed to discontinue its night train and the Northern Pacific its late afternoon train.

Depot Doldrums

Fewer local trains meant less revenue for the St. Paul Union Depot Company and therefore did not help to offset the costs of operating the almost new $15 million passenger terminal, although service consolidations and reduced terminal costs were of immediate benefit to the owning railroads. The reductions in revenue, though, were insignificant compared to those that followed in the wake of the 1929 market crash.

There were 297 arrivals and departures each day in 1927 and 421,194 tickets were sold. Just five years later, in 1932, 189 trains arrived and departed each day and 123,913 tickets were sold, a drop of 35 and near 70 percent, respectively. Great Northern's trains carried 8.5 million passengers in 1920. In 1931 there were less than a million. It was catastrophic. All nine railroads serving St. Paul Union Depot responded with drastic service reductions. The Great Northern's *Oriental Limited* was downgraded to a plug run in 1931, losing its Pullmans, diner, and observation car; that same year the Milwaukee discontinued the *Columbian*, its secondary Chicago-Seattle run. Further discontinuances on the Great Northern, Northern Pacific, Soo Line, Milwaukee, and the Omaha wiped out most of the few remaining branch-line locals originating at St. Paul Union Depot, leaving only main-line runs, which themselves were often downgraded with fewer or no amenities and slower schedules.

Twin Ports-Twin Cities pool service was cut back. On June 27, 1931, Soo Line trains 61 and 60 became a mixed train, operating between Dresser and Superior, Wisconsin, with a connection at Dresser to the Minneapolis-Ladysmith, Wisconsin, trains. The Soo Line also discontinued the parlor and café observation cars on trains 63 and 62. In 1931 Northern Pacific stopped trains 61 and 62 in St. Paul rather than continuing on to Minneapolis. Great Northern removed the diner and parlor cars on its morning trains and replaced the diner and parlor cars on its afternoon trains with a café-observation car.

The Chicago Great Western, teetering on bankruptcy, withdrew all of its through sleeping cars and diners. Its once fancy Twin Cities-Rochester-Chicago *Legionnaire* was downgraded in 1930 with a single Pullman-restaurant-sleeper car providing all meal and sleeping space. Through local service between Minneapolis-St. Paul and Rochester ended in 1931 and 1932, and the railroad closed its downtown ticket offices in St. Paul and Minneapolis.

The Union Depot Company cut back, but it couldn't reduce the scale of its operations, and

In the 1930s, struggling railroads, like the Chicago Great Western, shed all of their dining, sleeping, and lounge cars, leaving their passenger trains bereft of any amenities. Postwar prosperity brought none of them back. An abbreviated *Mill Cities Limited* splits the semaphore signals in 1949 or 1950 after leaving the depot at Sargeant, Minnesota.

Operating and maintaining the depot's sprawling yards and facilities made it almost impossible to trim costs. Fixed costs were awesome. Whether there were ten trains a day or one hundred, all of the depot's facilities had to be maintained.

therefore its expenses, in direct proportion to the declining number of passenger trains. It was a huge facility that had to be maintained. It required heat and light; its tracks had to be kept in good condition. Although the volume of mail and express was down by some 5 million pieces, the same number of mail handlers were needed. Moreover, the sheer size of the building and its thirteen miles of yard trackage made it nearly impossible to reduce the number of gatemen, switch tenders, train directors, and other operating personnel. Then there was the matter of the $15 million in mortgage debt acquired for construction and the fact that the facility was less than ten years old. All of these ongoing expenses and long-term obligations ultimately fell to the owning railroads, and one of them, the Minneapolis & St. Louis, was about to call it quits.

It was a difficult situation that confronted the Union Depot Company board of directors at its annual meeting on May 14, 1930. Less than a year had passed since the stock market crash, and it was unclear how far the economy would plunge. It moved cautiously, reducing wages by 5 percent. It imposed a freeze on hiring, eliminated a number of vacant positions, and deferred improvements, among them an expansion of the train yard communication system and the installation of an illuminated "Union Depot" sign at the front of the head house. It also declined participation in a proposed employee group insurance plan.

As the Depression deepened, the board at its May 13, 1931, meeting ordered further study of possible economies and force reductions. They were implemented in August of that year, producing a 10 percent reduction in overall payroll expense. In January 1932, a 10 percent reduction was ordered for all officers and management earning over $300 per month. That was followed in February by a 10 percent reduction for all classified and nonclassified employees, and in March there was a 10 percent reduction in pensions. At the May 1932 meeting, the board ordered a study of depot operations to include the advantages and savings achievable if responsibility for track maintenance and locomotive servicing were transferred to one of the owning railroads. It also called for an investigation as to whether the company should replace its steam switch engines with the newer diesel power, which was just emerging as a practical alternative to steam.

The Minneapolis & St. Louis was never a robust property. Most of the cities and towns it reached were already served by other, more prosperous competitors, but in the pre-automobile era it enjoyed a reasonable traffic in agricultural and forest products and people. In the 1890s passengers accounted for 35 percent of all revenues; by 1905 it was 51.6 percent. Most of its passenger business was local and therefore highly vulnerable to automobile competition, but it did field some first-rate limiteds with Pullmans, diners, and observation cars to Omaha, Chicago, and St. Louis through

Soon to be gone for good, a Minneapolis & St. Louis local *(second from right)*, departs St. Paul Union Depot. By 1933, when the Minneapolis & St. Louis exited the depot, it was so broke that from day to day it was unsure if it faced liquidation and a piecemeal sell-off or complete abandonment.

connections with the Illinois Central and the Wabash. By any measure its 1902 *North Star Limited* to St. Louis and Chicago was a very fine train.

The Minneapolis & St. Louis gained entry to St. Paul through an 1883 agreement with the Northern Pacific for joint operation of the latter's just completed (1886) "A" line between Minneapolis and St. Paul. James J. Hill resented the intrusion and used his influence to keep the Minneapolis & St. Louis from using St. Paul Union Depot. As a result, it sought solace from the Northern Pacific, which granted use of the basement of its office building for use as a temporary station until the Minneapolis & St. Louis could build its own at Fourth and Broadway. The Northern Pacific agreed to service the Minneapolis & St. Louis's locomotives and passenger cars. In 1902 Minneapolis & St. Louis maneuvered its way into St. Paul Union Depot, becoming one of the owning roads with a stake in the planning, construction, and operation of the new depot—until June 10, 1933, when it discontinued all passenger service to St. Paul and ceased using St. Paul Union Depot. It was inevitable. The Minneapolis & St. Louis had been in receivership since 1923, and with its passenger-train-operating ratio at 205.8 percent, the receiver had no choice. The bankruptcy judge ordered the receiver to effect economies, among them the termination of passenger service between Minneapolis and St. Paul.

An eight-year contretemps followed. As a stockholding tenant, and according to the terms of the operating agreement, the Minneapolis & St. Louis forfeited all of its capital stock in the Union Depot Company, but that still left approximately $11 million in mortgaged debt, some $1.2 million of that owed by the Minneapolis & St. Louis. The matter dragged back and forth until 1942, when the owning railroads refinanced the debt, wiping out the obligations of the Minneapolis & St. Louis.

A New Deal for the Passenger Train

Franklin Delano Roosevelt took the oath of office on March 4, 1933, three years and seven months after the October 1929 stock market crash and the beginning of the deepest and longest economic depression in American history. Plants were idle. Millions were out of work. Banks had no money. The ten-year-old St. Paul Union Depot was quiet and empty, its train announcements beckoning a few straggling passengers to still fewer trains with uncertain futures. The passenger train needed a New Deal: streamlining.

Streamlining grew out of the art deco movement, which emphasized bright colors and smooth, uncluttered lines as represented in station buildings such as Buffalo Union Terminal, Philadelphia's Thirtieth Street Station, Cincinnati Union Terminal, and Omaha's Union Pacific Station. It called forth new materials such as lightweight alloys, aluminum and plastics, and new techniques such as the shot-weld process for fabricating stainless steel. Its futuristic shapes reduced wind resistance and, when combined with lightweight materials, permitted greater speeds. Railroad car builders took note and incorporated these designs and new materials, along with advances in diesel engine technology, in a whole new class of trains.

Ralph Budd left the Great Northern, becoming president of the Chicago Burlington & Quincy in 1932, and turned his attention to the declining fortunes of its passenger business. After consultation with engineers at the Edward G. Budd Company in Philadelphia, owner of the patented shot-weld process, and General Motors, Budd persuaded his board to invest in a three-car, stainless steel speedster that would transform the American passenger train. Budd named the train *Zephyr* after Zephyrus, the god of the west wind, and on May 26, 1934, it debuted in a spectacular dawn-to-dusk

At St. Paul Union Depot, Burlington president Ralph Budd eyes the camera from the cab of the *Zephyr*, then on tour after its dawn-to-dusk race from Denver to Chicago. In 1934 the *Zephyr* was the first in a series of streamliners that brought Depression-era travelers back to the rails.

dash from Denver to Chicago, attaining a top speed of 112.5 miles per hour. In July it completed a test run between Chicago and the Twin Cities in six hours flat. A delighted Burlington board of directors immediately authorized the construction of two additional train sets that would be placed in a six-hour-thirty-minute schedule between Chicago and the Twin Cities. Following exhibition of one set at St. Paul Union Depot on April 19, the *Twin Zephyrs* entered regular service on April 21, 1935.

Not to be outdone, competitors Milwaukee Road and Chicago & North Western launched their own six-hour schedules, the Milwaukee's *Hiawatha* making its first run on May 29 and the North Western's *400* earlier, on January 2, 1935. Both trains were steam powered. The Milwaukee's *Hiawatha* featured brand-new, streamlined 4-4-2 Atlantic-type locomotives, specially constructed for *Hiawatha* service along with new streamlined coaches, diners, club cars, and a unique "beavertail"

The 1934 edition of the Milwaukee's *Afternoon Hiawatha* for Chicago descends the Short Line Hill and will arrive at St. Paul Union Depot in just a few minutes. Like the *Twin Zephyrs* and the *400*, the *Hiawatha*, with its high-speed running, abbreviated schedule, and new streamlined equipment, brought business back to the rails. Soon there would be a *Morning Hiawatha*, a *Midwest Hiawatha* between Chicago and Omaha, and a *North Woods Hiawatha* between Chicago and Peninsular Michigan, and after the war an *Olympian Hiawatha* for Seattle–Tacoma. New equipment would debut in 1937, 1939, 1942, and 1948.

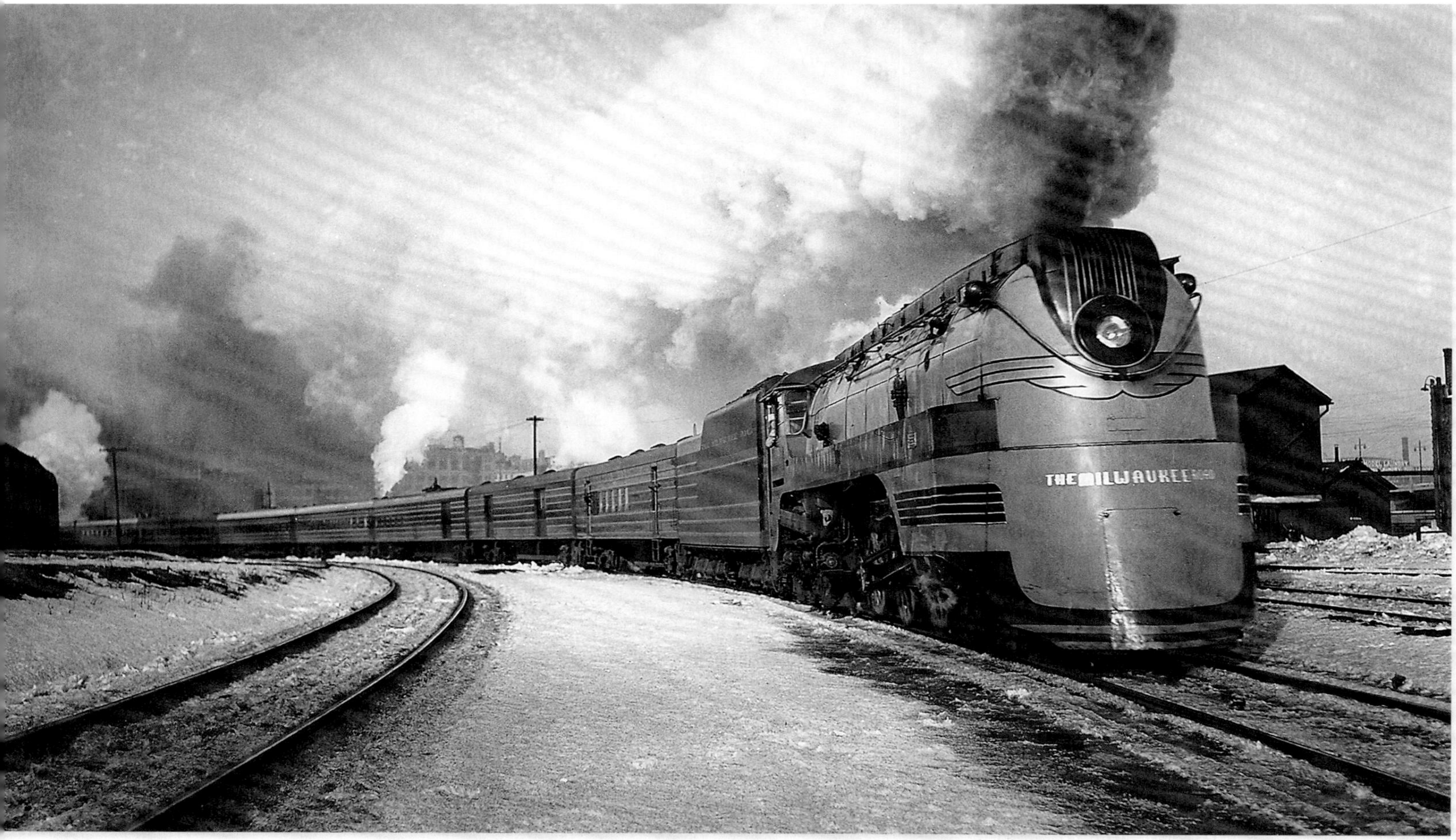
THE MILWAUKEE ROAD

From streamlined locomotive to beavertail observation car, the 1939 edition of the *Afternoon Hiawatha* makes an impressive display at St. Paul Union Depot.

Not to be outdone, Chicago & North Western introduced a new diesel-powered *400* streamliner in 1939. Three railroads now offered streamlined trains between St. Paul and Chicago. The *400* ascends Westminster Hill, heading north away from the depot and then east to Chicago.

parlor-observation car. The North Western's 400 used steam-powered 4-6-2 Pacific locomotives of the latest design and modernized passenger cars.

Acceptance of these ninety- to one-hundred-mile-per-hour trains was overwhelming. The railroads took a great risk, spending scarce Depression-era dollars on new passenger equipment and upgraded track, but it paid off in full trains and long lines at the ticket office. The *Zephyr*, the *Hiawatha*, and the 400 were regularly sold out, and the railroads had to operate an extra and sometimes two extra trains—in the case of the *Zephyr*—to handle the demand for space. This increase in ridership spilled over to other trains and schedules outside the Twin Cities–Chicago corridor. In 1937, two years after the new high-speed schedules were put into effect, St. Paul Union Depot sold 34,567 more coach and Pullman tickets than in 1932.

Consolidation

But this upturn wasn't enough. St. Paul Union Depot was still running far below capacity, and the owning railroads began looking for ways to cut operating expenses. The surest was to trim employment. The company had already thinned the ranks of operating personnel. It now began searching for economies in its overall organizational structure. Could some functions such as track and locomotive maintenance be handled by one of the owning railroads? The board of directors had looked at this before, but the findings were inconclusive. During 1937 and 1938, discussions were held with officials and the board of directors of the Minnesota Transfer Railway Company about merging the administrative and operating staffs of both organizations, with the goal of putting both companies under the control of one operating staff that would be headquartered at the St. Paul Union Depot.

The Minnesota Transfer Railway Company was incorporated in 1883 by the same railroads that formed the St. Paul Union Depot three years before. The Transfer Railway Company operated a large clearing yard in St. Paul's Midway that was used by the owning railroads to interchange freight cars among themselves. It also served a number of local industries in the Midway and owned track from a junction with the Milwaukee's Short Line at Merriam Park through to interchange connections with the Great Northern, Northern Pacific, Omaha, and Great Western at St. Anthony Park, then on to New Brighton, where it served a stockyard around the turn of the century and, later, the Twin Cities Army Ammunition Plant during World War II. Its offices and shops adjoined Cleveland and University Avenues.

The plan that was proposed in April 1938, and subsequently adopted by both boards of directors, called for merging and restructuring the operating managements of both companies. They continued as separate companies with their own boards of directors and presidents, but the rest of the operating managements were merged, and some thirty-two positions were eliminated with one vice president and general manager left in charge of both organizations.

An additional twenty-two positions—primarily clerical, administrative, and nonoperating, were abolished at the Transfer Railway Company, with their duties shifted to positions at St. Paul Union Depot. It was a painful but, at the time, necessary adjustment.

War and Peace

The depot was quiet, except for the rattling of dishes in the coffee shop and the occasional snorts of a switch engine shuffling mail cars. It was 1:30 in the afternoon on Sunday, December 7, 1941. The *Afternoon Hiawatha* had departed a half hour before, and there would be nothing until 3:00, when the arriving *Morning Zephyr* from Chicago was scheduled to slip beneath the waiting room on track 17 and come to a halt. It would be the first in a parade of arrivals and departures stretching all the way to midnight. But this wasn't a typical Sunday afternoon because around 1:35 a bulletin came through on the Western Union wire at the depot telegraph office that Pearl Harbor had been attacked. It was confirmed by a flurry of calls from dispatchers of the owning railroads and stationmasters at the Great Northern and Milwaukee Road stations in Minneapolis. Railroad and depot officials, who heard John Daly's announcement on the radio, pushed away Sunday dinners and rushed in to take charge. Security was immediately tightened. In the first few weeks following the attack, army units from Fort Snelling were detailed to patrol the yards. Military police appeared and were a regular presence until the war's end. Skylights over the ticket lobby were blacked out.

The next ten years were the depot's best. It was a refreshing turnabout given the retrenchments of the 1930s, which had seen the closing of the head house restaurant and the movement of second-floor mail-sorting operations across the street to the new post office. Passengers came back by the

Wartime passengers stand in line at the Pullman check-in desk before boarding an overnight train. All sleeping-car space was reserved. To confirm the space, passengers gave their tickets to the conductor who compared it with his space reservation forms and then collected the ticket. During the war there was great demand for sleeping-car space, and the Pullman conductor's job sometimes required diplomacy. Mistakes and duplicate sales were rare, but if they occurred, the Pullman conductor hoped there would be a no-show so he could accommodate both passengers. Otherwise, notice of any open, or unclaimed, space was sent to stations down the line to be sold to standby passengers.

thousands. A new coffee shop opened on the concourse, and part of the old restaurant and dining room was given over to the Twin City Model Railroad Club. The former mail-sorting area became a bowling alley, recreation center, and snack bar that was well patronized during the war years. Yet another part of the former restaurant became a USO canteen for servicemen and servicewomen. A dormitory sleeping area was created on the second floor for service personnel making late-night or early-morning train connections.

Gas and tire rationing and the unavailability of new automobiles, along with a red-hot economy, brought people back to the rails, putting tremendous pressure on railroads that were still recovering from the lean 1930s. Ancient cars and locomotives were pulled from scrap lines and returned to service. Boxcars were given seats and windows and pressed into service as passenger

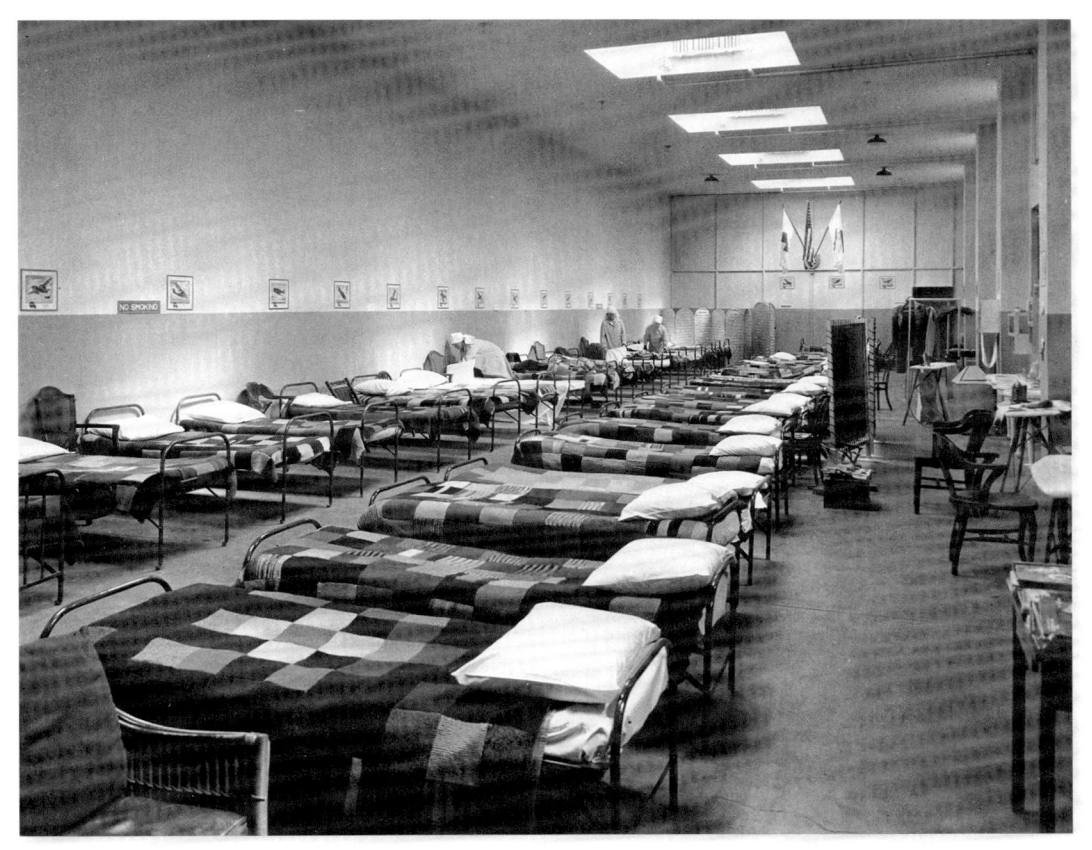

In 1940, war was still a year away, but the military draft had begun, and a servicemen's dormitory was opened on the third floor of the head house.

Departing St. Paul Union Depot, the Rock Island's Minneapolis–Kansas City *Kansas City Rocket* was one in a family of Rock Island streamliners that debuted just before World War II. A companion train, the *Zephyr Rocket,* a joint effort with the Chicago, Burlington & Quincy, offered overnight service from Minneapolis to St. Louis.

cars. The depot sold 237,804 coach and Pullman tickets in 1942 and 366,871 in 1944, compared to 157,082 in 1932 and 191,649 in 1937. Many trains had standing room only. People were forced to sit on suitcases. Fortunately, just before the war, the railroads had responded to the popularity of the new streamliners and placed additional streamlined equipment and trains in service. The Burlington *Zephyr* was expanded with additional cars. The Milwaukee added a *Morning Hiawatha* to its timetables along with more new cars and locomotives. The Chicago and North Western's 400 became a diesel-powered streamliner, and the Rocket Island added the *Rocket*s, a whole new lineup of diesel-powered streamliners, to its St. Louis, Kansas City, and Texas schedules. But even these couldn't accommodate the crowds wanting tickets, and rationing had to be imposed with military and defense personnel given priority over everyone else. Trains like the *Empire Builder* and the *North Coast Limited* routinely ran in multiple sections (separate trains), scheduled ten minutes apart, with as many as sixteen cars in each consist.

As part of the general mobilization, the Office of Defense Transportation was created on December 18, 1941, and given responsibility for regulating and coordinating all forms of transportation.

During the war the former dining room became a servicemen's canteen where they could relax while awaiting their train departures.

Volunteers at the Travelers' Aid desk helped thousands of servicemen sort out train schedules and itineraries.

Through a series of directives, it took steps to improve equipment utilization and discourage nonessential travel. All lounge and club cars were required to have seating or sleeping space. Rather than promoting travel, railroads were directed to ask passengers if their planned trip was really necessary. Special passenger trains and excursions were prohibited. The Great Northern closed its Glacier Park facilities for summer visitors. Near the end of the war, as military and defense traffic reached its peak, all sleeping cars were ordered removed from trains traveling less than 450 miles.

Some 40 million men and women served in the military during World War II and most of them traveled by rail, either in scheduled passenger trains or in troop trains that transported entire units with their equipment. To accommodate these "main moves," as they were called, the Office of Defense Transportation ordered 2,400 troop sleepers and 440 kitchen cars from Pullman. They were little more than boxcars outfitted with bunk beds and cooking facilities and were far removed from the luxury associated with Pullman travel, even though Pullman maintained them and assigned porters to each car and a Pullman conductor to the troop train itself. Troop moves originated at Fort Snelling and St. Paul Union Depot. Service personnel were brought from Fort Snelling by bus or truck and put aboard the train at the depot. A typical troop train ran sixteen to eighteen cars and was filled out with standard Pullman sleeping cars, troop sleepers, kitchen cars, and baggage cars. As many as 450 soldiers could be aboard, along with military police, officers, the military train commander, and Pullman and railroad personnel. Soldiers were assigned spartan accommodations in bunks or Pullman sections, whereas officers and the train commander had private space in Pullman bedrooms and drawing rooms.

By the end of the war, the owning railroads were infused with a new optimism about the passenger business. Wartime restrictions on new passenger cars and diesel locomotives were gradually lifted, and the railroads, flush with fresh earnings, began ordering hundreds of new passenger cars and diesel locomotives to replace war-weary equipment. Only a limited number of diesel locomotives

Some troop trains originated at St. Paul Union Depot, but mostly they were assembled at Fort Snelling. In June 1945, a train carrying soldiers destined for the Pacific and a possible invasion of Japan loads at Fort Snelling. The railroads moved millions of soldiers and quantum tons of freight and supplies during World War II. It was their finest hour.

The war is over, and returning servicemen are welcomed at St. Paul Union Depot.

had been available for wartime use, but their reliability, low cost of operation, endurance, and above all their pulling power convinced the railroads using them that the days of steam were numbered. After the war the industry would spend $500 million on new passenger cars and diesel locomotives.

In 1944 the Great Northern announced that it would reequip its *Empire Builder* as soon as new cars and diesel locomotives could be delivered and placed an order with Pullman Standard for dozens of new sleeping cars, diners, coaches, club cars, and observation cars, enough for five complete train sets. An order was also given to the Electro-Motive Division of General Motors for a fleet of diesel locomotives.

The new *Empire Builder* departed St. Paul Union Depot for the first time on February 23, 1947, becoming the first new streamlined transcontinental train to go into service after the end of World War II. The faster, forty-five-hour Chicago–Seattle schedule and new equipment were an immediate hit, so much so that the railroad reinstated its secondary train, the *Oriental Limited,* using the 1929 *Empire Builder*'s equipment. For the first time since the onset of the Depression, there were now two Great Northern passenger trains operating between Chicago and Seattle. The Great Northern reequipped its *Empire Builder* a second time in 1951, and its almost-new cars were used to replace the *Oriental Limited* with a second streamliner, the *Western Star.*

On June 29, 1947, the Milwaukee brought out its new *Olympian Hiawatha* on a similar forty-

With its observation car *Mississippi River* bringing up the rear, a brand-new 1947 *Empire Builder* drifts into St. Paul Union Depot.

five-hour Chicago–Seattle schedule and later reinstated its secondary train, the *Columbian,* which like the *Oriental Limited* had been discontinued early in the Depression. The Northern Pacific was more cautious, acquiring a number of new cars but not reequipping the entire *North Coast Limited* or speeding up its schedule until 1952–54.

The Burlington was the first to introduce the dome car to the Twin Cities, on its *Twin Zephyrs*. Cyrus Osborn, president of the Electro-Motive Division of General Motors, pioneered the idea. During the war, he was riding in the cab of a diesel locomotive through the Rockies and, taking note of the spectacular scenery, realized that if travelers could enjoy a similar view, more of them might take the train. He subsequently ordered a model built and showed it to Ralph Budd of the Burlington. Budd liked the concept so much that he ordered the *Silver Alchemy,* a 1940 stainless steel chair car, which had been used in *Twin Zephyr* service, to be rebuilt and given a dome. The refitted car, christened *Silver Dome,* emerged from Burlington's Aurora, Illinois, shops and was placed in service on the *Twin Zephyrs,* appearing at St. Paul Union Depot on July 23, 1945. It was the world's first Vista Dome car and was greeted with such enthusiasm that the Burlington ordered dozens more for the *Twin Zephyr* and its other postwar trains. Nationally, they became so popular that the Union Pacific, Santa Fe, and Southern Pacific introduced them on their major transcontinental trains.

At St. Paul Union Depot the *Twin Zephyrs,* the Great Northern's *Empire Builder,* the Northern

The interior of the 1947 *Empire Builder*'s lounge-observation car offered comfortable views of Glacier National Park.

Four years later, the Great Northern brought out a new *Empire Builder*, and the 1947 train became the *Western Star*, the second train on its Chicago–Seattle route. The *Western Star* replaced the *Oriental Limited*, which was restored to service in 1947 when the new, postwar *Empire Builder* made its debut. This is the Ranch lounge car. It offered light meals and bar service with a Western motif.

The Burlington's *Silver Dome* car, seen here in the Chicago coach yards, was the world's first dome car and a prototype for many more that followed it onto the rosters of Burlington and several other railroads. Domes came in many varieties: coaches, sleepers, lounge, even dining cars. They were very popular with the public and offered outstanding views of passing scenery. Dome cars were usually assigned to the *Twin Zephyrs* on their scenic runs along the Mississippi between Chicago and Minneapolis–St. Paul.

Pacific's *North Coast Limited,* and the Milwaukee's *Morning Hiawatha* and *Afternoon Hiawatha* and *Olympian Hiawatha* all offered domes, along with brand-new sleepers for overnight travel, full-service dining cars, club-café cars, and, bringing up the rear of the trains, observation cars with comfortable chairs and wide, wonderful windows.

The railroads promoted their trains and the advantages of rail travel in newspapers and magazines and on radio and television. Rocky, the Great Northern Railway's mountain goat mascot, urged travelers to "Go great, go Great Northern" on its *Empire Builder, Western Star, Dakotan, Winnipeg Limited,* and *Badger* and *Gopher* trains. Sue, the stewardess-nurse, welcomed everyone aboard a "happy train," the Northern Pacific's *Vista-Dome North Coast Limited*.

By 1957, with the exception of the Soo Line and the Chicago Great Western, all of the railroads serving St. Paul Union Depot had purchased and assigned modern postwar equipment to their important passenger trains. Steam locomotives were gone, except for the occasional excursion. The depot had also made improvements. Its interior had been cleaned and repainted. Tracks and switches

Not to be outdone, the Northern Pacific brought out a new *North Coast Limited* after the war and improved on it over the next several years, adding domes in 1954 and this Lewis and Clark Traveler's Rest lounge car. The *North Coast Limited* took travelers from Chicago to Seattle and Portland via Yellowstone National Park.

in the yard were renewed with heavier rail. There were new lights. The drugstore, newsstand, and coffee shop had been remodeled, and escalators had been installed between tracks 3 and 4, 15 and 16, and 17 and 18. There was even a drive-up ticket office on the Fourth Street driveway. The railroads and the depot had made a huge investment in the passenger business. But it wasn't enough.

Last Call

When railroad managements opened the books on their passenger services in 1957, they saw nothing but red ink. How could this be? The Interstate Commerce Commission used a formula to calculate the costs of passenger train operation that assigned expenses directly attributable to the operation of the trains themselves plus a portion of the common overhead associated with both freight and passenger service. In other words, if a specific train covered all out-of-pocket expenses and a percentage of the overhead, all was well, but defining these expenses was another matter and a cause of some dispute. Some argued the ICC formula was misleading and that as long as a railroad's passenger

Domes were popular with travelers because they offered an engineer's-eye view of the track ahead and the passing countryside. This dome car is on the Great Northern's *Empire Builder*.

Postwar streamlined coaches on the *Empire Builder* offered roomy, reclining seats.

service covered its direct operating expenses, then anything in excess of those expenses should be treated as a contribution to overhead. John Budd, president of the Great Northern, questioned how much expense might be eliminated if all passenger service was discontinued, saying, "Fifty-two per cent of all savings would go to the government in income taxes, while the remainder—if retained—would increase the return on investment by only one-tenth of one per cent."

As early as 1951 the Great Northern produced some $13 million in revenue, but according to the ICC formula it lost $18 million. Until 1953 passenger trains on Great Northern and several others were at least covering out-of-pocket costs. Then came 1954, and the bottom fell out. Under the ICC formula, the railroads nationally lost a whopping $669.5 million on their passenger trains.

By 1957, they were spending $161.86 for each $100 of revenue they grossed on passenger traffic and lost $723.4 million on the passenger business, almost as much as their entire net income. That same year the airlines were carrying more passengers than the railroads, and passenger losses for the railroads serving St. Paul Union Depot became unsustainable.

The numbers got lots of attention in corner offices and boardrooms and from shippers who

The Milwaukee was the third railroad offering passenger service between the Twin Cities and the Pacific Northwest. Its route closely followed the Northern Pacific's *North Coast Limited*, and they competed for the same passenger business. The Milwaukee's *Olympian Hiawatha* was a beautiful train, but as traffic declined, two passenger trains in the same market were one too many, and the Milwaukee discontinued the *Olympian Hiawatha* in 1961. This is the final train heading east through Missoula, Montana, on May 23, 1961.

complained that freight rates were indirectly subsidizing empty passenger trains. Meanwhile, Stratocruisers and Constellations went right on stealing more and more business travelers from the rails, Boeing 707s were about to take to the air, and President Eisenhower had just signed the Federal Aid Highway Act into law the year before. Still, some railroads retained an allegiance to the passenger train and tried to keep the faith. Managements at the Burlington, the Great Northern, and the Northern Pacific defended their passenger services and tried to preserve them and, at the same time, cut expenses by reducing some onboard services, combining trains, and discontinuing those that weren't covering their costs. The less-prosperous Milwaukee and Rock Island tried to do the same. The Soo Line modernized its older, prewar equipment and, with its parent Canadian Pacific, offered through transcontinental service to Vancouver, British Columbia, via Winnipeg and the Canadian Rockies. The Chicago Great Western, on the other hand, did nothing to promote its few remaining trains and dropped them as soon as mail contracts ran out or the regulatory opportunity presented itself. The Chicago and North Western, under the leadership of its new president Ben Heineman, took a much more aggressive stand and vowed to get out of the passenger business altogether. In six years, its passenger trains would exit St. Paul Union Depot for good. Soon the others would do the same.

The passenger train had reached the point of no return. Pessimistic railroad managements looked at declining passenger numbers and rising costs and decided the only way to cope with the passenger problem, as it came to be called, was to stop running passenger trains. The tipping point was the Federal Transportation Act of 1958, which stripped state regulatory authorities of their powers over discontinuing interstate passenger trains, making it easier for railroads who wanted to exit the business to get out. But it also started a decade-long fight between those who wanted to save passenger service and those who thought its usefulness was at an end. The fight ended in a draw when Congress created the National Railroad Passenger Corporation in 1970. It left the

The Union Depot Company continued to make improvements. Escalators were installed in 1957, making it easier for passengers to reach the train boarding platforms.

country with only a skeletal passenger train network, but it saved the railroads from certain bankruptcy had they been forced to continue operating passenger trains without some form of relief.

The passenger train had few friends in the late 1950s and early 1960s, certainly not at the Interstate Commerce Commission or among railroad CEOs. ICC commissioner Howard Hosmer in a 1957 report declared the passenger train a hopeless cause and stated prophetically that it would be gone by 1971. The Doyle Report, a transportation study for the U.S. Senate during the Kennedy administration, concluded: "The railroad intercity passenger service meets no important needs that cannot be provided by other carriers. . . . It serves no locations that cannot be adequately served by air and highway."

Southern Pacific president Donald Russell presided over some of the best passenger trains in the country until 1956 when, on a trip aboard his railroad's premier *Sunset Limited*, he counted only nineteen passengers in its four Pullmans and fifty-seven in the coaches. Russell resolved to rid his railroad of passenger trains. In St. Paul, Great Northern president John Budd strove for a middle course. Budd acknowledged the problem and looked for ways to reduce losses, but he was determined that the Great Northern Railway would provide good trains and good service as long as it was in the passenger business. Both the Great Northern and the Northern Pacific actively promoted travel to the 1962 Seattle World's Fair and were rewarded with increased traffic. The Great Northern also went after tour business for Glacier Park, as did the Northern Pacific for Yellowstone. When other western railroads and the Western Passenger Association sought fare increases in 1963, the Great Northern opposed them. By 1966, however, Budd conceded that passenger service appeared to be a lost cause and ordered the firm of Wyer, Dick and Company to make a study of the Great Northern's passenger trains and their future: "It does not seem to us that for the long pull there is any future for Great Northern passenger service and that over some period of time there should be a gradual phasing out of such service. Pullman passengers handled over the past few years have generally been decreasing, no doubt brought about by the severe competition from the airlines for the long distance traveler. Coach passengers handled over the past few years have held reasonably constant no doubt due to the high cost of air travel and the general unacceptability of bus travel. However, with the improved modern highway system and the deterioration of connecting rail service we anticipate a decline in coach passengers, as well. . . .

"The railroad problem is further complicated by the use of older physical facilities such as stations compared with the modern airline or bus terminals. The improvements that have taken place in the facilities for the bus and airline operations, many of which are government financed, have

Drive-up windows were popular in the 1950s, so why not a drive-up ticket office? Unfortunately, the Union Depot Company quickly discovered that people with cars rarely rode trains.

been an important competitive factor insofar as railroad passenger service is concerned and, in our opinion, will continue to be an important factor. . . .

"One of the basic problems in trying to improve the operation of Great Northern's passenger service is that it is not operated in a vacuum. It is influenced by the operations of other railroads, and, at the same time, it is restricted in many areas to improving its service unless such improvements were, at a minimum, carried out by other western railroads. . . . We doubt that many of the possible changes will be made by the railroad industry because a substantial part of the industry is generally against passenger service and 'wants out' as soon as possible. It is possible that the attitude on railroad passenger service has deteriorated to such point, both within the industry and within the eyes of the public, that it cannot be revived except by, perhaps, a massive government transfusion of public money along with changes in public policy. . . . Inasmuch as we believe there is a limited future for railroad passenger service, and little prospect of growth, which might cure its deficit problems, it eventually should be phased out."

Meanwhile, the St. Paul Union Depot Company began preparing itself for the inevitable end of passenger service, which was already well under way at the time of the Wyer, Dick report and would come some five years later. Earlier, Ben Heineman's Chicago and North Western had removed its Twin Cities–Omaha trains along with its overnight Twin Cities–Chicago *North Western Limited* in 1959, followed by the *400*, its star Chicago–Twin Cities streamliner, in 1963. The Chicago Great Western dropped its last Chicago–Omaha run in 1965. The Soo Line's *Winnipeger* came off in 1967.

By then pro-passenger Great Northern, preparing for the coming merger that would create the Burlington Northern, had combined its *Fast Mail* with the *Western Star* between St. Paul and Seattle, curtailed some off-season dining- and lounge-car service on the *Empire Builder* and the *Western Star*, and would go on to discontinue the *Red River* and the *Dakotan*, its St. Paul–Fargo trains; the *Winnipeg Limited*, its overnight St. Paul–Winnipeg service; and its morning *Badger* (Duluth–St. Paul)

The Soo Line ran some fine trains to Chicago, Duluth, Montreal, Vancouver, and Winnipeg, but its share of the passenger market was smaller than competing roads, and by the mid-1960s it was down to one train, the overnight *Winnipeger*, seen here approaching the Minneapolis Milwaukee depot. By 1967 the Soo Line carried only freight.

The Great Northern's Twin Cities–Fargo passenger business through St. Cloud and Fergus Falls evaporated as Interstate Highway 94 neared completion. Its remaining local train, the *Dakotan*, has just arrived at Fargo in February 1970 after making its final run. Today, the *Dakotan*'s route is a bike trail.

and afternoon *Gopher* (St. Paul–Duluth) runs. Between St. Paul and Chicago, the *Empire Builder*, the Northern Pacific's *North Coast Limited*, and the Burlington's *Morning Zephyr* ran as one combined train.

For its part, the Northern Pacific dropped sleeping cars and full dining cars on its *Mainstreeter* and observation cars on its *North Coast Limited*. It also did away with what had been primarily mail trains between St. Paul and Jamestown, North Dakota, and between St. Paul and International Falls and pulled off its last run to Duluth, an overnighter that carried few passengers. The Rock Island's famous Rocket fleet dwindled to a single Twin Cities–Kansas City train, the *Plainsman*, which ended in 1969.

The Milwaukee Road's Chicago-Seattle *Olympian Hiawatha* was at first combined with the *Morning Hiawatha* in 1957 and then discontinued completely in 1961. The *Afternoon Hiawatha* to Chicago came off in January 1970, followed by the overnight *Pioneer Limited* a few months later. Thereafter, with the disappearance of the Burlington's *Black Hawk* that same year, there was no longer any overnight service between St. Paul and Chicago.

In July 1962, with the winding down of passenger service, the St. Paul Union Depot Company board of directors ordered a complete review of personnel levels in all departments. It took no immediate action, but between then and 1969, when it called for major staff reductions, it began the process of downsizing depot operations and services in response to the declining number of passenger trains. By 1967 the depot had a lot of empty space, and it would get emptier and lonelier in the coming four years. The bowling alleys were gone, along with other tenants such as the Internal Revenue Service and the Pullman Company. Storage space that had been leased by the railroads for supplies for servicing passenger trains sat empty. The restaurant and coffee shop closed in 1969, replaced by vending machines located in the waiting room and on the concourse. Offices of the Minnesota Transfer Railway Company replaced the drugstore, barbershop, and newsstand in the ticket lobby. A small newsstand opened next to the baggage room, but it closed down in early 1971. By then, with most of the trains and employees gone, the depot was a place of ghosts and echoes.

With the end approaching, the depot company and the owning roads began looking at alternate uses for the property. As early as 1965 the Great Northern, one of the principal owning roads, made an independent study of vacating St. Paul Union Depot and relocating its passenger trains to another, smaller depot facility on Great Northern property. The study concluded that the costs and legal ramifications made it impractical. Meanwhile, discussions were held with St. Paul city officials about the depot's role in the Lowertown redevelopment program, which was just getting under way.

LAST CALL

In 1966 the board authorized spending $6,000 with the Metropolitan Improvements Commission for architectural drawings. A year later the board considered the Chicago Union Station redevelopment project and whether a similar plan might benefit the depot. This was followed in 1969 with the appointment of a real estate committee to study income-generating uses for the property, including air rights and the possible demolition of the depot complex.

Overshadowing all this were the nearly $9 million in bonds from a 1941 refinancing that were coming due in 1971. By 1970 the Burlington Northern merger was complete, and it and the Milwaukee were the only two owning railroads still using the depot for passenger trains;

By 1970 depot passengers wanting a cup of coffee or a soda could refresh themselves at a vending machine. The coffee shop was closed but available for rent. It never reopened.

A rather grimy *Western Star* makes its morning departure from St. Paul. It had been combined with the *Fast Mail* for many years and would carry on until Amtrak, but it was down to one sleeping car, a diner-lounge car, and three or four coaches.

On April 30, 1971, the final day before Amtrak, a porter on Great Northern's *Empire Builder*, says a last goodbye to another porter (hidden from view) on the *Morning Hiawatha* (right). Soon both trains will depart for Chicago and into history.

In the 1950s the Rock Island's *Twin Star Rocket*, going all the way to Houston and Dallas with luxurious sleepers, diners, observation cars, and connecting Pullmans, was switched into the *Golden State*, its Chicago–Los Angeles streamliner, at Kansas City. But in 1969 times have changed: the Rock Island is almost bankrupt, and the *Rocket* is now the *Plainsman*, a coach-only conveyance that is about to make its final departure from St. Paul Union Depot for Kansas City.

It is April 1971. In a few weeks these trains will make their final runs, and the depot will close for good.

It is the final day at St. Paul Union Depot. The waiting room is empty, and the arrival and departure board will soon come down. After ninety years, it's all over.

the Chicago & North Western, Soo Line, and Rock Island had discontinued their trains some years before. In a final disagreement, reminiscent of all the disputes over the years, they contended that the Burlington Northern and the Milwaukee, as the remaining users, should be solely responsible for the bonds even though the original agreement and the mortgage notes bound them to the debt as well.

On April 30, 1971, at 8:15 p.m. and 8:25 p.m., respectively, the *North Coast Limited* and the *Empire Builder* made their final westbound departures for Seattle and Portland, followed by the final *Afternoon Zephyr* from Chicago for Minneapolis at 11:40 p.m. The next day Amtrak took over and its *Empire Builder*, the only passenger train serving the Twin Cities, bypassed St. Paul Union Depot and began using the Great Northern Depot in Minneapolis. For the next two days, eastbound trains—the final *Empire Builder, Western Star, North Coast Limited,* and *Mainstreeter*—terminated in Minneapolis, and their St. Paul passengers took taxis to St. Paul where a darkened, deserted building and a handful of employees awaited them. One hundred and eight years after the *William Crooks* left St. Paul for St. Anthony, St. Paul Union Depot was silent, and the city of St. Paul was left without rail passenger service.

Finding alternate uses for St. Paul Union Depot proved problematical. The Union Depot Company and the Minnesota Transfer Railway Company maintained offices in the head house until 1974, when they were relocated to the Minnesota Transfer Railway Company's building near Cleveland and University Avenues in the Midway. Shortly before the end of passenger service, discussions were held with the U.S. Post Office about the use of the depot as a mail-processing center, but they were unsuccessful, and by 1971 all of the bulk-mail operations had been moved to a new site.

Meanwhile, to reduce costs, the Union Depot Company removed the old central heating plant and installed a smaller system in the head house, cutting off all heat to the concourse and waiting room. At the same time, the Burlington Northern Railway filled the yard and platform tracks with surplus passenger cars awaiting final disposition. The buildings were listed on the National Register of Historic Places in 1974 amid efforts to develop the property as a children's museum. When this failed, the U.S. Postal Service (which the U.S. Post Office Department was renamed in 1971) was approached about a possible sale of the entire site. Negotiations continued through 1976. A major sticking point was the Postal Service's proposal to demolish the concourse and the waiting room, which was opposed by the Advisory Council on Historic Preservation and the State Historic Preservation Office. Fortunately, a compromise was reached with the Advisory Council and the Preservation Office, and the Postal Service agreed to preserve and mothball them until such time as a

The rail bus was a 1960s attempt to merge the flexibility of a transit bus with a railcar. It made a demonstration tour, stopping at St. Paul Union Depot for Metropolitan Transit Commission officials. Unfortunately, its tiny wheels had a habit of derailing at speed.

Thousands of travelers passed through the depot and saw this mural every day, but by 1980 the effects of no heat and a leaking roof had taken their toll.

determination had been made about the future of the head house. In March 1977, the concourse, waiting room, and the train deck were sold to the Postal Service. All of the tracks and boarding platforms were removed, and the roundhouse building and yard office were razed.

The next six years witnessed a succession of plans and proposals, among them a children's museum, a river garden complex featuring offices and retail space in the head house, and new construction on the former train deck. About this time, Amtrak was making plans to vacate the Great Northern Station in Minneapolis, and although it eventually built a new station in the Midway, it considered constructing a new station below the waiting room as part of the proposed complex. Then in 1983, the head house was sold to a consortium of developers who moved forward with plans to renovate and restore the interior for restaurant and office use. These plans were not completely successful, and ownership of the building changed hands multiple times while the city government sorted through a variety of options, among them museums and offices. In 2005 the U.S. Postal Service announced that it would move its facilities to Eagan and offered the waiting room, the concourse, and the train deck to the Ramsey County Railroad Authority, which with Amtrak was making plans for a multimodal transit center that would include the depot complex. The Ramsey County Rail Authority purchased the property in 2008 and shortly thereafter acquired the head house, portions of which had been converted to condominiums.

With construction underway in 2011, the first phase of the depot's restoration and reuse as a multimodal transportation hub is scheduled for completion in late 2012, followed in 2014 by completion and opening of the Central Corridor Light Rail Line. As the depot begins its second century, there is hope that it will regain its standing as a major transportation hub for high-speed rail, commuter rail, bus, and light-rail services. The depot renovation is a down payment on that future.

Its builders thought there would be three hundred arrivals and departures a day, but fifty years later there are none. The trains and tracks are gone, and were it not for the U.S. Postal Service, the depot itself might have followed.

"Creative Destruction." The depot's train sheds and boarding platforms come down. The St. Paul post office needed parking space for its trucks, and they were in the way.

Workers torch the depot's sign. Its trains are gone. Soon it will lose its identity.

EPILOGUE
WHITHER THE PASSENGER TRAIN?

THE PASSENGER TRAINS THAT CALLED ON ST. PAUL UNION DEPOT were the pride of the railroads and the employees who ran them. Although the depot itself is being readied for a new role as a twenty-first-century transportation hub, a revival of the intercity passenger train is less certain. What is certain is that intercity and long-distance passenger trains in the postwar era carried great economic burdens, were not air and auto competitive, and were slowly bankrupting the railroads that ran them. For the railroads, Amtrak arrived as a blessed relief.

Passenger trains were slow. Although point-to-point speeds took a big jump in the 1930s with the introduction of new, high-horsepower steam and diesel locomotives and lightweight, streamlined cars, most of them plodded along with old, heavyweight cars and steam locomotives that dated back to World War I. This equipment was completely worn out and was replaced or extensively modernized and rebuilt after World War II. Passenger comfort and amenities improved, and there were some schedule speedups, but speeds exceeding eighty miles per hour would have demanded a massive investment in track and signal infrastructure, money the railroads didn't have.

In 1947, after a series of train wrecks, the ICC allowed train speeds over seventy-nine miles per hour only on lines equipped with automatic train stop (ATS) or automatic train control (ATC). These systems automatically halt a train if the engineer runs by a restrictive signal and fails to slow

There were no freeways in 1951, and the top posted speed on trunk highways was sixty miles per hour. Assuming an average travel speed of forty-five miles per hour, only twenty-two (29 percent) of the seventy-five passenger trains in Minnesota were competitive with autos. None of them would be competitive today.

AVERAGE PASSENGER TRAIN SPEEDS IN 1951

Railroad	Train	From	To	Miles between Stops	Speed
CB&Q	21-Morning Zephyr	La Crosse	St. Paul	43	61
CB&Q	23-Afternoon Zephyr	La Crosse	St. Paul	43	61
C&NW	401-Twin Cities 400	Eau Claire	St. Paul	85	60
CMStP&P	101-Afternoon Hiawatha	La Crosse	St. Paul	43	60
CMStP&P	15-Olympian Hiawatha	Minneapolis	Aberdeen	143	59
CMStP&P	15-Olympian Hiawatha	La Crosse	St. Paul	65	59
GN	1-Empire Builder	Minneapolis	Fargo	84	56
CRI&P	507-Twin Star Rocket	St. Paul	Manly, Iowa	26	56
CB&Q	49-Empire Builder	La Crosse	St. Paul	65	54
GN	20-Gopher	Minneapolis	Duluth	38	54
GN	27-Fast Mail	Minneapolis	Fargo	84	52
GN	11-Red River	Minneapolis	Fargo	30	51
CRI&P	561-Zephyr Rocket	St. Paul	Manly, Iowa	26	51
CMStP&P	5-Morning Hiawatha	La Crosse	St. Paul	22	51
CMStP&P	1-Pioneer Limited	La Crosse	St. Paul	43	48
C&NW	405-North Western	Eau Claire	St. Paul	28	48
NP	Limited	Minneapolis	Fargo	24	47
CB&Q	1-North Coast Limited	La Crosse	St. Paul	43	45
C&NW	47-Black Hawk 519-Dakota 400	Winona	Brookings, S.D.	29	45
CMStP&P	17-Columbian	Minneapolis	Aberdeen	29	45
GN	3-Western Star	Minneapolis	Fargo	28	45
C&NW	203-North American	St. Paul	Sioux City	24	45
CMStP&P	17-Columbian	La Crosse	St. Paul	21	43
CGW	28-Nebraska Limited	St. Paul	Mason City	17	43
C&NW	201-Nightingale	St. Paul	Sioux City	35	42
CRI&P	15-Mid Continent Special	St. Paul	Manly, Iowa	26	42
GN	24-Badger	Minneapolis	Duluth	6	42
CB&Q	51-North Coast Limited	La Crosse	St. Paul	43	41
NP	62-local	St. Paul	Duluth	7	41
Soo Line	3-Soo Dominion	Minneapolis	Fairmount, N.D.	38	40
GN	7-Winnipeg Limited	Minneapolis	Winnipeg	15	39
Soo Line	109-Winnipeger	Minneapolis	Winnipeg	24	38
Soo Line	62-local	St. Paul	Duluth	10	38
C&NW	515-Victory	Eau Claire	St. Paul	28	37
Soo Line	6-Laker	St. Paul	Owen, Wis.	18	37
CMStP&P	55 local	La Crosse	St. Paul	9	36
Soo Line	2-local	St. Paul	Owen, Wis.	7	36

Railroad	Train	From	To	Miles between Stops	Speed
NP	55-local	Duluth	Staples	9	35
C&NW	501-Viking	Eau Claire	St. Paul	8	34
CGW	24-Mill Cities Limited	St. Paul	Oelwein, Iowa	8	34
CB&Q	45-local	La Crosse	St. Paul	7	34
NP	3-Alaskan	Minneapolis	Fargo	11	32
Soo Line	7-local	St. Paul	Ladysmith, Wis.	11	32
C&NW	81-local	Worthington	Sioux Falls	8	32
GN	35-local	Duluth	Grand Forks	8	31
Soo Line	65-local	Duluth	Thief River Falls	8	31
GN	9-Dakotan	Minneapolis	Fargo	7	31
NP	11-local	Minneapolis	International Falls	7	31
CMStP&P	121-local	Austin	St. Paul	8	30
NP	57-local	Duluth	Staples	6	30
GN	185-local	Willmar	Huron, S.D.	9	29
GN	29-local	Minneapolis	Grand Forks	7	29
M&StL	2-local	Minneapolis	Fort Dodge	7	29
Soo Line	105-local	Minneapolis	Fairmount, N.D.	7	29
NP	13-local	Fargo	Grand Forks	10	28
GN	135-local	Crookston	Warroad	8	28
CMStP&P	5-local	Minneapolis	Aberdeen	7	28
GN	51-local	Willmar	Sioux City	7	28
CMStP&P	203-local	Austin	Madison, S.D.	6	28
CMStP&P	157-local	La Crosse	Austin	6	28
C&NW	515-local	Mankato	Brookings, S.D.	8	27
GN	105-local	Sauk Centre	Bemidji	7	27
DM&IR	1-local	Duluth	Hibbing	4	27
DM&IR	5-local	Duluth	Winton	3	27
CRI&P	17-Short Line Express	St. Paul	Manly, Iowa	16	26
CN/DW&P	19-local	Duluth	Winnipeg	15	26
C&NW	209-Mondamin	St. Paul	Sioux City	9	26
NP	29-local	Little Falls	Morris	7	26
C&NW	515-local	Winona	Mankato	7	24
NP	111-local	Staples	Breckenridge	6	24
DSS&A	8-local	Duluth	Marquette, Mich.	12	23
NP	66-Twin Ports Express	St. Paul	Duluth	6	23
M&StL	13-local	Minneapolis	Watertown, S.D.	7	20
GN	302-local	Pelican Rapids	Fergus Falls	5	19
GN	61-local	Minneapolis	Hutchinson	5	18
GN	305-local	Minneapolis	Milaca	6	17

An engineman races the *400* across Wisconsin at ninety miles per hour. Such speeds were a rarity.

or stop. The same order placed an upper limit of seventy-nine miles per hour on lines with conventional automatic block signals (ABS), and a forty-nine-miles-per-hour limit on lines with no signals. Most of Minnesota's main-line mileage already had ABS, but not ATC or ATS. Only the Chicago & North Western and the Milwaukee installed this equipment on portions of their Chicago–Twin Cities main lines. It was expensive, and railroads simply reduced passenger train speeds rather than add ATS or ATC. High maintenance costs and a reduction in the number of passenger trains eventually caused the North Western and the Milwaukee to remove their systems, reduce speeds, and lengthen schedule times.

Besides noncompetitive speeds, there were other forces at work, notably labor work rules and high overall costs, in part attributable to labor, excessive regulation, expensive-to-operate downtown terminals, subsidized competition, and a demoralized management. It was also partly due to the railroads themselves, who still thought and behaved like Gilded Age monopolies. Loath to cooperate, they warred constantly with each other, labor, and the ICC.

Passenger trains took lots of TLC. The Northern Pacific's *North Coast Limited* had its dome cars washed en route.

Consider labor productivity and work rules. Between St. Paul and Seattle the Northern Pacific's *North Coast Limited* changed engine crews (engineer and fireman) sixteen times and train crews (one conductor and two brakemen) ten times for a total of sixty-two employees over a distance of some 1,800 miles. Operating employees, enginemen and trainmen, worked only across districts or divisions. None of them worked a full eight hours. Their workday was determined by geography, not time on the job. This was the "basic day rule," which had been in effect since 1919 when passenger trains averaged just twenty miles per hour.

Besides the train crews, there were another twenty to twenty-five onboard employees—dining- and club-car personnel, coach and sleeping-car porters, a stewardess-nurse—who were there to take care of passengers' needs. There was even a traveling electrician to handle any maintenance issues that might occur. At division points, or every five hundred miles, a team of carmen would meet the train to inspect it, perform a brake test required by the ICC, fill water tanks, and fuel the locomotives. A typical summer-season *North Coast Limited* of the early 1960s ran to about fourteen cars and could accommodate approximately four hundred passengers. Assuming the train was full throughout the entire trip from St. Paul to Seattle, and it seldom was, that works out to roughly four passengers per onboard employee. With five trains on the road at one time, a pool of approximately 450 operating employees was needed to maintain daily service.

However, it was this high ratio of employees to passengers that gave long-distance passenger trains their cachet. Passengers who rode them expected a high level of personal attention and service from the crew, along with Pullman accommodations for overnight travel, elegant dining, club and observation cars, and dome cars for watching the scenery during daylight hours. All of this came at a very high cost that couldn't possibly be recouped from ticket revenues, especially when fewer and fewer tickets were being sold.

Work rules were another issue. One rule forbade road crews from doing their own switching en route or at terminals. Thus, if a car had to be added or one taken off, the road locomotive was cut off and pulled away, and a switch crew and locomotive were summoned to do the work. To this add all the maintenance employees, ticket and station agents, commissary workers, and other backroom employees associated with passenger trains, then add in depreciation and capital costs, and it's obvious why passenger trains were never profitable except maybe during the standing-room-only days of World War II.

Regulation in the form of the ICC and various state railway boards and commissions came along in the 1880s, when railroads had a monopoly on intercity freight and passenger transportation and used that monopoly to enrich themselves at the expense of the public interest. As early as the 1920s this was no longer the case. Yet all the nineteenth-century rules remained in effect until the Staggers Act of 1980 abolished the ICC and deregulated the industry.

In this environment, railroad managers couldn't manage because everything was subject to ICC or state regulatory review. Any change in tariffs required regulatory concurrence, making it impossible to use price as a marketing tool. One size had to fit all. Fare increases sometimes took months to gain approval. Some weren't granted at all, or a lesser amount was approved. Discontinuing money-losing passenger trains meant months of legal work and an ICC or a state hearing and investigation. There was no support or sympathy from the public. No one was riding, but people still liked to wave at the engineer from their automobiles.

Complaints about downgrading—removing dining, lounge, and sleeping cars—were frequent, despite the fact that such specialty cars lost huge amounts of money even when the trains were full. An unfavorable ruling meant the whole process had to start all over again. Meanwhile, the railroads had to continue providing the service and swallow the losses.

A classic example is the Northern Pacific's *Mainstreeter*, its secondary St. Paul–Seattle train and companion to the *North Coast Limited*. Introduced in 1954 as a streamlined replacement for the *Alaskan*, which ran with older prewar, heavyweight equipment, the *Mainstreeter* came with a full dining car, club-lounge car, and all-room Pullman sleeping cars. By 1967 most of its long-distance riders and its mail business had gone away, and in an effort to match service with demand and reduce expense, the railroad removed the diner, club-lounge car, and sleepers, substituting a buffet car with food and beverage service and a Slumbercoach. The Slumbercoach offered smaller private-room accommodations at coach fares without the frills and first-class fares of Pullman sleepers. Then in 1969, citing losses of $3.5 million, Northern Pacific applied to the ICC to discontinue the train. President Louis W. Menk was adamant: "The plain fact is that people are not using passenger service. Not many will spend 42 hours on a train when they can fly from the Twin Cities to Seattle in three, and few people will use the train for short trips when they can drive and have the car available at their destination." The ICC wasn't impressed. Finding that the railroad had downgraded the service when it removed the diner and sleeping cars, it turned down the petition to discontinue, never mind that no one was riding. The ICC noted that as few as four passengers used the Slumbercoach on some trips from St. Paul to Seattle, but it still found the operation of the train vital to public convenience and necessity. Three times the railroad petitioned to drop the service, and three times it was turned down. The *Mainstreeter* didn't go away until Amtrak.

The *Mainstreeter* was the train that wouldn't go away. Shorn of its mail business, it was losing gobs of money. The Northern Pacific tried to cut expenses and trimmed dining and sleeping-car services, but stubborn regulators considered this to be downgrading and ruled the railroad should spend even more money to attract fewer and fewer passengers.

In the postwar era, as business and residential development moved to the suburbs, railroads confronted declining passenger traffic with the additional burden of huge downtown passenger terminals that were increasingly expensive to operate and maintain. St. Paul Union Depot was one of them. Many were heavily mortgaged, still carrying their original construction debt. Costs loomed larger and larger as ongoing operating expenses had to be spread over a dwindling number of trains. Parking and downtown traffic made them inconvenient and inaccessible. For prospective passengers, they became just another reason not to take the train.

A few terminals, notably Pennsylvania Station in New York City, were architectural monuments that cried out for preservation but were lost when their railroad owners, in need of cash, demolished them and redeveloped the valuable real estate they occupied. Others, Michigan Central Terminal in Detroit and Washington Union Station, for example, were neglected and allowed to rot, becoming hangouts for vagrants and petty criminals. Some larger cities had suburban stations that shared both long-distance and commuter trains, but dispersing all intercity trains to them would have made it difficult, if not impossible, for passengers to transfer from one railroad to another. Ownership of downtown stations by public authorities was out of the question. There was no support for it, and

Peeling paint and water damage in the waiting room. The St. Paul Union Depot was showing its age.

there wouldn't be for another twenty years. By then the intercity network had dwindled to a handful of passenger trains running on borrowed time.

St. Paul Union Depot fared better than most. Its standing as a postal center helped, and four of its owners, the Great Northern, Northern Pacific, the Burlington, and the Milwaukee were still running some classy passenger trains. Even so, their attention was focused more on what to do with the place when the trains stopped running. At the end, it was an empty, lonely space.

In 1937 the railroads, the St. Paul Union Depot Company, and the Minneapolis Planning Commission studied the possible relocation of passenger traffic from the Milwaukee's Short Line to the Great Northern's line between St. Paul and Minneapolis, along with the closure of the Milwaukee's Minneapolis depot and the consolidation of all passenger services at the Great Northern Station. This was part of a much larger study of Twin Cities terminals that included the possibility of a joint passenger station in the Midway, reminiscent of Samuel Felton's ideas of some twenty years before. The railroads and the city couldn't agree on a course of action, and the plan quietly died.

Meanwhile, as railroads fought to discontinue money-losing passenger trains, public authorities were busy building new airports at taxpayer expense and handing out generous government subsi-

By the 1960s downtown passenger stations were an expensive anachronism and a financial albatross for the railroads that owned them.

dies to airlines to operate unprofitable routes. Between 1938 and 1959 the airlines received $441.3 million in cash subsidies to fly a handful of passengers every day to and from many of the same communities served by passenger trains that the railroads were trying to discontinue. Moreover, by the late 1950s government had spent almost $4 billion on civilian airports and $1.4 billion on the federal airways system. The disparity with highways was even worse. From 1921 through 1955 governments financed some $93 billion for highway construction and maintenance, a dribble compared to the billions that would follow as the interstate highway system was being built. Through all this the railroads were expected to maintain and operate passenger trains solely from passenger revenues, pay off debt, earn enough to cover the cost of capital, and just maybe turn a profit. It was impossible. Smart railroad managements knew it, saw the handwriting on the wall, and got out.

Mail and express provided substantial revenues for the railroads and terminal companies, like St. Paul Union Depot. However, it is unclear if these revenues, substantial as they were, actually covered the full costs of carrying mail. More likely, passenger trains were subsidizing the mails rather than the other way around. Compensation was based on the linear square feet of car space occupied by mail plus a charge per sack for handling. However, besides transportation, railroads were required to load and unload mail cars, sort mail sacks, and maintain mail-handling equipment and facilities. No consideration was given to the standby capacity needed to handle peaks such as the Christmas rush. Railroads were expected to provide all of the rolling stock needed to move the mails, even though a large percentage of these cars sat idle during the year. This was a great boon for the U.S. Post Office, but it did little for the railroads' bottom lines. Some railroads, notably the Chicago & North Western, looked at the economics, decided it was a bad deal, and proceeded to drop passenger trains that were still hauling large volumes of mail and express.

Unprofitable services, high costs, and heavy-handed regulation bred a cautious, conservative management that was slow to accept innovation much less challenge the status quo. Some outside-the-boardroom types talked about creating a national reservation bureau, owned by the railroads, that would take over all passenger ticketing and reservations, thus streamlining the process, reducing costs, and giving better service to the customers. It never got off the ground. There were also industry discussions about pooling passenger services, much as the Great Northern, Northern Pacific, and Soo Line did between the Twin Cities and Duluth. Why operate several daily long-distance trains via different routes between city pairs when an alternate day service would serve the market and reduce train miles? Nothing happened. Presumably there were worries about ICC and state regulatory disapprovals. No one wanted to complicate matters when it was easier to go before the regulators and just petition to drop the service.

Moving people is an entirely different business from hauling freight, yet organizationally the railroads made no distinction. There were no separate, fully self-contained passenger divisions with a vice president wholly responsible and accountable for everything from marketing to maintenance and operations. Running passenger trains is a specialty, yet it was commingled organizationally with freight. Despite the great pride and organizational identity that came with passenger trains, railroaders in the late 1950s and early 1960s knew that passenger trains had no future and that having anything to do with them was a dead-end job—a perception that proved largely correct.

Today, there are reasons for optimism. The railroad industry and the passenger train have seen many changes. Onerous work rules are gone, the regulatory environment has changed, and one agency is responsible for running intercity passenger trains. Best of all, the railroads are making money, and their attitude toward passenger service has shifted from outright hostility to mild enthusiasm. Passenger and freight trains are seen as coexisting with government infrastructure spending and improvements, benefiting both passenger and freight service. There is growing public acceptance of a balanced approach to transportation funding. Still, the question is asked: if passenger trains couldn't compete with Model Ts, Ford Tri-motors and DC3s in the 1920s and 1930s, and freeways and 707s in the 1950s and 1960s, how can they compete today, even at one hundred miles per hour? The answer is they can, and they are. Ridership is growing steadily on both intercity and long-haul trains, especially along the Northeast Corridor, as air and automobile travel become increasingly expensive and congested.

Passenger train advocates see the Chicago–Twin Cities corridor as a market for high-speed service. However, the current Amtrak route, which once saw one-hundred-mile-per-hour passenger train speeds, has been downgraded from two tracks to one, and all the high-speed signaling has been removed. It will take millions of dollars to upgrade track and signals and purchase passenger equipment, just to return to 1930s-era speeds and running times. Billions would be needed for European- or Japanese-style high-speed trains. Restoring Duluth service has also been mentioned. However, the railroad bridge that once carried passenger trains over the harbor into Duluth Union Station was removed. It would have to be replaced or an alternate high-speed route developed. Both the Chicago and the Duluth services are feasible but require huge sums. For that reason, in these days of shrinking public budgets and conflicting priorities and needs, the possibilities and the benefits of passenger rail service remain elusive. ❈

APPENDIX
Passenger Train Discontinuances in Minnesota, 1950–1971

This appendix lists passenger train discontinuances in Minnesota by railroad from 1950 until Amtrak in 1971, based on data from the Minnesota Historical Society's collection of Minnesota Railroad and Warehouse Commission records. Shown are the train numbers, the destinations served, the effective date (if available) of the discontinuance, and train names. Notes indicate if a particular service was converted to a mixed passenger–freight run or if only a portion of the train's route was discontinued. Most of the discontinuances in the early to mid-1950s were local runs, but eventually even the long-distance named trains disappeared. An asterisk marks routes that served the St. Paul Union Depot.

Great Northern

Train	Destinations	Date	Notes
131, 132	Fargo–Noyes	June 28, 1950	
49, 50	Morris–Browns Valley	July 17, 1950	
31, 32	Willmar–Sandstone	March 15, 1951	
105, 106	Sauk Center–Cass Lake	January 28, 1952	
135, 136	Crookston–Warroad	June 1, 1952	
197, 198	Breckenridge–Larimore	June 1, 1952	converted to mixed 341, 342
305, 306	Minneapolis–Milaca	October 15, 1952	
191, 192	Breckenridge–Aberdeen	August 1, 1954	converted to mixed 325, 326
29, 30	*St. Paul–Grand Forks	June 11, 1955	discontinued St. Paul–St. Cloud
301, 302	Fergus Falls–Pelican Rapids	March 2, 1957	
29, 30	St. Cloud–Grand Forks	May 18, 1958	
51, 52	Willmar–Sioux City	June 28, 1958	
60, 61	Minneapolis–Hutchinson	July 6, 1958	
35, 36	Duluth–Grand Forks	April 18, 1959	
185, 186	Willmar–Watertown	August 30, 1959	
51, 52	Willmar–Sioux Falls	February 15, 1960	
11, 12	*St. Paul–Grand Forks	May 22, 1960	to Fargo only
331, 332	Crookston–Fargo	July 10, 1960	
9, 10	*St. Paul–Minot	September 9, 1961	to Fargo only
345, 346	Barnesville–Crookston	September 16, 1961	
9, 12	*St. Paul–Fargo	May 27, 1962	
199, 200	Breckenridge–Minot	June 18, 1965	
325, 326	Breckenridge–Aberdeen	December 6, 1965	
11, 14	*St. Paul–Fargo	February 15, 1968	*Red River*
23, 20	*St. Paul–Duluth	February 1970	morning from Duluth; afternoon from St. Paul
7, 8	*St. Paul–Winnipeg	February 1970	*Winnipeg Limited*; new connection with *Western Star* at Grand Forks
3, 4	*St. Paul–Fargo	February 1970	*Dakotan*

Northern Pacific

Train	Destinations	Date	Notes
31, 32	Brainerd–Little Falls	August 19, 1953	
29, 30	Little Falls–Morris	January 11, 1954	
61, 62	*Minneapolis–Duluth	January 27, 1958	
111, 112	Staples–Oakes	May 1959	
55, 56	Duluth–Staples	June 1966	
65, 66	*Minneapolis–Duluth	January 5, 1967	
3, 4	*St. Paul–Jamestown	October 1967	
11, 12	Little Falls–International Falls	July 1968	
57, 58	Duluth–Staples	May 25, 1969	

Burlington

Train	Destinations	Date	Notes
45, 52	*Minneapolis–Chicago	January 1958	local
47, 48	*Minneapolis–Chicago	April 12, 1970	*Black Hawk*

Omaha, Chicago & North Western

Train	Destinations	Date	Notes
107, 106	Tracy–Burr	May 8, 1950	
83, 82	Worthington–Sioux Falls	March 5, 1951	
501, 508	Mankato–Winona	July 7, 1951	
209, 210	*Minneapolis–Sioux City	February 13, 1953	*Mondamin*
81, 80	Worthington–Sioux Falls	August 26, 1953	
201, 202	*Minneapolis–Omaha	December 10, 1956	*Nightingale*
501, 508	*Minneapolis–Chicago	March 1957	*Viking*
405, 406	*Minneapolis–Chicago	June 14, 1959	*North Western Limited*
511, 510	Duluth–Chicago	June 14, 1959	*Duluth Superior Limited*
203, 204	*Minneapolis–Omaha	October 19, 1959	*North American*
515, 514	Chicago–Rochester	October 21, 1960	*Rochester Special*
519, 518	Mankato–Rapid City	October 21, 1960	*Dakota 400*
519, 518	Mankato–Chicago	July 23, 1963	*Dakota 400*
401, 400	*Minneapolis–Chicago	July 23, 1963	*Twin Cities 400*

Milwaukee Road

Train	Destinations	Date	Notes
41, 40	Farmington–Wells	January 2, 1951	
103, 118	*Minneapolis–Austin	April 1, 1951	Sunday only
121, 118	*Minneapolis–Austin	April 28, 1952	
103, 122	Austin–Iowa Line	January 26, 1953	remnant of the *Minnesota Marquette*
205, 206	Farmington–Cologne	January 5, 1955	mixed train
315, 392	Glencoe–Hutchinson	January 5, 1955	mixed train
17, 18	Minneapolis–Ortonville	April 1, 1957	remnant of the *Columbian*
301, 302	Hastings–Stillwater	October 7, 1957	
5, 6	Minneapolis–Aberdeen	March 31, 1958	
157, 158	Austin–LaCrosse	March 31, 1960	through Chicago Pullman
15, 16	*Chicago–Seattle	May 22, 1961	*Olympian Hiawatha*
15, 16	Minneapolis–Aberdeen	April 16, 1969	remnant of the *Olympian*
55, 58	*Minneapolis–Chicago	August 7, 1969	
3, 2	*Minneapolis–Chicago	January 23, 1970	*Afternoon Hiawatha*
1, 4	*Minneapolis–Chicago	September 8, 1970	*Pioneer Limited*
57, 56	*Minneapolis–Chicago	March 28, 1971	*Fast Mail*

Rock Island

Train	Destinations	Date	Notes
57, 58	*Minneapolis–Des Moines	March 1, 1958	*Short Line Express*
17, 18	*Minneapolis–Fort Worth	October 30, 1966	*Twin Star Rocket*; through Texas service discontinued and became Minneapolis–Kansas City *Plainsman*
19, 20	*Minneapolis–St. Louis	April 8, 1967	*Zephyr Rocket*
15, 16	*Minneapolis–Kansas City	November 1967	*Kansas City Rocket*
17, 18	*Minneapolis–Kansas City	July 7, 1969	*Plainsman*

Soo Line

Train	Destinations	Date	Notes
1, 2	*Minneapolis–Chicago	February 15, 1953	
5, 6	Minneapolis–Enderlin	May 2, 1959	
65, 64	Duluth–Thief River Falls	May 16, 1959	
161, 160	Superior–Glenwood	May 2, 1959	mixed
7, 8	*Minneapolis–Sault Sainte Marie	March 5, 1960	remnant of the *Atlantic Limited*
62, 63	*Minneapolis–Duluth	June 1961	
13, 14	Glenwood–Portal	December 1963	remnant of the *Mountaineer*, which carried through cars for Vancouver. It was combined with Minneapolis–Glenwood trains 9 and 10: through cars were carried in Minneapolis–Winnipeg trains 9 and 10, and trains 13 and 14 were operated as a local mixed west of Glenwood until it was discontinued in the late 1960s.
3, 4, 5, 6	*Duluth–Chicago– Minneapolis	January 15, 1965	*Laker*
9, 10	*St. Paul–Winnipeg	March 25, 1967	*Winnipeger*

Chicago Great Western

Train	Destinations	Date	Notes
43, 44	Randolph–Rochester	August 16, 1950	motorcar
3, 4	Chicago–Oelwein	1956	a connection with Minneapolis–Kansas City trains 5 and 6, the *Mill Cities Limited*; direct, through service to and from the Twin Cities and Chicago lapsed in 1949
5, 6	*Minneapolis–Kansas City	April 27, 1962	*Mill Cities Limited*
13, 14	*Minneapolis–Omaha	September 29, 1965	

Minneapolis & St. Louis

Train	Destinations	Date	Notes
1, 2	Minneapolis–Des Moines	1954	day train
7, 8	Albert Lea–Albia	May 31, 1958	
3, 4	Minneapolis–Des Moines	March 21, 1959	
13, 14	Minneapolis–Watertown	July 20, 1960	

Bibliographic Resources

St. Paul Union Depot ran its final passenger trains on April 30, 1971, and began a forty-plus-year hibernation that will end once Amtrak moves in. That it survived as long, bereft of trains, as when it was an active passenger terminal is no small miracle. Were it not for the U.S. Postal Service and the strong preservationist instincts of St. Paul's civic leaders, it would have been razed and carted off to a landfill long ago and its site, overlooking the Mississippi River, given over to condominiums.

More surprising is that, unlike other important rail stations such as Penn Station, Grand Central Terminal, St. Louis Union Station, or Washington Union Station, the St. Paul Union Depot has attracted scant attention among architects and rail aficionados. Frank Lloyd Wright once visited and said some kind things, and there have been a few scattered articles in railroad publications, but there are no major works on the depot, something this book will remedy.

Fortunately, this anonymity can't be explained by an absence of good sources. With the exception of documents lost in the 1913 depot fire, the complete corporate archives of the St. Paul Union Depot Company (1879–1982) are preserved and available to researchers at the Minnesota Historical Society. There are forty-seven boxes in the collection, filled with annual reports, correspondence, meeting minutes, engineering studies, operating and financial agreements, accounting records, arbitrations, personnel and organizational policies and procedures, and government reports to the ICC and the Minnesota Railroad and Warehouse Commission. There is also an extensive collection of photographs in the Minnesota Historical Society's art and photo database. The corporate records of the Great Northern, the Northern Pacific, and the Soo Line, three of the nine railroads that owned the Union Depot Company, can be found in the Minnesota Historical Society's library along with those of the Minnesota Transfer Railway Company, an affiliate of the St. Paul Union Depot Company. The original plans and drawings for the depot, as well as construction photographs, are in the

Frost papers at the Andersen Library, University of Minnesota. All of these sources were explored in gathering materials for this book, and they are readily available for others who might wish to do additional research.

Special mention must be made of three articles by G. H. Wilsey, found in the St. Paul Union Depot collection, that offer excellent summaries of the current depot's design and construction. Wilsey was chief engineer for the St. Paul Union Depot Company in the 1920s when the depot was under construction.

Other sources deserve special mention as well. Among them is an article on the U.S. Railway Mail Service authored by the late John Borchert, professor of geography at the University of Minnesota. It appeared in the winter 1997 issue of the *Minnegazette,* edited by Aaron Isaacs. The *Minnegazette,* now *Twin City Lines,* is a members-only publication by the Minnesota Streetcar Museum. Similarly, my discussion of commuter trains and the St. Paul Union Depot drew on an article by Aaron Isaacs in the fall 2009 issue of *Twin City Lines,* which is devoted entirely to the commuter and suburban trains that once ran in Minneapolis and St. Paul.

Books of importance include Richard Prosser's *Rails to the North Star,* a compilation of the corporate histories and dates of construction of all the railroads built in Minnesota. Don Hofsommer's works on the Minneapolis & St. Louis and the railroads of Minneapolis are solid histories with good background and useful information on the St. Paul Union Depot Company. Mention should also be made of Stanley Mailer's *Omaha Road,* H. Roger Grant's works on the Chicago & North Western and the Chicago Great Western, and a series of books on the Milwaukee, Northern Pacific, Great Northern, Chicago Great Western, Chicago & North Western, and Rock Island by local railroad historian John Luecke. *Passenger Terminals and Trains* (1916), by John Droege, is a superb contemporary study of great stations and the passenger train just before they began their long decline. Droege was general superintendent of the New Haven Railway, one of the country's largest passenger-carrying railroads.

Finally, first-person history is the best history, and the author was able to interview the late William (Bill) Bannon, the last vice president and general manager of the St. Paul Union Depot Company, and John Jensen, its chief engineer. Both men recalled their experiences and the workings of the depot in the 1950s and 1960s, answering many questions and providing insights not found elsewhere. The author is especially grateful for their help.

"After the Passenger Gets There." *Railway Age,* May 21, 1951.

Beebe, Lucius. *Twentieth Century.* Berkeley, Calif.: Howell-North Books, 1962.

Belle, John, and Maxinne R. Leighton. *Grand Central: Gateway to a Million Lives.* New York: W. W. Norton, 2000.

Berg, Walter C. *Buildings and Structures of American Railroads.* New York: John Wiley & Sons, 1893.

Borchert, John. *America's Northern Heartland.* Minneapolis: University of Minnesota Press, 1987.

———. "The Heyday of the Railway Post Office in Minnesota." *Minnegazette,* Winter 1997.

Bradley, Bill. *The Last of the Great Stations: 40 years of the Los Angeles Union Passenger Terminal.* Glendale, Calif.: Interurban Press, 1979.

Byron, Carl R., with Robert W. Rediske. *The Pioneer Zephyr: America's First Diesel-Electric Stainless Steel Streamliner.* Forest Park, Ill.: Heimburger House, 2005.

DeRouin, Edward M. *Chicago Union Station: A Look at Its History and Operations before Amtrak.* Elmhurst, Ill.: Pixels, 2003.

———. *Moving Mail and Express by Rail.* La Fox, Ill.: Pixels, 2007.

Diehl, Lorraine B. *The Late Great Pennsylvania Station.* New York: Houghton Mifflin, 1985.

Donovan, Frank P., Jr. "Walk Right In." *Trains,* February 1954.

Doughty, Geoffrey H. *Burlington Route: The Early Zephyrs.* Lynchburg, Va.: TLC, 2002.

Droege, John A. *Passenger Terminals and Trains.* New York: McGraw-Hill, 1916. Reprint, Milwaukee: Kalmbach, 1969.

Frailey, Fred W. *Twilight of the Great Trains.* Waukesha, Wis.: Kalmbach, 1998.

Garrett, Klink, with Toby Smith. *Ten Turtles to Tucumcari: A Personal History of the Railway Express Agency.* Albuquerque: University of New Mexico Press, 2003.

Grant, H. Roger. *The Corn Belt Route: A History of the Chicago Great Western Railroad Company.* Dekalb: Northern Illinois University Press, 1984.

———. *The North Western: A History of the Chicago & North Western Railway System.* DeKalb: Northern Illinois University Press, 1996.

———, and Charles Bohi. *The Country Railroad Station in America.* Boulder, Colo.: Pruett, 1978.

———, Don L. Hofsommer, and Osmund Overby. *St. Louis Union Station: A Place for People, a Place for Trains.* St. Louis: St. Louis Mercantile Library, 1994.

Hidy, Ralph W., Muriel E. Hidy, Roy V. Scott, and Don L. Hofsommer. *The Great Northern Railway: A History.* Minneapolis: University of Minnesota Press, 2004.

Highsmith, Carol M., and Ted Landphair. *Union Station: A Decorative History of Washington's Grand Terminal.* Washington, D.C.: Chelsea, 1988.

Hofsommer, Don L. *Minneapolis and the Age of Railways.* Minneapolis: University of Minnesota Press, 2005.

———. *The Tootin' Louie: A History of the Minneapolis & St. Louis Railway.* Minneapolis: University of Minnesota Press, 2005.

"How Can Pullman Traffic Be Made More Profitable?" *Railway Age,* May 17, 1954.

"How to Put Passenger Service in the Black Ink." Editorial. *Railway Age,* May 21, 1951.

Isaacs, Aaron. "Commuter and Suburban Trains of Minneapolis and St. Paul." *Twin City Lines,* Fall 2009.

Johnson, Carla. *Union Pacific and Omaha Union Station.* David City, Neb.: South Platte Press, 2001.

Kirkpatrick, O. B. *The Station Agent's Blue Book.* Chicago: Order of Railroad Telegraphers, 1928.

Kuebler, William R., Jr. *The Vista Dome North Coast Limited.* Hamilton, Mont.: Oso, 2004.

Larson, Agnes M. *The White Pine Industry in Minnesota: A History.* Minneapolis: University of Minnesota Press, 2007.

Luecke, John C. *The Chicago and North Western in Minnesota.* St. Paul: Grenadier Publications, 1990.

———. *The Great Northern in Minnesota: The Foundation of an Empire.* St. Paul: Grenadier, 1997.

———. *More Chicago Great Western in Minnesota.* St. Paul: Grenadier, 2009.

———. *The Northern Pacific in Minnesota.* St. Paul: Grenadier, 2005.

———. *The Rock Island in Minnesota.* St. Paul: Grenadier, 2011.

Mailer, Stan. *The Omaha Road: Chicago, St. Paul, Minneapolis & Omaha.* Mukilteo, Wash.: Hundman, 2004.

Martin, Albro. *James J. Hill and the Opening of the Northwest.* St. Paul: Minnesota Historical Society Press, 1991.

Middleton, William D. *Manhattan Gateway: New York's Pennsylvania Station.* Waukesha, Wis.: Kalmbach, 1996.

Morgan, David P. "Fast Mail." *Classic Trains,* Fall 2006.

———. "Who Shot the Passenger Train." *Trains,* April 1959.

"New Service Bureaus Speed Sale of Reserved Space." *Railway Age,* May 18, 1953.

"Now Tickets Are Streamlined Too!" *Railway Age,* July 30, 1951.

Official Guide of the Railways. National Railway Publication Co. June 1941, July 1956, March 1959, July 1962.

Ploss, Thomas H. *The Nation Pays Again: The Milwaukee Road.* T. H. Ploss, 1984.

"Progress in Ticketing and Handling of Reservations." *Railway Age,* May 19, 1952.

Prosser, Richard S. *Rails to the North Star.* Minneapolis: University of Minnesota Press, 2007.

Schwantes, Carlos A., James P. Ronda. *The West the Railroads Made.* Seattle: University of Washington Press, 2008.

Schwantes, Carlos Arnaldo. *Going Places: Transportation Redefines the Twentieth-Century West.* Bloomington: Indiana University Press, 2003.

Scribbins, Jim. *The 400 Story: Chicago and North Western's Premier Passenger Trains.* Minneapolis: University of Minnesota Press, 2008.

———. *The Hiawatha Story.* Milwaukee: Kalmbach, 1970.

Shaw, Robert. "Decline and Decay of REA." *Trains,* July 1979.

Stilgoe, John R. *Metropolitan Corridor Railroads and the American Scene.* New Haven, Conn.: Yale University Press, 1983.

———. *Train Time: Railroads and the Imminent Reshaping of the United States Landscape.* Charlottesville: University of Virginia Press, 2007.

Stout, Greg. *Route of the Rockets: Rock Island in the Streamlined Era.* Hart, Mo.: White River, 1997.

Welsh, Joe. *Pennsy Streamliners: The Blue Ribbon Fleet.* Waukesha, Wis.: Kalmbach, 1999.

Wilsey, G. H. "St. Paul Union Depot Completes Third Section." *Railway Age* 76, no. 17 (March 29, 1924): 827–30.

———. "First Unit of St. Paul Union Station Completed." *Railway Age* 68, no. 21 (May 21, 1920): 1442–46.

———. "St. Paul Union Depot." Special issue, *Bulletin of the Minnesota Federation of Architectural and Engineering Societies* 11, no. 1 (January 1926).

Withers, Bob. *The President Travels by Train: Politics and Pullmans.* Lynchburg, Va.: TLC, 1996.

Zimmerman, Karl. *Domeliners: Yesterday's Trains of Tomorrow.* Waukesha, Wis.: Kalmbach, 1998.

Illustration Credits

The University of Minnesota Press gratefully acknowledges the following institutions and individuals who provided permission to reproduce the illustrations in this book.

Author's collection: pages 51, 52, 90, 100, 115 (above), 115 (below), 119, 139 (above), 139 (below), 145.

Burlington Northern Santa Fe Photo Archives: page 239.

Collection of Aaron Isaacs: pages 29, 68, 72 (left), 72 (right), 125 (below), 136 (above), 163 (above), 174 (above), 184 (above), 200 (above), 201, 205.

Collection of Bill Raia: page 230.

Collection of Don L. Hofsommer: pages 178, 180, 182, 185 (above), 185 (below), 186 (above), 186 (below), 189, 195, 208, 249 (below), 265.

Collection of J. M. Gruber: pages 227, 228, 229 (photographs by Robert Graham); 242 (photograph by Owen Leander).

Collection of Roger W. Bee: page 222 (above).

Collection of Steve Glischinski: pages 135, 158 (above), 158 (below), 249 (above) (photograph by William D. Middleton).

Environmental Data Resources, Inc.: page 57.

Great Northern Archives, Collection of Stuart Holmquist: pages 80, 121 (below), 210 (above).

Great Northern Railway Company Record Collection, Minnesota Historical Society: pages 35, 123 (above), 240, 241, 244 (above), 244 (below).

Kalmbach Publishing Company: page 154 (photograph by Philip R. Hastings).

Lowertown Redevelopment Corporation Records, Minnesota Historical Society: pages 110 (above), 110 (below).

Minneapolis–St. Paul Newspaper Negative Collection, Minnesota Historical Society: pages 7, 8, 150, 168, 169, 176, 262 (above).

Minnesota Historical Society: pages x, xiv, xv, xxii (photograph by *St. Paul Dispatch and Pioneer Press*), 3, 4 (photograph by *St. Paul Dispatch and Pioneer Press*), 10, 12 (photograph by Kenneth M. Wright Studios), 13, 14, 16 (photograph by Benjamin Franklin Upton), 21, 23, 25, 26, 28, 31 (photograph by William W. Wales), 34, 36, 40 (photograph by Joel Emmons Whitney), 42 (photograph by Edward Augustus Bromley), 44 (photograph by Humphrey Lloyd Hime), 45, 46 (above), 46 (below) (photograph by Louis D. Sweet), 50 (photograph by William Henry Illingworth), 55 (above), 55 (below) (photograph by George W. Floyd), 56,

ILLUSTRATION CREDITS

58, 59, 61, 62 (photograph by Albert Charles Munson), 66 (photograph by the *St. Paul Dispatch*), 69, 73 (photograph by Helmut Kroening), 74 (photograph by the *Minneapolis Star*), 76, 77, 79, 84, 87, 88 (photograph by Charles P. Gibson), 91 (above), 91 (below), 92, 93 (photograph by Underwood & Underwood), 94 (photograph by Charles J. Hibbard), 95 (above), 96 (photograph by Charles J. Hibbard), 97 (below) (photograph by the *Minneapolis Star Tribune*), 112, 121 (above), 128 (photograph by *St. Paul Dispatch and Pioneer Press*), 129 (below), 130 (photograph by the *St. Paul Daily News*), 133, 134 (photograph by *St. Paul Dispatch and Pioneer Press*), 136 (below), 137 (photograph by Richard R. Wallin), 140–41 (photograph by Mehl & Kromer), 142, 144 (above), 144 (below) (photograph by Kenneth Melvin Wright), 148 (above) (photograph by *St. Paul Dispatch and Pioneer Press*), 148 (below), 151, 156 (below) (photograph by *St. Paul Dispatch and Pioneer Press*), 157, 160 (photograph by Charles P. Gibson), 162 (photograph by Edward Albert Fairbrother), 166 (photograph by *St. Paul Dispatch and Pioneer Press*), 175 (below) (photograph by *St. Paul Dispatch and Pioneer Press*), 181, 191, 192 (photograph by Northwest Airlines), 193 (above) (photograph by the *Minneapolis Star Tribune*), 193 (below) (photograph by *St. Paul Dispatch and Pioneer Press*), 210 (below), 211 (above), 211 (below), 212, 213, 214 (below), 215, 216 (photograph by the *Minneapolis Star Journal*), 217, 219, 220, 222 (below), 224 (photograph by the *St. Paul Daily News*), 226 (photograph by the *St. Paul Daily News*), 233 (photograph by William John Kellett), 235 (photograph by William John Kellett), 237, 243, 248.

Museum of the Rockies: pages 132, 196, 214 (above), 234, 245, 262 (below) (photographs by Ronald V. Nixon).

Northeast Minnesota Historical Center, University of Minnesota Duluth Library, Duluth: pages 48 (above), 48 (below) (photographs by Paul B. Gaylord).

Northwest Architectural Archives, University of Minnesota Libraries: pages 108, 120 (above), 123 (below), 124 (below).

Parrot Graphics: maps on pages 17, 18, 19 (all from Richard S. Prosser, *Rails to the North Star: A Minnesota Railroad Atlas*), 187, 188 (above), 188 (below).

Photograph by Dennis C. Henry: page 257 (above).

Photographs by Byron Olsen: pages 95 (below), 163 (below), 164, 200 (below), 251 (below), 252 (above), 252 (below), 255 (above), 266, 267.

Photographs by Jim Heuer: pages 253 (above), 253 (below).

Ramsey County Rail Authority: page 113 (below).

St. Paul Pioneer Press: pages 9, 60, 81, 101, 117, 118, 120 (below), 124 (above), 125 (above), 126–27, 129 (above), 146, 149, 153, 155, 156 (above), 165, 167 (above), 167 (below), 174 (below), 175 (above), 177, 184 (below), 198, 203, 232, 236, 238, 246, 251 (above), 255 (below), 257 (below), 258.

Wayzata Historical Society Archives Collection: pages 33 (above), 33 (below).

Winona County Historical Society: page 22.

index

Aberdeen, Bismarck & Northwestern, 64
Advisory Council on Historic Preservation, 254
Afternoon Hiawatha (train), xix, 95, 227, 228, 229, 242, 250
Albert Lea, Minnesota, 32
"A" line, 73, 225
American Railway Express, 192
Amtrak, xviii, xix, 96, 143, 247, 254, 256, 259
Anoka, Minnesota, 20, 42
Armstrong, W. C., 6, 105, 106
Austin, Minnesota, 14, 43, 45, 46

Badger (train), xx, 176, 185, 242, 248
Barnesville, Minnesota, 32
Bartlett, Samuel, 32
Bishop, Judsen, 53
Bismarck, North Dakota, 47
Black Hawk (train), xviii, 250
Blue Bird (train), xviii, 132
Borup & Champlin, 11, 37
Brainerd, Minnesota, 32, 47
Breckenridge, Minnesota, 52
Broadway Limited (train), 154
Brook Park, Minnesota, 185
Budd, John, 245, 247
Budd, Ralph, 96, 103, 104, 209, 213, 217, 218, 219, 226
Buffalo Union Terminal, 225
Buffington, L. S., 40, 54, 55
building superintendent, 146
Bureau of Railway Economics, 7

Burlington. *See* Chicago, Burlington & Quincy
Burlington, Cedar Rapids & Northern, 64, 83

Canadian Pacific, 64
Cardigan Junction, 77, 78
Carlton, Minnesota, 47, 48
Central Corridor Light Rail Line, 256
Chaska, Minnesota, 36, 37
Chicago & Alton, 92
Chicago & North Western, xix, xviii, 20, 47, 64, 227, 230
Chicago, Burlington & Northern, 63, 76
Chicago, Burlington & Quincy, xviii, 20, 37, 63, 64, 76, 83, 90, 86, 96, 135, 137, 146, 147, 191, 226
Chicago Great Western, xviii, 3, 5, 20, 37, 63, 77, 82, 84, 90, 92, 96, 131, 132, 221
Chicago, Milwaukee & St. Paul, 3, 20, 45, 46, 51, 54, 64, 70, 71, 82, 90, 91, 198, 272
Chicago, Milwaukee, St. Paul & Pacific, xix, 36, 37, 64, 135, 147, 209, 227
Chicago, Rock Island & Pacific, xix, 15, 20, 37, 64, 71, 83, 90, 92, 94, 196
Chicago, St. Paul & Kansas City, 63
Chicago, St. Paul & Minneapolis, 47
Chicago, St. Paul, Minneapolis & Omaha, xix, 5, 20, 32, 36, 37, 47, 64, 82, 96, 135, 140
Chrysler, Walter P., 93
Cincinnati Union Terminal, 225
City Beautiful, 108
Clark, Frank B., 53
Clark, James T., 78

280

coach yards: Great Northern Mississippi Street, 162, 163, 164; Northern Pacific, 162, 164
Columbian (train), xix, 94, 221
Commodore Vanderbilt (train), 154
Commonwealth Electric Company, 118
Como Shops, 139
Congdon, H. P., 144
Cooke, Jay, 38, 47, 49
Coolidge, President Calvin, 152
creative destruction, 8, 257
Credit River, 43

Dakotan (train), 242, 248
Dayton's Bluff, 49, 50, 87
depots and small-town stations: design and construction, 23, 26–27, 28, 29, 32–35; functions, 23, 24, 25–26, 27–29, 33–34; joint facilities, 36–37; location, 31, 32; role and importance to community, 21–22; station agent, 23–25, 30
Division Street Tower, 174, 175
dome car, 239, 244
Doyle Report, 247
Dubuque, Iowa, 63
Dubuque Packet Company, 38
Duke and Duchess of Windsor, 152, 153
Duluth, Minnesota, 47, 48
Duluth, Missabe & Iron Range, 37
Duluth Union Depot, 37

Eastern Express (train), 43, 46
Eastern Railway Company of Minnesota, 64
Eberhart, Governor Albert O., 66
Edward G. Budd Company, 226
Eisenhower, Mamie, 8
Eisenhower, President Dwight D., 8
Electric Short Line Railway, 214
Electro-Motive Engineering Corporation, 132
Ellis, Harry, 25
Empire Builder (train), 154, 175, 180, 209, 210, 213, 214, 234, 238, 239, 240, 241, 244, 252, 254
excursions, 140–41

Fargo, North Dakota, 32
Faribault, Minnesota, 43, 44, 46
Fast Mail (train), xx, 154, 170, 176, 248, 251
Federal Aid Highway Act of 1921, 215
Federal Aid Highway Act of 1956, 246
Federal Transportation Act of 1958, 246
Felton, Samuel, 3, 90, 92, 93, 98, 99, 102, 104, 131
Foley Brothers Construction Company, 118
Fort Snelling, 13, 44, 70, 71
Fort Snelling State Park, 44
400 (train), xix, 227, 230
Frost, Charles, 94, 96, 98, 102
Frost and Granger (architectural firm), 107
Fulton Asphalt Company, 118

Gardner, Webster, 11, 12
General (train), 154
General Motors, 226, 238
George Grant Construction Company, 118
Gilbert, Cass, 32, 34
Gilded Age, 12
Glacier National Park, 32, 152
Glenwood, Minnesota, 32
Golden State (train), xix, 252
good roads movement, 7
Gopher (train), xx, 242, 250
Grainger, Alfred, 107
Grand Army of the Republic, 65
Grand Central Terminal, 1, 6, 83
Great Encampment, 65
Great Northern, xx, xviii, 3, 5, 6, 11, 20, 32, 33, 35, 37, 52, 64, 70, 71, 86, 90, 96, 104, 131, 135, 137, 147, 196, 209, 238, 245, 247, 250, 252
Great Northern Station, 5, 37, 96, 97, 147, 256
Great Railroad Excursion, 15, 43
Great Western. *See* Chicago Great Western
Great Western Limited (train), 132
Griggs, Alexander, 38
Griggs, Chauncey, 38

Harriman, Edward H., 92
Harvey, Fred, 165
Heinemann, Ben, 248

*Hiawatha*s, xix, 7, 227
Hill, James J., 3, 5, 11, 12, 32, 33, 35, 37, 52, 53, 64, 73, 80, 86, 89, 93, 96, 114, 190
Hill, Louis, 86, 190
Hinckley, Minnesota, 47
Homestead Act, 41
Hosmer, Howard, 247
Hubert, Minnesota, 23
Hudson, Wisconsin, 47
Hudson's Bay Company, 12
Hunt, Jarvis, 102

immigrant trains, 21
interlocking plants, 85
International Falls, Minnesota, 34
Interstate Commerce Commission, 243, 259, 263, 264
Inver Grove, Minnesota, 67, 76

Jackson Street roundhouse, 137
Jackson Street Shops, 139
Johnson, W. C., 90

Kittson, Norman, 38
Kittson Trading Post, 12, 13

LaCrescent, Minnesota, 43, 51
Lake Elmo, Minnesota, 75
Lake Minnetonka, 30, 67, 70
Laker (train), xxi
Lake Superior & Mississippi, 47, 48, 49, 50, 51, 74
Lake Superior Museum of Transportation, 10
Larpenteur, Auguste, 15
Legionnaire (train), xviii, 132, 221
Lehman Brothers, 206
Life on the Mississippi (Twain), 60
Lincoln, President Abraham, 41
Litchfield, Minnesota, 193
Little Falls, Minnesota, 32, 34
Little Falls Chamber of Commerce, 32, 34
Lower Levee, 16
Lowertown, 49, 50, 51, 130

mail and baggage foreman, 14, 146
Mahtomedi, Minnesota, 75
main moves. *See* troop trains
Mainstreeter (train), xviii, xx, 176, 250, 254, 264, 265
Mankato, Minnesota, 32, 36, 43
McGregor & Western, 43
Melrose, Minnesota, 52
Mendota, Minnesota, 46, 67, 70, 71
Merchant Bank Building, 130
Merriam Park (station), 71
Merrill, Sherburne S., 53
Mesaba Electric Railway, 214
Metropolitan Improvements Commission, 251
Metropolitan Transit Commission, 255
Michigan Central Station, 1
Midway News, 89, 99
Mill Cities Limited (train), xviii, 132, 222
Milwaukee & St. Paul, 43, 44, 45, 51
Milwaukee Depot, 37, 94, 147
Milwaukee Road. *See* Chicago, Milwaukee, St. Paul & Pacific
Minneapolis & Cedar Valley, 15
Minneapolis & Duluth, 49
Minneapolis & Pacific, 64
Minneapolis & St. Croix, 64
Minneapolis & St. Louis, xxi, 5, 20, 30, 36, 37, 49, 64, 73, 83, 90, 96, 223, 224, 225
Minneapolis, Anoka & Cuyuna Range, 214
Minneapolis, Northfield & Southern, 20, 22, 214, 216
Minneapolis Planning Commission, 267
Minneapolis, Saulte Ste Marie & Atlantic, 64
Minneapolis, St. Paul & Saulte Ste. Marie, xxi, 20, 64, 71, 77, 78, 79, 83, 90, 135, 147, 196, 219, 248
Minnehaha Trail, 44
Minneapolis Tribune, 53, 54
Minnesota Belt Line Railway & Transfer, 67
Minnesota & Northwestern, 63
Minnesota & Pacific, 15, 20
Minnesota Central, 16, 42, 43, 44
Minnesota Enabling Act, 15
Minnesota Railfans Association, 141

Minnesota Railroad and Warehouse Commission, 20, 216, 270

Minnesota railroads: consolidation and mergers, 20, 63–64; growth and expansion, 20, 41–50, 63; maps, 16–18; planning early construction, 11–20

Minnesota Transfer Railway Company, 231, 254

Minnesota Valley Railroad, 42, 43

Mississippi Street coach yards, 138

Mondamin (train), xx

Montevideo, Minnesota, 32

Morgan, J. P., 92

Morning Hiawatha (train), xix, 94, 154, 227, 231, 243, 242, 252

Morris, Shepherd & Dougherty (construction company), 118

Mountaineer (train), xxi, 94

Murphy, Harry, 202

National Railroad Passenger Corporation. *See* Amtrak

National Register of Historic Places, 254

Nebraska & Lake Superior, 47

Neiler, Rich & Company, 118

Nightingale (train), xx, 172, 176

Nixon, Vice President Richard, 152

North American (train), xx, 156

North Coast Limited (train), xviii, xx, 5, 6, 154, 175, 190, 234, 239, 242, 243, 245, 250, 254, 263

Northern Pacific, xviii, xx, 5, 6, 20, 23, 34, 37, 38, 41, 47, 48, 49, 51, 64, 70, 73, 74, 75, 82, 90, 96, 135, 147, 191, 196, 219, 239, 247, 250

Northfield, Minnesota, 43

Northland Transportation Company, 217, 218

North Redwood, Minnesota, 26, 29

North Star Limited (train), xxi, 225

North St. Paul, 67, 75

Northwest Airlines, 7

North Western Limited (train), xix, 176, 248

Office of Defense Transportation, 234, 236

Official Guide, xix, 1, 2, 51, 71

Olympian (train), 94, 154, 190, 209, 227, 239, 242, 245, 250

Omaha. *See* Chicago, St. Paul, Minneapolis & Omaha

Oriental Limited (train), 6, 209, 210, 211, 212, 213, 221, 238, 239, 241

Osborn, Cyrus, 239

Otis Elevator Company, 118

Owatonna, Minnesota, 43, 46

panic of 1857, 47

panic of 1873, 49

panic of 1907, 92

passenger trains: automobile competition, 7, 215; bus substitution, 217, 218; decline, 209, 213, 214, 215, 221; downgrading service, 264, 265; downtown terminals, 266, 267; future possibilities, 269; labor, 263; mail revenues, 268; pooled service, 218–20; postwar optimism, 238–243; regulation, 263–64, 218–20; speeds, 259–62

Paul Bunyan State Trail, 23

Pembina, North Dakota, 12

Pennington, Edmund, 99

Pennsylvania Station, 1, 6

Perlman, Alfred, 206

Phalen Creek, 47, 49

Pierz, Minnesota, 3

Pillsbury, Charles, 55

Pillsbury A Mill, 55

Pioneer Limited (train), xix, 94, 170, 250

Plainsman (train), xix, 250, 252

Prairie du Chien, Wisconsin, 13, 14, 46

preemption laws, 12

Pullman Avenue, 23, 76

Pullman Company, 111, 142, 143

Pullman conductor, 154, 159

Pullman porter, 154

rail bus, 255

Railway Express Agency, 97, 114, 191–94, 204–7

Ramsey, Alexander, 15

Ramsey County Railroad Authority, 256
Ranch lounge car, 241
Red Bird (train), xviii
redcaps, 144
Red River (train), xx, 248
Red River trails, 12, 13
Redwood Falls, Minnesota, 29, 30
Reed & Stem (architectural firm), 1
Rice, Edmund, 11
Rideaux, Charles, 144
roadmaster, 146
Rockets (trains), 234
Rock Island. *See* Chicago, Rock Island & Pacific
Roosevelt, President Franklin Delano, 152, 155
Root River Valley & Southern Minnesota, 15
Rossler, Bob, 33
Russell, Donald, 247

Sargent, Homer E., 53
Sears, Richard, 29
Sears Roebuck & Company, 30
Seattle World's Fair, 154, 247
Seven Corners, 51
Shakopee (engine and car), 42
Shakopee, Minnesota, 36, 37
Short Line, 72, 82
Silver Alchemy (car), 239
Silver Dome (car), 242
Smith, Donald, 38
Smith, George H., 53
snow, melting, 155
Solana, Minnesota, 28
Solway, Minnesota, 25
Soo Line. *See* Minneapolis, St. Paul & Saulte Ste. Marie
South St. Paul, Minnesota, 67
Sperry report, 78-85
Staples, Minnesota, 32, 34
State Historic Preservation Office, 254
stationmaster, 144, 145
Statistical Review of the Railroad Year 1924, 7
steamboats, 12, 14, 62
Stephen, George, 38

Stevenson, Adlai, 5
Stickney, Alpheus B., 53, 92, 93
Stillwater, Minnesota, 13, 47, 49, 67, 74, 75
Stillwater & St. Paul, 49
St. Anthony, Minnesota, 11, 13
St. Cloud, Minnesota, 32, 35, 179
St. James, Minnesota, 32, 43
Stone Arch Bridge, 69, 70
St. Paul & Chicago, 43
St. Paul & Duluth, 51, 54, 74
St. Paul & Pacific, 16, 20, 30, 31, 38, 42, 49, 51, 52, 70
St. Paul & Sioux City, 43, 51, 64
St. Paul Association of Commerce, 102
St. Paul Citizens Terminal Depot Committee, 5
St. Paul Dispatch, 86
St. Paul, Minneapolis & Manitoba, 11, 32, 37, 38, 39, 52, 64
St. Paul Park, Minnesota, 67, 146
St. Paul Pioneer Press, 65
St. Paul Southern, 214
St. Paul, Stillwater & Taylors Falls, 47, 51, 64
St. Paul Union Depot (1880 facility): 1884 fire, 1889 improvements, 63; 1900-1902 improvements, 85-86; calls for expansion and new station, 86; description, 54, 57-61; dispute over location, 54; need for depot, 49-52
St. Paul Union Depot (1920 facility): 1913 fire, 89; 1914 plan and proposal, 100-105; closing, 254-56; construction, 117-29; depot services and amenities, 165-68; disputes over need for depot, 90-93, 145; floor, site plans, and track layout, 109-17; improvements, 246, 248; operations, 146-55, 170-77; planning for new depot, 90, 105-6, 108; World War II, 231-38
St. Paul Union Depot Company: corporate organization, 145; disputes and arbitrations, 133, 138-43, 223-25; incorporation, 51-53; operating agreements, 131-38; operating organization, 143-46; restructuring, 222-23, 231; search for alternate uses of depot, 248, 250-56

streamlining, 225
suburban passenger trains: map, 67; routes and railroads, 70–78; St. Paul Union Depot, 70; streetcar competition, 67, 70; and U.S. mail, 78
Sunset Limited (train), 247

Tacoma, Washington, 48
Taft, President William Howard, 66
Taylors Falls, Minnesota, 67
Taylors Falls & Lake Superior, 74
telautograph, 147, 149
telegraph office, 150
Texas Rocket (train), xix
Thorpe, B. J., 89
tickets and reservations, 28–29, 155–61
Toltz Engineering Company, 118
Tracy, Minnesota, 32
train director, 148
trainmaster, 146
train shed, 61, 123
Transit Railroad Company, 15
Transportation Act of 1958, 246
Trauning, Hattie, 144
Travelers' Aid, 168, 236
Traveler's Rest lounge cars, 243
troop sleepers, 236
troop trains, 152, 236, 237
Truman, President Harry S., 151, 152
Twain, Mark, 41
20th Century Limited (train), 154
Twin City Model Railroad Club, 167, 168, 233
Twin City Rapid Transit Company, 20, 22, 55, 70, 72, 75, 215
Twin Star Rocket (train), xix, 252

Union News Company, 143, 165
Union Pacific, 136
U.S. Civil War, 15, 20, 42
U.S.–Dakota War, 15, 42
U.S. Railway Administration, 192
U.S. Railway Mail Service: catching mail on the "fly," 185–86; costs and profitability, 202–4; decline, 203–4; importance, 179; RPOs, 178–83, 194, 197; RPO routes, 186–90; schedules, 185, 189; sorting, 199, 200–201; St. Paul Union Depot, 4, 5, 11, 178, 184, 184, 194, 197
U.S. War Department, 105

Victory (train), xix
Viking (train), xix

Wallace, John F., 99
Warren & Whitmore (architectural firm), 1
Waseca, Minnesota, 32
Watertown, South Dakota, 30
Wayzata, Minnesota, 30, 31, 32, 33
Wayzata Historical Society, 33
WCCO radio, iii
Western Passenger Association, 247
Western Railroad of Minnesota, 49
Western Star (train), xviii, xx, 154, 176, 238, 241, 248, 254
Western Union, 25
West St. Paul, Minnesota, 43
West Wisconsin (railroad), 47, 51
White Bear Lake, Minnesota, 47, 49
Wilgus, William J., 98
William Crooks (locomotive), 10, 11, 13, 20, 43, 254
Willmar, Minnesota, 32
Winnipeger (train), xxi, 94, 248, 249
Winnipeg Limited (train), xx, 242, 249
Winona, Minnesota, 20
Winona & St. Peter, 43
Wisconsin Central, 64, 83
Worthington, Minnesota, 32
WPA, 129
Wright, Frank Lloyd, 108
Wyer, Dick & Company, 204, 247
Wyoming, Minnesota, 74

Yellowstone National Park, 152

Zephyr (train), xviii, 154, 164, 174, 175, 226, 227, 230, 231, 234, 239, 242, 250, 254
Zephyr Rocket (train), xix, 234

JOHN W. DIERS has worked in management in the transit industry for thirty-five years, including twenty-five years at the Twin Cities Metropolitan Transit Commission, where he started as a bus driver–dispatcher, then moved on to administrative assistant to the general manager, division superintendent, chief of radio communications, and manager of maintenance administration. He also worked with ATE Management and Services as general manager of the transit system in Racine, Wisconsin. He is now an independent consultant on transit operations and a writer and researcher on transportation history. He has written for *Trains* magazine and is coauthor, with Aaron Isaacs, of *Twin Cities by Trolley: The Streetcar Era in Minneapolis and St. Paul* (Minnesota, 2007). He has served on the board of the Minnesota Transportation Museum and on the editorial board of the Ramsey County Historical Society. He is president of the Scott County (Minnesota) Historical Society.

ALSO PUBLISHED BY THE UNIVERSITY OF MINNESOTA PRESS

The Boomer: A Story of the Rails by Harry Bedwell

Twin Cities by Trolley: The Streetcar Era in Minneapolis and St. Paul by John W. Diers and Aaron Isaacs

Minnesota Railroads: A Photographic History, 1940–2012 by Steve Glischinski

Twilight Rails: The Final Era of Railroad Building in the Midwest by H. Roger Grant

The Great Northern Railway by Ralph W. Hidy, Muriel E. Hidy, Roy V. Scott, and Don L. Hofsommer

The Hook & Eye: A History of the Iowa Central Railway by Don L. Hofsommer

The Minneapolis & St. Louis Railway: A Photographic History by Don L. Hofsommer

Minneapolis and the Age of Railways by Don L. Hofsommer

The Tootin' Louie: A History of the Minneapolis & St. Louis Railway by Don L. Hofsommer

Minnesota Logging Railroads by Frank A. King

The Missabe Road: The Duluth, Missabe and Iron Range Railway by Frank A. King

Union Pacific: Volume I, 1862–1893 by Maury Klein

Union Pacific: Volume II, 1894–1969 by Maury Klein

Dining Car to the Pacific: The "Famously Good" Food of the Northern Pacific Railway by William A. McKenzie

Rails to the North Star: A Minnesota Railroad Atlas by Richard S. Prosser

The 400 Story: Chicago & North Western's Premier Passenger Trains by Jim Scribbins

The Hiawatha Story by Jim Scribbins

Milwaukee Road Remembered by Jim Scribbins

		OR OTHER		
	Station	SELLING AGENT STAMP HERE	Fare $	
	Date Sold			
	Good Commencing Date of Sale Otherwise Date Shown Below		BAGGAGE ☐	
			19	
	TICKET SELLER NO.		NON-TRANSFERABLE VOID IF DETACHED	

TICKET — Sold Subject to Tariff Regulations — *F.J. ___* Passenger Traffic Manager

PRINTED IN U.S.A. BY RAND McNALLY

VIA SHORT LINE Good IN COACHES ONLY for One Passage within Six (6) Months in addition to date of sale stamped on back. Ⓢ Subject to tariff regulations

Form 1-16
W. F. Burke
Gen. Passenger Traffic Mgr

3994

ROUTE NO.

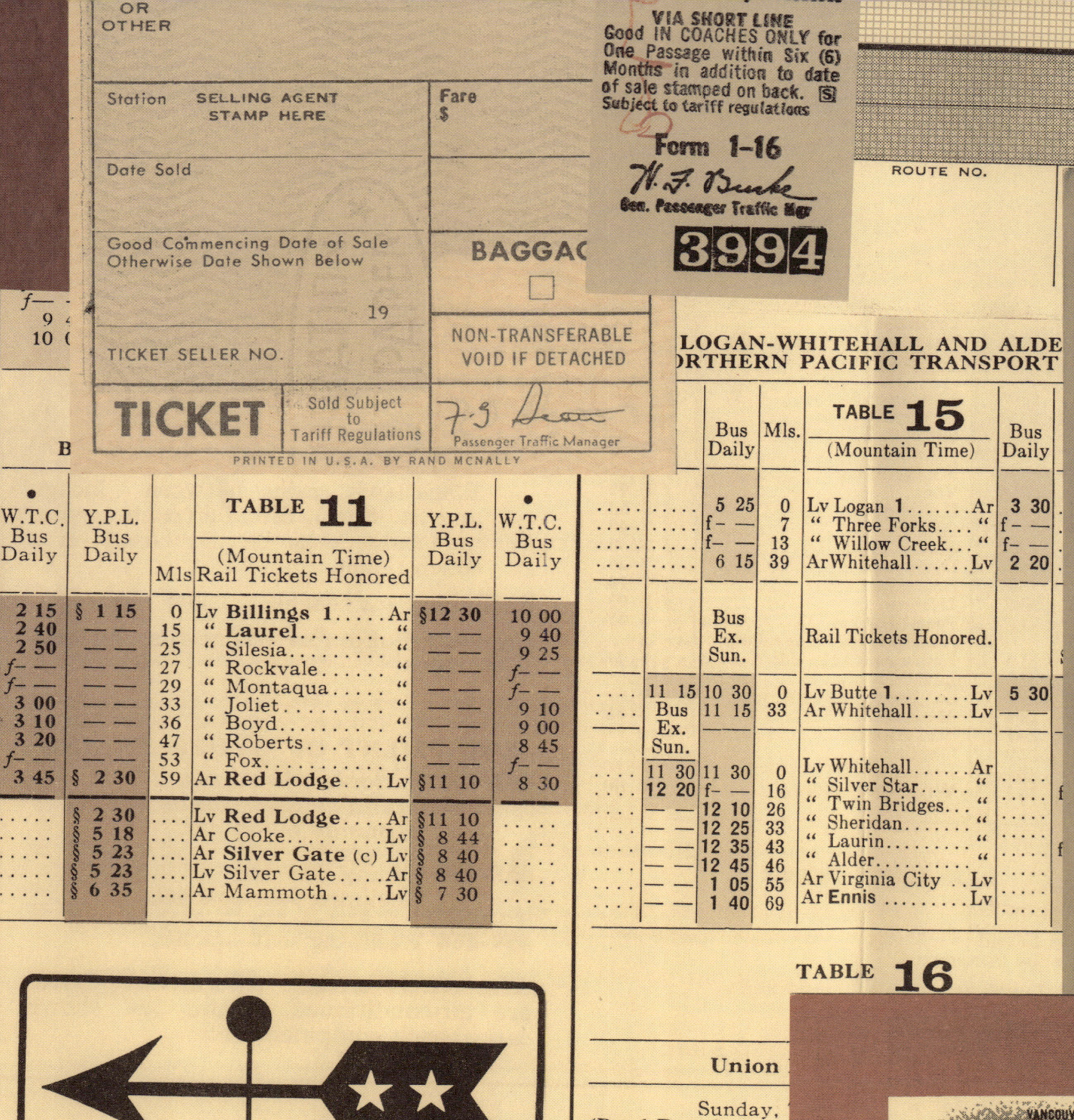

LOGAN-WHITEHALL AND ALDE[R]
[NO]RTHERN PACIFIC TRANSPORT

TABLE 11

W.T.C. Bus Daily	Y.P.L. Bus Daily	Mls	(Mountain Time) Rail Tickets Honored	Y.P.L. Bus Daily	W.T.C. Bus Daily
2 15	§ 1 15	0	Lv Billings 1....... Ar	§12 30	10 00
2 40		15	" Laurel........ "		9 40
2 50		25	" Silesia....... "		9 25
f—		27	" Rockvale...... "		f—
f—		29	" Montaqua..... "		f—
3 00		33	" Joliet........ "		9 10
3 10		36	" Boyd......... "		9 00
3 20		47	" Roberts....... "		8 45
f—		53	" Fox.......... "		f—
3 45	§ 2 30	59	Ar Red Lodge... Lv	§11 10	8 30
....	§ 2 30	....	Lv Red Lodge... Ar	§11 10	....
....	5 18	....	Ar Cooke....... Lv	§ 8 44	....
....	5 23	....	Ar Silver Gate (c) Lv	§ 8 40	....
....	5 23	....	Lv Silver Gate... Ar	§ 8 40	....
....	6 35	....	Ar Mammoth.... Lv	§ 7 30	....

TABLE 15

Bus Daily	Mls.	(Mountain Time)	Bus Daily
5 25	0	Lv Logan 1........ Ar	3 30
f—	7	" Three Forks.... "	f—
f—	13	" Willow Creek... "	f—
6 15	39	Ar Whitehall...... Lv	2 20

Bus Ex. Sun. — Rail Tickets Honored.

11 15	10 30	0	Lv Butte 1........ Lv	5 30
Bus Ex. Sun.	11 15	33	Ar Whitehall..... Lv	

11 30	11 30	0	Lv Whitehall..... Ar	....
12 20	f—	16	" Silver Star..... "	.... f
—	12 10	26	" Twin Bridges... "	....
—	12 25	33	" Sheridan....... "	....
—	12 35	43	" Laurin......... "	.... f
—	12 45	46	" Alder.......... "	....
—	1 05	55	Ar Virginia City.. Lv	....
—	1 40	69	Ar Ennis......... Lv	....

TABLE 16

Union [...]

Sunday, [...]
(Read Down)

* 7 30	Lv Butte [...]
9 25	Lv Dillon. [...]
12 45	Ar Idaho F[...]
2 05	Ar Pocatel[...]
7 00	Ar Salt La[...]
5 00	Ar Los Ang[...]

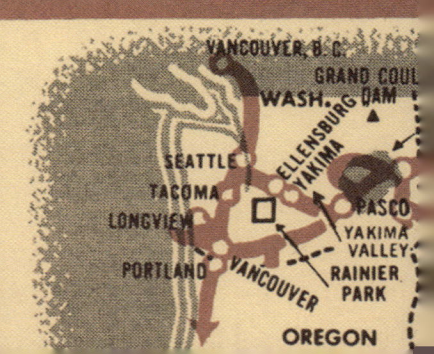

← ★★ **DISCOVER AMERICA**